About the author

DAISAKU IKEDA was born in Tokyo, Japan, on January 2, 1928, to a family of seaweed farmers. He lived through the devastation of World War II as a teenager and witnessed its senseless horror, which left an indelible mark on his life. His four older brothers were drafted into military service, and the eldest was killed in action. These experiences fueled his lifelong quest and passion to work for peace and people's happiness, rooting out the fundamental causes of human conflict.

In 1947, at the age of nineteen, he met Josei Toda, educator and leader of the Soka Gakkai lay Buddhist society, whose activities are based on the teachings of the thirteenth-century Buddhist reformer Nichiren. Ikeda found Toda to be a man of conviction with a gift for explaining profound Buddhist concepts in logical, accessible terms. Challenging poverty and ill health, he continued his education under the tutelage of Toda, who became his mentor in life.

In May 1960, two years after Toda's death, Ikeda, then thirty-two, succeeded him as president of the Soka Gakkai. He dedicated himself to encouraging the group's members in the process of personal transformation and societal contribution. Under his leadership, the movement began an era of innovation and expansion, fostering individuals committed to the promotion of peace, culture and education. In 1975, Ikeda became the first president of the Soka Gakkai International (SGI), now a global network linking some twelve million members in over 190 countries and territories.

Ikeda is a prolific author of some 100 works ranging from discourses on Buddhism to children's books, poetry and essays. He was named Poet Laureate by the World Academy of Arts and Culture in 1981, and an English-language volume of his antiwar poems, *Fighting for Peace*, was a finalist in the US-based Publishers Marketing Association's 2005 Benjamin Franklin Awards. He is also an avid photographer with a particular love of scenic landscapes and natural beauty. In recognition of his contributions as peacebuilder and educator, Ikeda has been awarded over 300 academic honors from universities in more than forty countries.

Journey of Life

Selected Poems of

DAISAKU IKEDA

I.B. TAURIS
LONDON · NEW YORK

Published in 2014 by I.B.Tauris & Co Ltd
6 Salem Road, London W2 4BU
175 Fifth Avenue, New York NY 10010
www.ibtauris.com

Distributed in the United States and Canada
Exclusively by Palgrave Macmillan
175 Fifth Avenue, New York NY 10010

Original copyright © Daisaku Ikeda, 1945–2007
English translation copyright © Soka Gakkai, 2014

The right of Daisaku Ikeda to be identified as the author
of this work has been asserted by him in accordance
with the Copyright, Designs and Patents Act 1988.

ISBN 978 1 78076 969 1 (hb)
ISBN 978 1 78076 970 7 (pb)
eISBN 978 0 85773 562 1

A full CIP record for this book is available from the British Library
A full CIP record is available from the Library of Congress
Library of Congress Catalog Card Number: available

Cover image: Llanddwyn Island cliffs and lighthouse, Anglesey,
Wales. Photo by Eli Pascall-Willis (Photolibrary/Getty Images)

Designed and typeset in Monotype Dante by illuminati, Grosmont
Printed and bound in the UK

Printed and bound in the UK by TJ International Ltd, Padstow, Cornwall

Contents

Foreword

This inaugural volume of *Selected Poems of Daisaku Ikeda* is the first of a three-volume compilation of his poems translated into English from the originals in Japanese. Whereas the two forthcoming volumes of *Poems* will be arranged to highlight specific aesthetic practices and thematic concerns associated with Ikeda's poems and the audiences to which he has traditionally addressed his thoughts in verse, the contents of this volume, which span the years from 1945 to 2007, are intended to provide readers already familiar with his poetry, as well as those encountering it for the first time, an overview of the subjects to which he has devoted attention through the inspiration, complemented by individual imagination, that flows from his "poetic heart and mind."[1]

Because the discourse in which Ikeda has most often addressed the public is either the energetic prose of his books, essays, speeches and lectures, or the very personal prose—sometimes vernacular, but always scholarly yet accessible—with which he has engaged in dialogue with conversational partners and correspondents from around the world, readers new to his poetry will possibly stand amazed at his facility in multiple verse forms and the range of his poetic interests in evidence throughout this volume. Here, readers will find lyrical verses celebrating nature's splendor through subjects large and small; poems addressed to Ikeda's fellow citizens of Japan on a wide variety of subjects; poems addressed to the various constituencies of the Soka Gakkai community in Japan as well as in the United States, Italy, Germany, Malaysia and other nations; poems dedicated to mothers and women generally, where Ikeda's theme is personal empowerment that transcends gender boundaries and the limitations those boundaries erroneously ascribe to women; and poems of personal introduction offered out of respect for world leaders such as Rajiv Gandhi, Nelson Mandela and Corazón Aquino with whom it has been Ikeda's privilege to interact and for authors and artists such as Nataliya Sats, Walt Whitman, Yehudi Menuhin, Oswald Mtshali and Esther Gress, whose poetry, music or educational practices in the arts have served Ikeda as sources of inspiration that piqued his own imagination.[2] Now in his eighties, and having spent his years engaged in genuine lifetime learning and public advocacy to improve the human condition—by advancing the cause of world peace, championing the preservation of the natural environment with which humankind was originally blessed and institutionalizing the forms of value-creating education central to the lay Nichiren Buddhist Soka Gakkai organization over which he has presided since 1960—across the poems gathered here Ikeda admirably demonstrates his unwavering commitment to nurturing the development of a humanistic global culture.

A significant feature of this volume is the Translator's Note, which fully describes the process whereby the fifty poems that follow have been translated from Japanese into English. Although some of these poems were previously translated from Japanese and published in English by the scholars of East Asian literature Burton Watson and Robert Charles Epp, final translations of all poems printed in this volume, including those few by Watson and Epp, have been overseen by a team of Soka Gakkai-associated translators in Tokyo whose consistent purpose has been to provide poetic texts that are faithful to Ikeda's authorial intent, even when recovering that intent has required the team to prepare new texts that now supersede those of earlier printed translations. While most of Ikeda's earlier poems—those written between 1945 and the mid-1970s—tend to disclose the poet's preoccupation with the natural environment which he approaches with a lyricism reminiscent of nineteenth-century

British and American romantic writers, it would be naïve to read Ikeda exclusively through any one aesthetic, critical, historical or political lens. Indeed, we know that as a young man he was a voracious reader who encountered in pre- and post-World War II Japanese anthologies not only selections from Plato's *Dialogues,* Dante's *Divine Comedy,* Pascal's *Pensées,* Milton's *Paradise Lost,* Emerson's essays, Lord Byron's poems and Max Weber's essays on the sociology of religion, but also, in whole or in part, Walt Whitman's *Leaves of Grass* and a wide range of Eastern and Western historical and realist fiction that included, for instance, Daniel Defoe's *Robinson Crusoe* (1719), Edward Bulwer-Lytton's *The Last Days of Pompeii* (1834), Nikolai Gogol's *Taras Bulba* (1835), Alexandre Dumas' *The Count of Monte Cristo* (1845–46), Victor Hugo's *Les Misérables* (1862), Henrik Ibsen's *A Doll's House* (1879), Lu Xun's Chinese vernacular novella *The True Story of Ah Q* (1921–22) and Eiji Yoshikawa's modern Japanese retelling of Luo Guanzhong's fourteenth-century Chinese *Romance of the Three Kingdoms* (1939–43).[3]

As much as the enormous range of the young Ikeda's reading may have shaped his consideration of what might be his place in postwar Japanese society, it also influenced his appreciation of the larger emerging world community into which he and his contemporaries would be invited to take part after 1945. Under the guidance of Josei Toda (1900–58), the educator and peace activist whom he credits as the great mentor of his early life and, in spirit, of his later career, Ikeda immersed himself in studies of the Lotus Sutra and in the value-creating educational philosophy of Tsunesaburo Makiguchi (1871–1944), the educational theorist and religious reformer whose opposition to Japan's militarism led to his imprisonment and death during World War II. Toda's generosity as a mentor and his modeling of productive citizenship in postwar Japan encouraged Ikeda to locate and cherish the spiritual—as opposed to the nominally religious—content of all human experience, adhere to the public and private practice of greeting the ideas and opinions of others with humility and respect, and engage in earnest, candid dialogue with his countrymen as well as with persons hailing from distant nations as means to effect mutual understanding and live in peaceful coexistence.[4]

Although multiple printings of his major prose works demonstrate his competency in that genre, poetry has served Ikeda as an equally significant vehicle to address his ideas and personal convictions to the world. If in his early years he ever wondered about the variety of poet he wished to become, no explicit evidence of his thoughts on the subject has been found. In his own Preface to *Songs from My Heart,* an early collection of his poems translated into English, he likens his casual practice of poetry to Goethe's claim about his: "All my poems are occasional poems, suggested by real life, and having therein a firm foundation." Yet while Ikeda, too, acknowledges that his poems "spring from real life, ... from the daily whirlwind of activities that I, like any ordinary person, find myself engaged in," he emphasizes the importance of feeling to all of them—of "feelings that have come to me in the course of my association with friends or ... with young people," of feelings born out "of basic human emotions" and the honest expression of them—which, he then states, may well be "the true definition of poetry, regardless of the form it happens to take."[5]

Enlarging on his view that feelings or emotions, and the honest expression of them, constitute "the true definition of poetry," a decade after *Songs from My Heart* appeared in print Ikeda had the occasion to develop further his thoughts on poetry in an essay addressed to the World Congress of Poets, which convened in Bangkok in November 1988. Under the title "A plea for the restoration of the poetic mind," he presented the case for poetry as "the spiritual bond that links humanity, society and the universe." Invoking the fundamental duality attributed to the human mind by Pascal in *Pensées* and other writings, Ikeda argued for the supremacy of the "sensitive" dimension of the mind marked by intuition and sensibility over the "geometric" dimension marked exclusively by rationalism and overreliance on the significance of matter. In a world that he characterized as wallowing in "unchecked egoism, ephemeral hedonism, compulsive destruction, despair[,] … nihilism, [and the tragedy of] … the isolated and alienated human spirit," Ikeda dismissed rationalism, material science and technology's overwhelming of civilization with new forms of matter that lessen the flow of human sensitivity necessary for "the wholesome development of civilization," and he asserted that poetry, whose wellspring is that portion of the human heart that is "spirit" and "invisible," has the capacity to link "all … in the great circle of the universe." Introducing the "poetic mind" and the "poetic heart" and treating them as identical, he wrote of the poet's heart/mind:

The gaze of the poet is directed at the heart, at the mind. He does not see … things as mere matter. He converses with the trees and the grasses, talks to the stars, greets the sun, and feels a kinship with all that is around him. In all these things he sees life and he breathes life into them, seeing in the myriad changing phenomena of this world the unchanging principle of the universe. And the poet is free of the fetters imposed by institutions and ideologies; he perceives the unlimited potential of the individual that transcends the trappings of society. He recognizes the bond that links all humankind and intricacies of the invisible web of life … [T]he wellspring of this prolific spirit [is] the "poetic mind."

The poetic mind is the source of human imagination and creativity. It imparts hope to our life, … gives us dreams, and infuses us with courage; it makes possible harmony and unity and gives us the power … to transform our inner world from utter desolation to richness and creativity.[6]

Ikeda's conviction that the poetic heart/mind "is the source of human imagination and creativity[,] ... imparts hope to our life, ... gives us dreams, ... infuses us with courage [and] ... makes possible harmony and unity [as it] gives us the power ... to transform our inner world from utter desolation to richness and creativity" at once provides us with a personal definition of his sense of the purpose and intended outcome of his poetry, and, at the same time, joins his poetic theory and practice to that of poets from the Enlightenment to the present. For instance, writing toward the end of the Enlightenment, the German "Novalis" (Friedrich von Hardenberg) affirmed poetry's relevance in any and all political states, saying, "Poetry heals the wounds inflicted by reason."[7] Then, at the height of the British romantic period, poets such as John Keats and Percy Bysshe Shelley more formally theorized the aesthetic and political power of poetry. Keats emphasized the aesthetic virtually to the exclusion of the political, arguing, for instance, that "Poetry should surprise by fine excess and not by Singularity—it should strike the Reader as a wording of his own highest thoughts, and appear almost a Remembrance."[8] In *A Defence of Poetry* (1821), Shelley drew attention to the ways in which poets have always been energized as well as humbled by "the electric life which burns within their words." However, far more than Keats, Shelley also recognized that some political theorists have feared the capacity of poetry's moral and emotional electricity to lead readers, particularly young ones, to question the conventional values of their elders and thus foment revolution; and he pointed to Plato's exile of poets from the ideal political state he envisioned in *The Republic* as the supreme illustration of that fear in practice. Noting that, because it "is a mirror which makes beautiful that which is distorted," poetry also has the capacity to "[redeem] from decay the visitations of the divinity in man," Shelley challenged political theorists by straightforwardly acknowledging the subversive power of poetry that Plato so feared. In Western literature's boldest rejoinder to positions such as Plato's, at the conclusion of *A Defence* he proclaimed, "Poets are the unacknowledged legislators of the world," thereby marrying the aesthetic and healing power of poetry, which draws from and appeals to the imagination, to the revolutionary power of poetry, which draws from the conviction of political or social urgency out of which a poet may write.[9]

Shelley's position, which has withstood all challenges for two centuries, still rings true among poets and theorists closer to our own time. Writing for the literary journal *The Dial* in the aftermath of World War I, the American modernist poet Marianne Moore asserted in 1926, "Poetry, that is to say the poetic, is a primal necessity."[10] Although his emphasis was more on the aesthetic power of poetry than on the political, writing for the *Saturday Review* in mid-century the British playwright, novelist and literary theorist W. Somerset Maugham agreed with Moore, saying, "The crown of literature is poetry. It is its end and aim. It is the sublimest activity of the human mind. It is the achievement of beauty and delicacy."[11] Finally, as the twentieth century neared its end, the African-American poet Gwendolyn Brooks told an interviewer in 1986, "I always say that poetry is life distilled." Like her poetry, in an important way Brooks' statement of her poetic practice returns us to Shelley, for in her recognition of poetry as "life distilled" she reminds us that poetic art is not designed to warm us only in our joyous moods, but to rouse us as well to action during those moments in which we need clarification of the sometimes confusing, if not also literally terrifying, events of the world around us, even if, in turn, that clarification counsels us to break with our own current or past cultural practices or those of our nation.[12]

With his emphasis on the poetic heart/mind, and his confidence that the genuine poet "perceives the unlimited potential of the individual that transcends the trappings of society" because he "is free of the fetters imposed by institutions and ideologies," Ikeda candidly acknowledges his adherence to a tradition of poetic practice that extends from the Enlightenment to today. It is a tradition that ignores those cultural and national distinctions and resists those institutional and ideological positions that, at the expense of feeling, have preoccupied bureaucratic minds across the centuries. With Ikeda, the freedom and feeling of the genuine poet reign supreme; as he has said, "A person who sees himself and others as fellow beings ... and who knows the pain, the anguish, and the pathos of others," can never be "cold and calculating."[13] The generosity of spirit with which Ikeda invests the poet has its origin in his own character, for sure, but it also has a source in a late essay by Ralph Waldo Emerson, of which Ikeda is quite fond. In "Poetry and Imagination" (1876), Emerson remarked, "The poet should rejoice if he has taught us to despise his song; if he has so moved us as to lift us,—to open the eye of the intellect to see farther and better" than he.[14] Emerson is certainly not ridiculing either the poet or the poet's reader here; rather, he is celebrating the capacity of all good readers of poetry to be poets themselves, and the capacity of genuine poets to inspire and move their readers to look within themselves for the license to read and write their world as a poem and thus eclipse the poet and the poetry that once inspired them. This is the spirit in which Ikeda has personally overseen the production of this first comprehensive volume of his poems in English translation, and it is the spirit in which he graciously invites readers into it. That his position with respect to readers of this volume and the two that will follow it should echo Emerson is not a surprise to the present writer. In *Creating Waldens: An East–West Conversation on the American Renaissance,* a series of eighteen conversations on Emerson, Henry David Thoreau and Whitman and the aesthetic, spiritual and political world of the American Renaissance that they so dominated, Ikeda said:

I believe that if a poet can perceive the infinite possibilities of humanity, his poetry naturally becomes a song in praise of humanity. The perception of those possibilities is really the perception of interconnectedness, like that between friends, between humanity and nature, and between humanity and the cosmos. Poetry crystallizes the surprise and emotion of awakening to such connections.[15]

Ronald A. Bosco

---

1. Daisaku Ikeda, "A plea for the restoration of the poetic mind," *World Tribune* (Santa Monica CA), December 12, 1988, p. 3. As discussed below, in this essay Ikeda is reported to have used the expressions "the poetic heart" and "the poetic mind" synonymously; however, these are actually two alternate translations of the term *shigokoro*, the *kokoro* of *shi* (poetry). *Kokoro* is a particularly rich term in Japanese, indicating at once the affective, volitional and even rational aspects of the inner life. Not acknowledging the possibility of a heart–mind disjunction in the poet, Ikeda writes that the poetic heart/mind "is the source of human imagination and creativity. It imparts hope to our life, ... gives us dreams, and infuses us with courage; it makes possible harmony and unity and gives us the power ... to transform our inner world from utter desolation to richness and creativity."

2. For a sample of lyrical verses celebrating naturalistic subjects large and small, in this volume see "Blossoms that scatter" (1945), "Fuji and the poet" (1947), "Weeds" (1971), "Pampas grass" (1971), "Pampas grass, the poet's friend" (2007) and "In praise of morning glories" (2007). Among the major poems in this volume in which Ikeda addresses his fellow Japanese citizens and various constituencies of the global Soka Gakkai community are "The people" (1971), "Arise, the sun of the century" (1987), "Youthful country with a shining future" (1988), "Be an eternal bastion of peace" (1988), "The sun of jiyu over a new land" (1993), "Standing among the ruins of Takiyama Castle" (2000) and "Salute to the smiling faces of the twenty-first century" (2001). For poems to women that address personal empowerment that transcends gender boundaries, see, especially, "Mother" (1971), "Salute to mothers" (1995) and "May the fragrant laurels of happiness adorn your life" (1999). For poems of personal introduction offered out of respect for Gandhi, Mandela and Aquino, see "The lion's land, Mother India" (1987), "Banner of humanism, path of justice" (1990) and "Shine brilliantly! Crown of the Mother of the Philippines" (1991), respectively; for poems dedicated to Nataliya Sats, pioneer of children's theater in Russia, Walt Whitman, American poet, Yehudi Menuhin, famed violinist, Oswald Mtshali, South African poet, and Esther Gress, Danish poet laureate, see "Mother of art, the sunlight of happiness" (1990), "Like the sun rising" (1992), "Cosmic traveler, our century's premier violinist" (1992), "The poet—warrior of the spirit" (1998) and "Together holding aloft laurels of the people's poetry" (2000), respectively.

3. For these and other of his youthful readings, see Daisaku Ikeda, *Wakaki*

hi no dokusho (The Readings of My Youthful Days) (Tokyo: Daisan Bunmeisha, 1978) and Daisaku Ikeda, *Zoku, wakaki hi no dokusho* (The Readings of My Youthful Days, continued) (Tokyo: Daisan Bunmeisha, 1993).

4. Ikeda celebrates the breadth and enduring value of Toda's legacy to him and to others in "My mentor, Josei Toda" (1986), printed in this volume.

5. Daisaku Ikeda, "Preface," in *Songs from My Heart,* trans. Burton Watson (New York and Tokyo: Weatherhill, 1978), p. 7.

6. Daisaku Ikeda, "A plea for the restoration of the poetic mind," p. 3.

7. Friedrich von Hardenberg, *Detached Thoughts,* quoted in *Dictionary of Quotations in Communications,* ed. Lilless McPherson Shilling and Linda K. Fuller (Westport CT: Greenwood Press, 1997), p. 165.

8. John Keats, to John Taylor, February 27, 1818, in *The Letters of John Keats,* ed. Hyder Edward Rollins, 2 vols. (Cambridge MA: Harvard University Press, 1958), vol. 1, p. 238.

9. Percy Bysshe Shelley, *A Defence of Poetry,* in *English Romantic Writers,* ed. David Perkins, 2nd edn. (New York, London, Tokyo: Harcourt Brace, 1995), pp. 1146, 1134, 1143, 1144, 1146, respectively.

10. Patricia C. Willis, ed., *The Complete Prose of Marianne Moore* (New York: Viking, 1986), p. 169.

11. W. Somerset Maugham, "Comment," *Saturday Review* (New York) July 20, 1957, p. 70.

12. Kevin Bezner, "A life distilled: An interview with Gwendolyn Brooks" (1986), in *Conversations with Gwendolyn Brooks,* ed. Gloria Wade Gayles (Jackson: University Press of Mississippi, 2003), p. 124.

13. Daisaku Ikeda, "A plea for the restoration of the poetic mind," p. 3.

14. Ralph Waldo Emerson, "Poetry and imagination," in *The Collected Works of Ralph Waldo Emerson,* ed. Alfred R. Ferguson, Joseph Slater, Douglas Emory Wilson and Ronald A. Bosco, 10 vols (Cambridge MA and London: Belknap Press of Harvard University Press, 1971–2013), vol. 8, p. 38.

15. Ronald A. Bosco, Daisaku Ikeda, and Joel Myerson, *Creating Waldens: An East–West Conversation on the American Renaissance* (Cambridge MA: Dialogue Path Press, 2009), p. 116.

Translator's note

This volume represents the largest and most comprehensive collection of Daisaku Ikeda's poetry in translation to date. Earlier publications, such as translations by Watson,[1] Epp[2] and Gebert,[3] offered more limited selections of his work, focused on particular periods, such as his earlier works, or on a specific theme, such as his thoughts on war and peace.

In contrast, this volume includes poems covering a span of more than sixty years: 1945 to 2007. As such, it contains works written in a wide range of styles, voices and modes. In selecting the poems for inclusion in this volume, an effort was made to ensure that this sample would be as representative as possible in terms of period, style and, in the case of the many poems addressed to specific individuals or groups, the nature of the recipient.

Part of Ikeda's view of literature is that there is an indissoluble relationship between the author and the work; that the words provide an important window on the inner life of the writer. In light of this, it is probably appropriate to offer a cursory biographical portrait of the author, relating this to a chronology of poetic production.

Daisaku Ikeda was born in Tokyo in 1928. His family had been engaged in cultivating and harvesting *nori* (edible seaweed) in Tokyo Bay for generations. The family had enjoyed relative prosperity until a massive earthquake struck the Tokyo region in 1923, producing widespread devastation and shifting the seabed of Tokyo Bay, thus greatly reducing the *nori* harvest. Soon after Ikeda was born, his father became bedridden with rheumatism, plunging the family deeper into poverty. Ikeda himself had a weak constitution and, as a result, from early in life he gravitated toward reading and literature as opposed to more strenuous physical activity. He has written that his early ambitions included becoming a writer of fiction or a reporter for a newspaper or magazine.[4]

The first poem in this collection, "Blossoms that scatter," was written in April 1945, when Ikeda was seventeen. It was written in the wake of the firebombings that had leveled much of Tokyo just months before the end of World War II. The war had had a devastating impact on Ikeda's family— his four older brothers had been drafted and sent to the Asian front; of them, his eldest brother was killed in action in Burma, although the family would not be informed of this for several years.

In August 1947, Ikeda encountered Josei Toda (1900–58), who was then engaged in rebuilding the lay Buddhist movement, the Soka Gakkai, that he and Tsunesaburo Makiguchi (1871–1944) had founded in 1930. Their Buddhist beliefs led Makiguchi, the organization's first president, and Toda to criticize the wartime policies of the Japanese militarist government and, as a result, they were arrested in July 1943 as "thought criminals." In November 1944, Makiguchi died of malnutrition while still imprisoned. Toda managed to survive the ordeal and was released in July 1945, just prior to the Japanese surrender. This encounter with Toda proved decisive for Ikeda, as he came to regard the older man as his personal mentor, and it was through Toda that Ikeda took faith in Nichiren Buddhism and became active in the Soka Gakkai. "Fuji and the poet" and "Morigasaki Beach" were both written in 1947 and capture the thoughts of the nineteen-year-old author. A much later poem, "My mentor, Josei Toda" (1986), offers a portrait of this crucial relationship.

Throughout the 1950s, Ikeda dedicated himself to supporting Toda's work as he developed the Soka Gakkai into the largest and most dynamic Buddhist movement in postwar Japan. Such poems as "Offering prayers at Mount

Fuji" (1950) and "Travelers" (1952) were written during this period.

Toda died on April 2, 1958. In May 1960, Ikeda succeeded Toda to become the third president of the Soka Gakkai. He continued to lead efforts to expand the movement, which grew from a membership of some 750,000 households at the time of Toda's death to more 8 million households in 1970.

This involved a demanding schedule of travel, both within and, increasingly, outside Japan, as Ikeda traveled to offer encouragement to nascent Soka Gakkai memberships in Europe, the Americas and Asia. Ikeda's prose efforts during this period were dedicated to providing contemporary exegesis and interpretation of the writings of Nichiren (1222–82), the founder of the school of Buddhism practiced by the members of the Soka Gakkai. In 1968, he began a multivolume novelization of the history of the organization under the leadership of Josei Toda titled *The Human Revolution*. "Daybreak" (1966) is one of a handful of poems published during the decade of the 1960s.

Also under Ikeda's leadership, the scope of the movement's activities expanded beyond the purely religious, to include engagement in the fields of peace, culture and education. To this end, Ikeda founded a number of institutions, including a research institution (1962), a concert association (1963), a political party (1964), junior and senior high schools (1968), a four-year university (1971) and an art museum (1973). These multifaceted endeavors were inspired by the Soka Gakkai's long-standing interpretation of Nichiren's writings and life as a paradigm of bringing the tenets of Buddhism to bear on the real-life challenges of living in society.

Starting in the early 1970s, it became increasingly common for Ikeda to use poetry as a medium for expressing his understanding of Buddhist concepts and for encouraging people encountered in the course of fulfilling his responsibilities. The collection "To my young friends" (1970–71) comprised short poems written to various individuals, often commemorating an encounter or exchange. Likewise, the poems "The people," "Weeds" and "Mother" (1971) were dedicated, respectively, to the youth and women memberships of the Soka Gakkai.

Long-simmering tensions with the Nichiren Shoshu priesthood, with whom the Soka Gakkai was associated, came to a head in the late 1970s over the respective roles of ordained and lay practitioners, with the priesthood asserting its inherent superiority over the laity. For several years Ikeda was compelled to maintain a low profile within the organization and its activities. In the early 1980s, he again chose the medium of poetry to publicly reaffirm his mentoring bonds with the youth membership of the organization. As had been the case with "Mother" and "The people," lyrics based on "Song of the crimson dawn" and "Youth, scale the mountain of kosen-rufu of the twenty-first century" (1981) were set to music and gained enduring popularity among the Soka Gakkai membership.

Beginning in the early 1970s, Ikeda's travels increasingly took on the aspect of a kind of citizen diplomacy. During 1974 and 1975, for example, he met with the respective leaders of China (Zhou Enlai), the Soviet Union (Alexei Kosygin) and the United States (Henry Kissinger) in an effort to reduce Cold War tensions. These efforts accelerated during the 1980s and often involved the use of poetry, translated into the recipient's language, as a vehicle for a highly personalized style of diplomacy. Poems written to such public figures as Indian Premier Rajiv Gandhi (1987) might commemorate an earlier encounter or, as in the case of South African President Nelson Mandela (1990) or Philippine President Corazón Aquino (1991), serve as a form of greeting and recognition, presented at the time of their first meeting. A similar pattern pertains for poems written for such cultural figures as the Russian theatrical producer Nataliya Sats (1990) and the violinist Yehudi Menuhin (1992).

The Soka Gakkai International (SGI) was established in 1975, with Ikeda as president, to coordinate among a growing number of Soka Gakkai organizations around the world. Ikeda's travels increasingly included meetings with SGI members and organizations in different countries, and his encouragement was often expressed in the form of poetry. This can be seen in the poems offered to the SGI memberships in Italy (1987), Malaysia (1988), Germany (1991) and the United States (1987, 1993).

The conflict with the Nichiren Shoshu priesthood re-surfaced in the early 1990s, taking the form of a decisive split when, on November 28, 1991, and despite Ikeda's repeated calls for dialogue, the high priest of the sect excommunicated more than twelve million Soka Gakkai International members worldwide, an event now celebrated by the SGI as the Day of Spiritual Independence. Ikeda reflects on this conflict in "The noble voyage of life" (1999). Other poems such as "The path to a peaceful world, a garden for humankind" (2000) and "Eternally radiant champion of humanity" (2001) express harsh critiques at those forces of authority, both religious and secular, which Ikeda sees as being indifferent or detrimental to the happiness of the common person.

During the 1990s, Ikeda sought to give enduring institutional form to the SGI's commitment to peace and human flourishing by founding a number of international policy and research institutions. Both the founding and second presidents of the Soka Gakkai had been educators, and although Ikeda never had the opportunity to meet Maki-guchi, he had learned of the latter's vision of humanistic education through his own mentor, Josei Toda. In the early 1950s, Toda and Ikeda had discussed the idea of founding a university that would embody these ideals; the founding of Soka University in Japan in 1971 was now followed by the establishment of Soka University of America in 2001. "Standing among the ruins of Takiyama Castle" (2000) gives expression to Ikeda's sentiments for the students and graduates of these educational institutes and the educational enterprise more broadly.

Ikeda's poetic output has continued to be prolific in recent years, with more than 200 long-form poems penned in just the years between 2000 and 2006. Through his poetry, he continues to address not only specific groups or individuals, but also larger themes such as peace ("August 15—The dawn of a new day" (2001), "The promise of a majestic peace" (2003)) and the mission of poetry and poets ("The poet—warrior of the spirit" (1998), "Together holding aloft laurels of the people's poetry" (2000) and "Salute to poets" (2007)); as well as to write poems that might be described as humanist reflections on nature ("Pampas grass, the poet's friend" and "In praise of morning glories" (2007)).

ABOUT THE TRANSLATIONS

This volume comprises renderings into English by three different translators: Burton Watson, Robert Epp and a team of Soka Gakkai-associated translators. The reader will quickly notice three quite different styles of translation. This is in part an inevitable outcome of translating between languages as grammatically distant and historically un-related as Japanese and English, something which inevitably involves a considerable degree of interpretative intervention on the part of the translator. But at the same time it is also a testament to the rich multivalence of Ikeda's poetic language, the range of voices and registers in which he writes.

Translations and translators are always guided by an implicit understanding of the function and nature of human language; the possibilities and problems of facilitating the movement of linguistic, intellectual and affective content between different languages and cultures; and the scope of the translator's respective responsibilities to the author and the reader. Professors Watson and Epp are well-known translators who have written about these issues generally as well as how they apply specifically to the translation of Ikeda's work.⁵ The comments here will thus be limited to the poems for which the Soka Gakkai translation team was responsible.

The ideal that has been pursued here has been to create a text that is not passively subordinate to the original, but which has the maximum possibility of finding a meaningful place in the lives of English readers. To this end, we have sought to reproduce, to the degree possible, the native reader's experience of these poems.

To do this is of course to add an additional subjective ambition to the already subjective undertaking of translation. This is further complicated by the nature of poetry, which seeks to express things that lie behind, between and around words, not simply what is contained stably within them.

The setting of such a goal, however, was felt to be necessary if these translations were to fulfill even minimally the ethical obligations due to author and reader. Both modern and classical Japanese (a grammar Ikeda has often employed) leave a great deal unstated: the language regularly makes no singular/plural distinction; there are technically no tenses, only grammatical features to indicate whether an action is considered completed or ongoing; the subjects of sentences are often only implied. The reader is expected to supply these elements, to see or feel a scene evoked by very sparse descriptors. A translation that refrained from providing any of the elements brought to the original by a native reader would remain obscure to the point of incomprehensibility.

Since poetry is not simply a matter of what is said, but how it is said, these translations also seek to reproduce the rhythms and timbres of Ikeda's poetic voice. As noted, he at times adopts a distinctly and self-consciously literary style, using the classical grammar that permits the kinds of compression typically associated with such Japanese poetic forms as *haiku* and *waka*. (The 1987 poem dedicated to the

novelist Eiji Yoshikawa, for example, is written in this style.)
At other times he adopts a simple vernacular voice. But
his language maintains a certain stately rhythm, perhaps
reflective of his sense of the dignity of ordinary language
and experience.

A final aspect of Ikeda's poetry that should be touched
on is what might be termed its addressive nature. As noted,
many of the poems are dedicated or addressed to particular
individuals, groups or even whole societies. This is in part
the inevitable outgrowth of his responsibility, as the leader
of a religious movement, to offer guidance and encourage-
ment to those who seek it from him. But it may also be
understood as reflective of his Buddhist appreciation that the
universal is contained within the particular, and that larger
messages are most effectively conveyed when addressed to a
specific audience.

Linguistically, this is facilitated by the relational nature
of Japanese, the many expressions for "I" and "you" which
can indicate various degrees of human relatedness, from
rigid formality to warm intimacy. Ikeda typically addresses
his reader with intimacy, using terms that indicate bonds
of trust and affection. He even at times writes in the first
person on behalf of his addressee as an expression of
solidarity and shared purpose. This could also reflect the
Buddhist worldview in which "self" and "other" are not
irreconcilable opposites, but necessary and complementary
parts of a larger whole. Needless to say, the relative poverty
of English in this regard, where we have only "you" and "I,"
complicates the work of attempting to express the textured
sense of relationship that is central to the reader's experi-
ence in Japanese.

All these factors have, it is felt, necessitated a less re-
strained "reading into" (or "out of") the original if there was
to be any hope of enabling the English reader to see what
Japanese readers see, to feel and hear what is felt and heard
in the original.

While Ikeda's language may at times be complex or even obscure, it is clear that he does not wish to simply leave his reader with literary puzzles for private contemplation. His desire is to have an impact on his addressee/reader. In many cases he clearly seeks to elicit quite specific emotional valences, such as pity or outrage, or to inspire some form of action.

This freer style of translation would seem to accord with Ikeda's own preferences. Considering Ikeda's long history as an avid reader of literature and poetry in translation, it is evident that he has not valued the literal or word-for-word transposition of the original so much as the generation of a new, parallel text in the target language—one capable of provoking the mood and sentiment of the original and, ideally, facilitating a sense of encounter between author and reader.

For Ikeda, the fourth- and fifth-century translations of Buddhist scriptures from Sanskrit into Chinese by Kumarajiva (344–413), in particular his translation of the Lotus Sutra, realize the highest possibilities of translation. The enduring popularity and influence of this translation, revered for centuries throughout East Asia, is testament to its success in conveying that most intransmissible of moods—enlightenment—and in facilitating that rarest of encounters—with the Buddha, in particular the Buddha residing within each of us (for that is the Lotus Sutra's central message).

Also following the historic example of Buddhist translation, every effort has been made to render specialized Buddhist terminology into language that will be accessible to the uninitiated reader. There are a few exceptions, which are noted in the glossary at the end of this volume. Perhaps the most important term which has been left in Japanese is kosen-rufu, a term originally from the Lotus Sutra that can be translated as "to proclaim and spread widely" and which indicates the propagation of Buddhist teachings. Within the Soka Gakkai, the sense of this term has been extended to indicate the process of working for the realization of a peaceful society through the promotion of such core Buddhist values as respect for the sanctity of life.

Readers' reactions to texts are subjective and vary widely, but they are not random. The process of developing these translations has benefited from the feedback and guidance of a number of sensitive native readers of Japanese, as well as extended editorial exchanges in English. This dialogic process recapitulates the methods employed by Kumarajiva, about which Ikeda has written eloquently.[6] Through dialogue, different perspectives are revealed and become available to the participants in the exchange; in the work of translation, dialogue enables participants on all sides of a linguistic divide to deepen and broaden their awareness of the reactions elicited by particular words, expressions and turns of phrase, as well as to the poems as a whole. It expands the realm of possible expressions within the target language while anchoring it in a more certain and accurate reading of the original.

The desire that readers of these translations will experience them as an encounter, and that this, the product of dialogue, will mark the start of a further dialogue, is one the translators feel confident is shared by the author.

These translations are based on the texts contained in the Japanese complete works of Daisaku Ikeda (*Ikeda Daisaku zenshu*). In cases in which a poem was presented by Ikeda to a public figure, the English translation used at that time has been treated as the definitive text. Names of contemporary Japanese individuals are given in the English order of personal followed by family name. For historical figures, the traditional Japanese name order (family name first) is used. Finally, diacritical marks that indicate differences in pronunciation that would not be meaningful to the average reader of English are not used in this volume.

ACKNOWLEDGMENTS

These translations would not have been possible without the collaboration and support of a large number of individuals. At times we have worked from excellent earlier translations, shaping them to fit the tone adopted for this volume. As mentioned, the interpretation of the original and the choice of English expression have been developed through numerous dialogues and exchanges. The number of people to whom thanks are due is so great, the timeframe over which the translations evolved so long, and the risk of inadvertent omission so onerous, that I must confine myself to a general, but heartfelt, expression of appreciation.

Andrew Gebert
on behalf of the translation team
March 2014

1. Daisaku Ikeda, *Songs from My Heart*, trans. Burton Watson (New York, Tokyo: Weatherhill, 1978).
2. Daisaku Ikeda, *The People*, trans. Robert Epp (Santa Monica: World Tribune Press, 1972); Daisaku Ikeda, *Hopes and Dreams*, trans. Robert Epp (Santa Monica: World Tribune Press, 1976).
3. Daisaku Ikeda, *Fighting for Peace*, trans. Andrew Gebert (Berkeley: Creative Arts Book Company, 2004).
4. Daisaku Ikeda, *My Recollections*, trans. Robert Epp (Santa Monica: World Tribune Press, 1980), p. 19.
5. Burton Watson, "Translator's Note" in Ikeda, *Songs from My Heart*, p. 9; Robert Epp, "Translator's Note" in Ikeda, *Hopes and Dreams*, pp. 7–10.
6. Daisaku Ikeda, "Kumaraju o kataru" (Discussion on Kumarajiva), in *Toyo Gakujutsu Kenkyu*, vol. 22(1), pp. 89–113 (1983).

Poems

Blossoms that scatter

Cherries in bloom that the air raid spared
blue sky above them   fallen petals jumbled

for a background the gutted ruins of reality
and the pitiful people who cannot look up to them

bitter are their long wanderings
the road of parent and child

amid the waves of little shacks, flowers in bloom
cherry blossoms—is theirs the hue of dawn?

Ah, there is a simile in this existence
men of power and men of peace

"blossoms that scatter, blossoms that remain
to become blossoms that scatter"—so sings a man

blossoms of youth, how many million—
why must they scatter? why must they scatter?

In distant southern seas, ill-fated cherries
full bloom not yet on them, their branches are in pain

and my friends remaining, their hearts, before we know it,
wounded by the loss of the world of the ideal

Are all things impermanent? are they eternal?
without even knowing, must we scatter?

Blossoms that scatter, blossoms that remain,
bloom forever, in spring send out your fragrance on
    the storm!

Written in April 1945, shortly before Japan's surrender at the end of World War II, when the author was seventeen. This translation, by Burton Watson, first appeared in *Songs from My Heart* (1978).

Fuji and the poet

There was a poet, a poet who sang
of this mountain's unmatched harmony and splendor.

> Forgive me, Fuji.
> Tonight as I look up at you
> I find myself weeping, without reason.

There was a poet who focused the light of his seasoned skill
on this ultimate of the Earth's forms, and wept.

> A day without wind.
> In the dear and dreamlike emptiness of the sky,
> a cloud is born to long after Fuji.

A poet who loved Fuji through the cycles of great art
that burned in the depths in his life.

Bokusui elevated himself to converse with Fuji
and solemnly sing its infinite melodies.

Fuji under clear skies.
Shining Fuji.
Snow-clad Fuji.
Towering Fuji.

Fuji's crisp outline against the winter sky.
Fuji under rainclouds.
Rough-skinned Fuji.
White-robed Fuji.

Fuji at daybreak.
Cloud-capped Fuji.
Fuji in the bright light of dawn.
Fuji tonight.

Fuji under leaden skies.
Expansive Fuji.
Fuji in the white garb of spring.
Fuji exposed in autumn.

High in the skies he sings his praise
for this mountain of goodness, justice and philosophy.

Written in 1947, when the author was nineteen.

"Forgive me, Fuji": trans. from Wakayama, *Umi no koe* (Voice of the Sea) in *Wakayama Bokusui zenshu*, vol. 1, p. 34.

"A day without wind": Ibid.

Wakayama Bokusui (1885–1928): a writer of traditional-style Japanese poetry, admired for his elegant and romantic style.

Morigasaki Beach

On the shore at Morigasaki, together with a friend.
The smell of the ocean; waves striking and retreating.
Time passes. Two nineteen-year-olds,
uncertain of their paths, discuss philosophy.

My friend is troubled, beset by poverty.
He declares he will follow the Christian way.
His eyes gleam intensely in the moonlight.
Waves beat the shore to that strong pulse.

Grasses grow thick on the collapsed embankment.
Not knowing the name of the insects that sing,
I suggest we compose poetry this evening,
the music around us like ancient court times...

But my friend is silent—How should I live
so that my soul may ascend to the moon
that shines above these impenetrable gardens?
He wipes his tears and sighs.

My friend lost in solitary sadness.
I have vowed, I say, to live for limitless aspirations,
however painful that pursuit.
My friend smiles—I'll do that too.

Although different from the far-off world
my friend seeks, I have my own way and path.
Watched over by the moon, let us weave
verses without end, 'til hair turns white.

May you find happiness, my friend!
Who knows when we will meet again?
Without a word, we take our separate ways.
Undulating silver waves—Morigasaki.

Written in August 1947, when the author was nineteen, around the time of his first meeting with Josei Toda. Morigasaki Beach is located on Tokyo Bay near the author's home in Ota Ward, Tokyo. The poem has been set to music and has become a favorite song within the Soka Gakkai.

.

Offering prayers at Mount Fuji

The time of humanity's awakening is here!
The dawn! The dawn!
First light of the day everlasting,
melodies of sacred teachings,
rhythmic vitality of life
brimming with vast and magnificent strength.

Mount Fuji, like the dawn,
brings restoring richness to our lives.
It enfolds a soul, eternally enduring.
Its solemn form like a wise philosopher
arising from deepest meditation.
Its peaceful aspect remains unmoved
by the bravest north winds.
With the accumulation of propitious snows
it paints a picture of sacred purity.
Under the fierce heat of summer's red emperor
it never neglects to refresh us
with fragrant breezes and tranquil green.
Mount Fuji! How transcendent is your perfectly formed
    beauty!

History's pages pile up
thousands, tens of thousands deep.
The trampling march of fire and steel
continues unchecked and unabated.
On which of life's shores have we touched land?
Humanity's passage is driven
by the maddened lashing of storm-torn sails.
Earth remains adrift on sad and tragic currents.
People yearn for indications
of a firm and certain direction.

Abiding on the parched earth, the people of medieval
    Europe
drew forth the clear waters of Scholasticism
and were revived.
Struggling in anguish through harsh trials, the Jewish people
kept faith in the coming of the Messiah
and were filled with the vital breath of life.
Exhausted by wandering on confounded paths, the people
    of Asia
encountered the sage philosopher of Eagle Peak
and brought their lives to new flowering.

The times pass on, new eras arrive.
The rich robes of the past are now threadbare.
The billowing waves of a defiled age
rage ever more ferociously.
Ah, let us offer our prayer and pledge
to the sacred peak of Mount Fuji,
that we may bring succor to the suffering.

Untold numbers of people
have extolled Mount Fuji.
But I have no taste for the exaggerated claims
of narrow particularism.
In the burning house of our all-consuming age
I stand, unadorned, fearing no refutation.

I will offer my praise to distant Mount Fuji,
just as the world's two billion people
turn themselves to face the sun's noble beams
or bathe in Luna's delicate light.
Now from Mount Fuji comes the stirring chime
of the sacred bell, resounding with
the tones of freedom, peace and dignity.

The time has come
to awaken to the realities of the inner life,
inspired by the echoing bell of lasting peace
that sounds from beautiful, sacred Mount Fuji.

How incomparable, Mount Fuji!
Preserving the writings of the great sage,
home to the eternal guide and master!
How majestic, this sublime peak!
Heritage unbroken over so many seasons,
key to reveal the secrets of the cosmos!
The doors to the jeweled throne
—without rival or parallel—
have now been thrown open!

The sacred bell echoes and sounds.
The dawn is here! The dawn!
The time of humanity's awakening
is finally at hand!

First published in the January 1950 issue of the magazine *Daibyakurenge*. This translation is based on a revised version published in 1991.

Eagle Peak (Skt Gridhrakūta): a mountain near the city of Rājagriha in Magadha in ancient India; sometimes called Vulture Peak. Said to be the place where Shakyamuni preached the Lotus Sutra.

I offer this to you

My friend!
Why do you suffer so?
Why do you
weep so profusely?
Why are you so filled
with anguish?

Suffer if you must.
Your suffering will nourish
young buds
as they break through
the fragrant earth
and stretch toward the sky.

Weep if you will.
Your tears are unavoidable
until the day comes
—after the long season of rains—
when you look up
to see the sun.

It is good to struggle.
Because unless we pass
through the dark depths of night
we cannot greet
the noble dignity
of the dawn.

This poem appeared as an entry in the author's diary, dated January 8, 1951.

Travelers

Travelers pass,
Searching today and tomorrow
For new roads to happiness.

I cannot know their hearts;
Perhaps they are loaded with grief,
Perhaps they are lightened with joy.

Merely to survive the chill of dawn
Or the heat of evening,
These travelers are forever on the move;
Though buffeted, they hold to the road.

Where do these countless travelers
Come from, you ask, where do they go?
They come from sojourns with tragedy
To seek out paths of hope.

The poet Wakayama Bokusui writes,
  How many hills and rivers must we cross
  To reach a land without loneliness?
  We set out again today…

The people of such a land
Have dreams,
Gardens which joy can flower in,
Arenas for democracy,
Unerring ideals,
A stage for all to act upon.

Travelers, advance and I shall follow
On Man's endless trek
From paths of wrath to paths of joy.

Written in August 1952 while the author was returning from a visit to
Osaka. This translation, by Robert Epp, first appeared in *The People* (1972).

Wakayama Bokusui (1885–1928): a writer of traditional-style Japanese poetry,
admired for his elegant and romantic style.

"How many hills": trans. from Wakayama, *Umi no koe* (Voice of the Sea) in
Wakayama Bokusui zenshu, vol. 1, p. 45.

Spring breezes

The sudden shower has passed,
the spring breezes rustle

Blossoms of the cherry-apple
wake from sleep,
one petal dancing

By the rocks in the garden
the shimmering
heat waves rise

On the surface of the pond
a leaf boat
glides quietly along

I pray that
the spring breezes of good fortune
blow in the hearts of all

Written in the 1950s. This translation, by Burton Watson, first appeared in
Songs from My Heart (1978).

Autumn wind

By the roadside, tangled clumps of bush clover,
clear winds of autumn spring up—
among the delicate leaves,
pink and white blossoms, gentle princess faces peering
Each coming day, each coming day
was a day of trial,
panting for breath,
walking the green road, climbing upward,
on the plains, winds reveling with the pampas grass,
alone, quietly roaming the Miyagino plateau,
recalling the song of the falling star, autumn wind on
    Wu-chang Moor,
the general who died forlorn there, Chu-ko Liang

Autumn wind,
wind sighing with the wine cup of one who weeps at
    parting,
wind sighing with the tears in the heart of one pained,
wind with its melancholy chant to the traveler

As the crimson sun of evening dips and sinks from sight,
bell crickets sing
and the autumn wind departs

Written in the 1950s. This translation, by Burton Watson, first appeared in
Songs from My Heart (1978).

Miyagino plateau: part of the Hakone National Park in Kanagawa
Prefecture.

Wu-chang Moor (Wuzhang Plain): the site of a battle between the Shu Han
general Chu-ko Liang (Zhuge Liang) and the forces of the rival state of
Wei, as famously described in the Chinese classic *The Romance of the Three
Kingdoms*.

Daybreak

Dawn is the
heart of a child,
the hope of youth.

Under a finally whitening sky
a single line of dazzling light
runs the length
of the horizon.
The sun lifts itself
perfectly round and red
painting a masterwork
of sublime artistry.
The morning sun
strides into the expansive sky
proud, dignified,
ablaze with passion and joy.

Indifferent to days
of rain and storm,
the sun rises
with the unfaltering rhythm
of the cosmos.
Its bright rays
find pride and purpose
in offering all people
everywhere, equally,
the strength and courage to live.

The sun pours
its brilliant beams
on all regions,
sweltering or frozen.
Faithful to its nature
holding nothing back,

its earnest prayer—
may all things grow!

My child!
Arise each day
together with the sun!
Study hard
with the sun in your heart.
And when the sun sets
in the evening,
take quiet rest
for tomorrow's dawn!

———————————

Composed for the January 1966 issue of *Kibo no tomo*, a magazine for young boys and girls.

The crisp day we parted

At that crisp moment of parting,
Wind crackled over the plateau;
Waves of pampas grass rippled white,
Flickering the evergreen memories of those days
Since that summer we shared—

One instant in our flash of life,
Under the cryptomerias
On the shores of the Inland Sea—
Like meeting a friendly face
In the window of a passing train.

Once our hearts opened to each other—
Innermost heart to innermost heart—
Such transparent purity,
Lucid as the glitter of the autumn sky,
Is my life's greatest joy.

Even if our eyes should never again meet
As on that crisp day we parted,
I shall believe through the eternity of each moment
In the reality of heart calling to heart,
A reality
    etched forever in my memory.

On that crisp evening when we parted,
Moonlight bound our hearts together
And cast a shadow as a parting gift
Over the winecup we shared as friends.
Autumn winds now sweep across that plateau.

Presented to Daizo Kusayanagi (1924–2002), political and social affairs critic,
writer and journalist, in September 1967. Mr. Kusayanagi had interviewed
the author on several occasions in the late 1960s. This translation, by Robert
Epp, first appeared in *Hopes and Dreams* (1976).

To my young friends

"That person seems to be
   enjoying life
      yet is just and correct."
Thus I would like to be spoken of—
   as a person enjoying the unrestrained
      trust of others
         a uniquely magnanimous person
   as I bring this life
      to a close.

☞

The blossoming cherry
   the rustling bamboo.
The faces of people
   the voices of youth…
Loving all these things
   I tread the path
      of happiness.

☞

I don't much desire
   the ordinary forms
      of happiness.
I want rather
   the magnificent light
      that arises from a lifetime
         culminating in
      the fulfillment of mission.

☞

I have graduated
    the age that dreams
        of a rose-tinted future.
    I have learned
        that the energy of happiness
    exists in the process of living today
        roots sunk firmly
            in reality's soil.

In order to spread my wings
    and soar through life
        true to myself
    I want to avoid
        self-pity and complaint
            even on the saddest days.

A life without laughter
    is like a flower that refuses
        to burst open in bloom.
However intense the conflicts
    of society
        I want to maintain
            my ability to laugh.

With a sense of determination
    and setting forth
        seeing today as a time
            for new endeavors
    I open and delve into
        the book of life.

They say there is much
    fraudulence in the world
        masquerading as wisdom.
    I wish to live my life
        with integrity and grace
            abiding by the principles
            of humanity
        in pleasant conversation
            and meaningful labor.

No matter how long it may take
    to bring the grand enterprise of
        my life to fruition
    I will continue without cease
        and with undiminished passion.

It is fine to doubt
    to struggle in earnest anguish.
But do you end up a mere
    captive of the darkness?
Or do you charge into the dark
    making it the impetus
        for your own construction
            and transformation?
    It is the final outcome
        that matters.

I have just one thing
    I'd like to say:
    To give up
        is to be defeated by oneself.
    Knowing this, I continue to take
        small but significant steps
            advancing single-mindedly
            toward the fulfillment
                of my destiny.

⤺

I hear people say
    they don't fear death.
        I don't want to become
            such a person.
For it is the fear of death
    that deepens our joy in living
        and demarcates civilization
            from barbarity.

⤺

I will live out my life
    as a human being
    who struggles and is true
        to myself.
I have no wish to become
    a person famed
        for character or action
    to whom the epithet
        "hypocrite" attaches.

⤺

I have absolutely no desire
    to be a hero or a genius.
For I believe that
    the most valid way of life
        is one that is steadfast and
            beautifully balanced.

⁀

Rather than live as a
    brief and high-minded flower,
        I want to live
            a weed-like life
                of tenacious vitality.

⁀

The end point of his success:
    a sense of emptiness.
The ultimate goal of my life:
    a friend's high flight.

⁀

Today once more
    I will continue
        the victorious
            procession of life
        sharing the anger and laughter
            of my fellow citizens.

⁀

I will become someone
   who has deeply experienced
      the pains of the world
         and knows its ways.
   For only from this arise
      words and actions
         that are valuable
            incisive and just.

The dawning sky
   a pure white rose
      a fairytale princess…
Strive never to forget these things
   even in an era
      of disordered humanity.

⁖

To challenge others,
   to confront oneself…
We do this because we know
   it is the obvious means
      of clarifying the realities of
         right and wrong
         noble and base.

⁖

I will not apologize
   or attempt to justify myself.
   Because I am confident
      that I am energetically opening
         my path in life
      faithful to my own sound judgment
         and belief.

⁖

There is no dreariness
    in my environs.
There are at all times
    vigorous and lively exchanges—
        the seeking spirit of youth.

Even if my dearest friend
    gave up on revolution
I will continue to advance
    transcending all limitations
        together with the winds of spring
        the winds of autumn
    rooted in the view
        of society and the cosmos
        to which I hold true
    maintaining at all times
        the magnanimous stance
            of a pioneer.

I have no interest
    in passing my golden years
    in some splendid fashion.
    So long as I can anticipate
        with a smile
            the completion of my purpose
        the human revolution that is
            the theme and subject
                of my life
    I will see that as a
        magnificent, glorious
            use of my remaining time.

I know clearly
    how fine it is
        to spread one's wings
    and sail into worlds
        of human happiness,
    how superior this is
        to the desperate, bloodshot eyes
            of the arrogant inhabitants
                of society's upper crust
            as they seek after status.

Even in this humble structure
    I stand on my own stage
        reciting poetry
            in the palace
                of my heart.

Anyone can repeat slogans
    about the dignity of life.
But what degree of humility
    and joy do you find
        in the fated existence
            of your self
    solemnly alive on this Earth
        in one small
            corner of the cosmos?
    That will determine
        whether your life is one
            of imitation or of creation.

Life is a succession
    of painful realities.
But I have built a golden life of the spirit
        beyond the power of
            anyone to destroy.

⤳

While his way of life may be affluent,
    there is much wasted effort
        and needless consumption.
My daily life
    abounds with joys
        and my heart is never
            without employment.

⤳

I am not obsessed
    with the fast flight of time.
Yet in order to construct
    a lifetime of glory,
        pursuing the path of humanity,
    I deliberately focus
        on the fleeting span
            of each passing day.

⤳

Your anguish, I believe,
    is of a still shallow nature.
Read history!
    Placing yourself at the
        juncture of centuries,
    ponder the future direction
        of your life!

⤳

I will live out my life
    with courage to the end,
because I know
    the mistaken fears
        so common to
    a life of theorizing
        and formality.

Someday
    death will visit
        and the time of parting
            will come.
But the bonds I share
    extend eternally
        and I therefore feel
            no deep or bitter
                remorse.

Today has its terminus
    but I will never disembark
        before arriving in grand style
    at a death that culminates a life
        free from regret.

There is no need for
    each little action
        to be analyzed.
I take pleasure in my work
    and invite others to consider
        the entirety of my life.

Nameless and unknown
I will not be recalled
by later ages.
Yet I perceive
that my lights will shine
brilliant and eternal
in the causal history
of my inner being.
And so I have chosen to be
a person of faith
living boldly, generously.

Nothing is more foolish
than to weep for one's fate
and be swept away by it.
Only by maintaining
an attitude of joyfully
challenging destiny
can we transform
the fundamental orientation
of life.

With this one day
that is today
as my touchstone,
singing a primordial song,
I initiate action
that is pure and exuberant
despite the pain.

I want to urge you
  in the midst of days
    of turmoil and sweeping change
  to live out your incomparably
    valuable life
      always finding some time
        each day
      to squarely confront
        your inner being.

    ☙

I didn't choose a quiet path
  lined with flower beds,
    but advance instead
    along this thorny way
  because I wished to create
    a life eternally marked
      by hot, impassioned tears.

    ☙

The sun rises.
  Today once more
    to author a new page
    of my own history
  I set out from home
    silent in thought.

    ☙

What is success,
   or its lack?
I have come to see it
   as the degree to which
      the development of one's
         standing in society
      is accompanied
         by the cultivation of
            the inner life.

⁕

Even if I am called
   uncompromising
      that doesn't bother me
         in the least.
   Everything hinges on how
      I can manifest in society
         not some minor talent,
      but the resilient power
         of my inner determination.

⁕

People often say that I am earnest
   and given to taking on
      unnecessary burdens.
To which I reply:
   No need for worry.
      I have my own plan and
         order of construction.

⁕

Skepticism—
    knowing that it was
        the first step ushering in
            the dawning of modernity,
    I do not deny the heart
        its full range of motion.
It is only after experiencing
    doubtful weeding and selection
            that we can be fully grounded,
        sublimely confident
            in our humanity.

A life of simple honesty
    is good, I think.
But foolishness
    is detestable.
Never forget the simple honesty
    of a tree that rises
        into the sky
    silent and uncomplaining
        in the scorching heat.

I don't want to lose myself
    in the world of abstract thought.
For I know that
    when conceptual abstraction
        goes bad
            the treasure of lived reality
                —that which should be truth—
            gets pared away
                and discarded.

In a dissembling society
    the presence of
        masked persons
    does not frighten me.
I know that because
    I uphold the highest
        and greatest law,
I cannot be caught
    in the snares
        of power and crowns.

⌒

The famous
    are not necessarily assured
        a peaceful death.
The people we are most deeply moved by
    are those who can point
        to the deepest roots
            of both life and death.

⌒

I wish to be someone
    capable of concentrating
        the energies of the spirit.
    But I do not want
        to be stubborn,
            for obstinacy
        shuts out the breezes
            of new awareness.

⌒

If you wish to rebel
    go ahead and rebel.
The question is:
    To what degree will that rebellion
        serve as the rule and rhythm
            of your growth?

Come what may
    I will burn the flame of life
        singing with the sun
            through the daylight hours.
    And on a still and moonlit way
        pausing for a friend to rest,
            I will ponder my meaning
                as a human being.

I have no time
    for world-weariness, nor for flight.
Each day I proudly continue
    my efforts to bring
        the work of self-transformation
            to crystalline completion.

There are times when I am obedient,
    times when I rebel.
There are times of gentle waves,
    times of fierce tempests.
The special gift of youth
    lies in responding to contradiction
        with keen perceptiveness.

People laugh, calling youth
    who sharply challenge
        falseness and hypocrisy
            naïve, "green."
    All the more reason young people
        should charge ahead
            filled with even deeper
                inner struggle and outrage.

Reading your letter
    I was deeply moved, in tears.
    There I found the sparkling light
        of human truth.
Let me also send a letter
    to a friend.
However poorly written
    I will entrust my very being
        to penning a letter
            at once anonymous and historic.

To you I wish to say:
    Live out your life
        with the undefiled purity
            of youth.
    Be someone who
        when commanded to flee
            responds with utter firmness:
                "I will not."

I read books
  and I write.
I happily engage
  in discussion and debate.
I choose not to reject
  even the harshest criticism.
I want to maintain
  a spirit of passionate seeking,
    the ability to respect those
      who forthrightly point out
        my failings.

Self-respect informs me
  there is no need
    to bow before any person.
And yet my head lowers
  in heartfelt gratitude
    for the unchanging wellsprings
      of your friendship.

More than anywhere
  it is in the earnest exchanges
    of struggling friends
  watched over beautifully by the moon
    that our lives flower
      eternally fragrant.

While seeking a way of life
  as a woman of the new era,
I wish to live to the very fullest,
  youthful and true
    to my core convictions.

Even if you are considered
    an ordinary woman
        in your gentleness and beauty
            that should not bother you.
    For you know
        better than anyone
        the ideals and courage
            that lie within.

Looking out
    at the falling snow,
befriended by the plum tree
    in the garden,
        today once more
    I set out to work
        for the sake of
            the vulnerable.

For my own sake
    I wish to bloom
        strongly, beautifully.
    Therefore I strive
        to elevate the scale and scope
            of my being.

The sun is obscured
    by clouds,
        the wind has risen.
But I have
    the promised safety
        and comfort
            of tomorrow.

Always breathing
    new life
        into the home,
    fulfilling my responsibilities
        as its master,
    never falling behind
        the greater movements
            of society,
    I turn with daily certainty
        along the orbit of the sun.

⌒

When a ship moves
    there is the churning sound
        of the propeller,
    waves rise against the bow.
If we remain inert
    we will not meet with criticism.
But having set out on the fated ship
    of religious revolution,
        I will continue to advance
    considering it an honor
        to be washed over
            by waves of slanderous abuse.

⌒

You dance
    on a stage lit
        by brilliant lights.
I run
    in the struggling shadows
        of that stage.

These short poems, written in 1970 and 1971, were addressed to various
individuals as the author's personal encouragement to them. They are
selected from *Wakaki tomo e okuru* (To My Young Friends), published in 1971.

39

Pampas grass

Beyond the bamboo thicket
a scattering of thatched-roof houses.

Someone seems to be playing a *biwa*,
its notes sounding high and low.

Clumps of pampas grass stand tall and straight,
listening in stillness.

Could a prince who gave his life for the realm,
a princess who languished for love,
have emerged from the world of shadows
to take this form?

Have the prince and princess,
who would have been lonely by themselves,
brought with them their many retainers
arrayed in spike-plumed finery?

Fields of pampas grass
will not grow among the bustle and pomp
of the capital.
In their flowing green trousers,
have they come to rest and set down roots
among the mountains,
fatigued from wandering across open plains?

Pampas plumes ready to open!
With your wire-thin legs,
your arms of silver,
your faces of gold,
to whom do you call out
so persistently?
Do you yearn to clasp the sleeve
of one now gone?

The wind blows over the path
of flourishing and decline.
The pampas shed tears of jeweled dew
opening their plumes
in the face of frigid gusts.

Childhood memories—
harvest moon like a painting.
Now, even our dreams of moon-viewing
bring only sadness.

How would the Man'yo poets of old have sung such
    feelings?
How would the Kokin era poets have written of them?

Hakone Road at dusk.
Mount Fuji capped with snow
looms in vague majesty.

But for this field of pampas grass
—like delicately stroked patterns
of gold-tipped brush on lacquer—
these scenes from your lives
would have been lost.

The path of glory and decay
is swept by the autumn wind.

Pampas grasses!
Do you quietly reflect on your
now aged state?
Do you choose to live in high-minded dignity
by roadsides and embankments,
shunning the paths trod by youth?
Or do you live taking in the sight
of those who, in the springtime of life,
flower and rise to new heights?

First published in the book *Shonen ni kataru* (Advice for Children), in April 1971.

biwa: a stringed instrument resembling a lute.

Man'yo: indicates the eighth century when the *Man'yoshu* (Collection of Ten Thousand Leaves), the earliest poetry collection in Japan, was compiled. It was a time when not only the nobility but ordinary people as well freely expressed their feelings in the form of short poems.

Kokin era: indicates the ninth and early tenth centuries, the period succeeding the Man'yo period. *Kokin* is an abbreviation of *Kokinwakashu* (A Collection of Poems Ancient and Modern), an important anthology which includes numerous sophisticated poems by aristocrats.

Hakone: a town in Kanagawa Prefecture, neighboring Tokyo, noted for its scenic beauty.

The people

Like the surging of a vast sea
stretching to the far horizon—the people

Joy, sorrow descending on them
in roaring torrents, yet each day making some little joke,
going their way together, living on—the people

From the beginning
there's been nothing to surpass the strength and shout
    of the people
from the beginning
nothing to outrun the pace of the people's wisdom
from the beginning
nothing to rival the banners of the people's justice

Yet in the past
and today as well
the history of the people and their struggle
has been bathed in tears of suffering and want

A poet put it this way:
"While ignorance and misery remain on earth
we will never give up our fight!"

You dark wielders of power,
can you not hear the lonely sighs
of the people troubled and sickened by you?
Wise ones of the world,
can you not perceive
that a single atom
is bursting with the laws of the entire universe?
Are the masses in their long and distant wanderings
only meek, subservient objects in your sight?

"The people"—
it is a word I love

People!
why do you believe
it is your fate
solely to still the storm of the heart
and be crushed beneath the stones of tyranny?

Why do you not
cast off your ancient chains?
Have you not the right to emerge from the history
    of the dead,
to become heroes of the history of the living?

Blood that has flowed cannot be redeemed
tears that have been shed are beyond recall
Ah, but
do not be silent!
You must not resign yourselves!
You must not grow weary!
To put an end to the refrain of this stupid history
dominated by a handful of men in power,
to silence once for all this pitiful weeping,
in dancing waves of people,
for the sake of the people of the future
you must gain victory!

Now is the time
to ring down the curtain on this rainbow farce
played out by elder statesmen with their plots for power,
the generals rattling their sabers,
the glittering rich and mighty alone
You, looking up to the skies,
roaming the earth,
will be the leading actors on the stage now,
creating as you go a wholly different drama of history

People!
you alone are reality
Outside of you there is no real world

The age will not forget to wait and pray
for the true movement of the people

It will not forget that you alone
are the great sea into which all things flow,
the furnace, the crucible in which all things,
emerging from chaos, are refined
for the sake of a new birth,
and you are the touchstone
to distinguish truth from falsity in all things

Science, philosophy,
art, religion,
all undertakings
must be directed toward the people

Science without you is coldhearted
philosophy without you is barren
art without you is empty
religion without you is merciless

You should look down on those who sneer at you,
not be bound by those who analyze and judge others coldly,
ignore those who hate the earthy smell about you

You who work away in silence,
you with your strong muscles, browned by the sun—
I can hear the pure, rapid beating
of the heart in your breast

I will spend my life exerting myself for your sake
Though at first sight I seem to stand in isolation,
I want to make it my proud and only mission
to fight on and on for you alone,
always in your behalf

I will fight,
you will fight,
fight until the day when,
on this earth,
your rough hands will tremble
and the joy of life shines forth in your simple faces

I will fight!
You must fight too!
Wherever you may be,
holding fast to a steady tempo
today again I fight!

Presented to the members of the Soka Gakkai young women's division on
September 28, 1971. This translation, by Burton Watson, first appeared in
Songs from My Heart (1978).

Weeds

They live
rank on rank of them in their green nakedness
they live vigorously
never flinching from the autumn frost, unbending in will,
through the supple resilience that is their heaven-given nature
they live on in joy

They live   greedily they live
never the least air of gloom about them
to the life-giving springs of the great earth their mother
calling out in answer
multiplying their friends as they live on

In the light of the heavens they live discordantly
giving thanks to the dews and springs of the earth
they live serenely

Sternly they battle with their surroundings
freely they take delight in their surroundings
day by day they carve out a life of fullness
with the drought, the gale, the drenching rain,
the morning dew, the sunset, the stars that fill the sky
they live on, dancing and singing

The burning heat relentlessly torments them,
the parching dryness, when one drop of water is a precious
    pearl,
the desperate fight—
The sudden storm in its madness would destroy them
but though they sway and bend to the ground
their chests swell with pride

The squalls attack, washing them, trying to down them,
but though their front ranks, their rear ranks are swamped,
unenraged they pick themselves up from the water

Waves of ordeal are never easy to bear
Sustained endurance in the face of life and death,
the unfaltering resistance that alone conquers all,
they who know no surrender
they who exude a thriving vitality
and they whose smiling faces never change—
even deserts are a waterside to them
even foul mud is an oasis
even barren fields are a longed-for paradise

And at last there comes to them
a time of rest

Morning dews gently call them to waking
little birds beat drums in the sky
and the light of the sun fills the grassy fields

The crimson setting sun colors them,
from the far edge of the horizon bidding them farewell,
praising them for their day's labor
and they, sitting straight up, sink into meditation

The Milky Way as it flows down the sky
speaks to them each night of dreams,
grieving over the impermanence and misfortune
of history's thousand changes, the ten thousand
    transformations of life

Who is aware of the awakening
of these tiny lives?
Who salutes them from the heart?

They know nothing of hothouses
they would not wish for the tedium of the potted plant
no thoughts of flower shows occupy them
They go unadmired
unpicked—
needless to say no one would buy them

But listen
to their untroubled soliloquy,
to their intense confidence and pride!

"All artifice, all human skill,
seen in the light of the highest value, which is to live,
are mere phantoms!"
that I know is what they say to one another as they tremble
    and sway

"Such elaborate protection
such delicate love
we have no need for"

"We do not fear the gale
we do not grieve at isolation
or resent our fate"

"We leave the nightingale to his plum tree
leave the moon to lodge in the pine
to the willow we leave the spring showers"

"For the nameless
there the mission and the flowering of the nameless
for the wild, that which belongs to the wild
With our own hands
we will open up our own road
This is the beautiful road
of our green existence"

In a theater where there is no applause
endlessly, earnestly they go on giving expression
to the beauty of their gratuitous revels and parades
Ah, their name is "weeds"

How great you are
How sturdy you are
How merry you are

Green friends, who live wholehearted,
come here!
let me share my seat with you

I will watch steadily over your trials
I alone am moved to praise your vigorous truth
I want your form to be
the guideline that governs my whole life

Gazing upward at the flowing stars,
live in your own free way!
If that be the proper path,
then with the elements of your true nature just as they are
keep on forever living as you have lived

Beauty of gregariousness
strength of the indigenous
wisdom that adapts itself to circumstance

This is the unadorned world of the common people
the republican world of the human tribe
this indeed is the yearned-for world of the Serene Light

In this sky and earth from antiquity
endlessly following the rainbow,
as though sprung up from the earth,
the vigor of life!

The weeds, immersed in joy,
today again live their lives
vigorously attaining to a love that is equal, they live
in ranks, forgetting ascetic practices,
today again they live through their lives!

Presented to the members of the Soka Gakkai young men's division on October 3, 1971. This translation, by Burton Watson, first appeared in *Songs from My Heart* (1978).

Mother

Mother!
Ah, Mother!
What a richly mysterious
power you possess!

Mother,
Ah, Mother!
Your very existence
potently generates
understanding and harmony.
You are an unmatched master
of conversation.

In societies poisoned
with spreading gray stains,
in vast asphyxiating cities
tormented by sullied noise,
in a planet bereft
of brightly lit paths
—closed off and
lacking all exit or escape—
you keep us rooted
in the great embracing earth.
Without you
we would end up wandering forever,
without direction or purpose.

Mother!
Mother!
You are simple
and persistent.
You are observant
and uncompromising.
You are honest
and obstinate.

But the image of your face
is the homeland of the heart
for all people everywhere.

The quiet smile of Mona Lisa.
Glimmering Venus...
And yet it is in the ordinary face
of one who has met
all the challenges
of daily life,
this brave visage
eroded and worn
by society's breaking waves,
this small, familiar
and glorious face
triumphant
through all grief and joy—
it is in this mother's face
that we find a beauty
formed by life's history.

Why do people sit up straight
and take account of themselves
before this figure?
Why do they kneel down
before this sublime fragrance?
It is surely due
to the depth and breadth
of your seemingly incomprehensible
yet oceanic love.

Your crystal laugh
brings an inexplicable
sense of ease and peace.
Times without number,
the seemingly contradictory fruit
of your acute perceptions
has brought theory
—lost in the maze

of abstract dispute—
back to the true and focused path.

No philosopher's reasoning
can surpass you.
The teachings of the saints
are to you but variations
on the theme.
There may be many
who exceed you in cleverness—
but only in the realm
of superficial appearance
and apparition.

The proof of this is that
those who find their way blocked
never fail to heed the tones
of your serene and earnest voice.
There they discern the basis
on which to construct once again
their talents and skills.

The afflictions of our age
grow steadily more grave.
In Vietnam, Cambodia, Laos…
frantic cries
of misery and cruelty
echo without end.

Why do people
—all equally human
all equally children—
battle and fight?
What a pathetic destiny
has humankind!
People and their civilizations
have yet to find liberation
from this foolish enterprise.

The horrifying, meaningless
and unjust work of destruction
that is war...
It has its exaggerated
—its counterfeit—
nobility of purpose.
It has its logic
and justifications,
its dignity, honor
and bare-knuckled pride.

But the instinctive wisdom of
Mother calls out
to humankind: Why?
—for the sake of vain medals,
for empty honors,
for the sake of the powerful
and their demands for sacrifice—
why should you allow
your precious life to be taken,
to become another corpse
forgotten by the wayside?
Remember
the crackling warmth
of the hearth.
Sing again the songs
your mother taught you.

Mother awaits
the revival
of those healthful days
when as children,
eyes brimming
with pristine tears,
we rested in her embrace;
the peaceful cradled nights
when she performed
her soul songs for us,

as we dreamed with easy breath
and ventured through fabled gardens...

Mother was always
and at all times
our faithful attendant.
She was a storyteller from the future,
gifted singer, master performer,
potent ally.

I am certain she is hoping
that we will not give ourselves
unnaturally adult airs,
or act with odd arrogance,
but will recognize
and remember
the purehearted origins
from which we arose.
When we do, on that day,
the embattled horizons
will be wrapped
in the dazzling green
of peace.

People may find it easy
to sneer and call this
a soft and sentimental wish.
They may laugh
and ask how
such a fragile prayer
could possibly lead
the human throng
out of the dark, dense,
chaotic woods into which
we have strayed so deeply...

But Mother,
the philosopher, calls out:
People!

Think quietly and deeply.
Behind each of you
is a mother
single-mindedly yearning
for your growth!
The American soldier in Vietnam
has a mother,
fiercely concerned
for her child's life.
The Vietcong soldier
trapped in smoking ruins,
has an agonized mother,
praying for the safety
of her child,
awaiting his return.

The compassionate
love of mothers
knows nothing
of fettering language,
of the high ice walls
of nationality,
of the conflicts and
struggles of ideology.
The love of mothers,
like the narrow path
between lush green fields,
is the one emotion
connecting all people everywhere.

I hope that we can find
the time and attention to cast
even a moment's reverent glance
at the grieving pleas
of mothers.

It is only in the consonant duet
of mother and child
that our deepest human qualities

are polished
and brought to a brilliant luster.
This alone can move us
toward genuinely hopeful progress
and revolution.
At that time,
humanity will come together
in dialogue and trust
as sibling children
of a distant mother
to embark on an enduring march
of unprecedented cultural flourishing.

Mother!
Dear Mother!
It was heartrending
to watch you persevere
through the blizzards of fate,
pitiable to see your repeated
grieved beseeching.

I am compelled to pray
for your lasting health,
that you may live to see the day
when your hopes
and prayers
take wing and rise
soaring into the skies.

Mother!
Mothers!
Never permit the power
of your gentle love
to be isolated,
cut off from others.
Around a blind, unthinking love
the shadows of unhappiness
will gather.
Only the love

of compassionate mothers
linked in solidarity,
with purpose and reason,
will set the crucial,
transforming point of light
in an otherwise miserable
and barbaric future.

This patient labor
of igniting lights
is the only real means
to defend the sanctity of life
against the assaults of the world.

The history of women
has been darkened
by torment,
extinguished smiles,
and pained, despairing tears.
The time has now come
to relegate that history
to an ancient, fossil past.

From now, from today,
with the wisdom and philosophy
that you yourself have gained
through your self-transformation,
bring the sought-for sun
to your home and family,
your clear and cheerful voice in song
to the constricted gloom of society,
the easy performance
and unmatched brilliance
of your songs of peace
to a world that yearns
for spring!

When this sustained
and energetic cadence

reaches and refreshes
the distant shores
with vibrant waves of light,
you, Mother, will preside forever
over an era
of humanity
revived and restored!

Presented to the members of the Soka Gakkai women's division on October 4, 1971. Portions of this poem have been set to music and have become a favorite song within the Soka Gakkai.

Song of the crimson dawn

Ah, the crimson dawn is breaking!
Shining young heroes,
pathfinders, pioneers!
Strike the morning bell
and make it sound!
What are these raging
arrogant billows to us?
Those of wicked intent
will never know glory.
The justice and truth
of the Bodhisattvas of the Earth
is marked by the banner
of the common people.

Let those who are swayed
by censure or praise
fall away and be forgotten.
We will continue to ascend
this bright and regal path.
We disciples have gathered
around our father and mentor.
He urges us to grow
into trees that will tower
high above him.
Ah, the golden glistening
sweat of youth.
Cast a rainbow across
the indigo blue sky
of our vow.

Protect without fail
the castle of kosen-rufu
constructed by our now aged parents.
Rising into the
dazzling light of the far horizon

youthful wings
beat with fresh vigor.
Together singing
the poems and songs
of ten thousand leaves
let us advance.
With proud and dignified step
let us advance,
into the new century!

In November 1981, two years after stepping down as president of the Soka Gakkai, the author was visiting Shikoku where young men's division leaders were composing lyrics for a song. At their request, Ikeda revised their draft and worked together with them to polish the song to completion.

indigo blue sky: a reference to the passage "From the indigo, an even deeper blue"—a well-known phrase from a Chinese classic that refers to a student or disciple surpassing their teacher.

ten thousand leaves: a reference to the *Man'yoshu* (Collection of Ten Thousand Leaves), the earliest poetry anthology in Japan, compiled in the mid-eighth century when not only the nobility but ordinary people as well freely expressed their feelings in the form of poems.

Youth, scale the mountain of kosen-rufu of the twenty-first century

A renowned mountaineer
when asked his reasons for climbing,
said of the mountain:
"Because it is there!"

We are now climbing
the mountain of the twenty-first century,
the mountain of kosen-rufu!

Beloved youth!
Holding aloft the banner
of the correct teaching of the Mystic Law,
bravely scale the mountain
of the twenty-first century,
in this way establishing a truly
autonomous and satisfying
way of life.

To this end,
continue to ascend
step by step, one by one,
the mountains large and small
that rise before us each day.
For the value of a deeply fulfilling youth
can only be found within those
who strive to surmount
the harsh realities
of their own lives and of society!
Only when you dedicate yourself
to pursuing this path
of your own profound choosing
can you develop,
with quiet strength,
a sense of self

inexpressibly expansive
like vast, unbounded plains.
Only then can you live out
the entirety of your life
with unshakable confidence!

Young people who are my disciples!
Live on—
for the cause of the Great Law
that is eternal, absolute and indestructible!
Live on—
to accomplish the noble mission
for which you were born!
Live on—
to ring the bell of peace in the world
and raise the flag of justice in society,
the goals which are our creed!

Again today, the sun rises.
It rises majestically—
in the morning of spring cherry blossoms,
in the burning heat of summer days,
in the autumn of red–gold leaves,
despite brooding skies and blowing snows.
Together with the sun,
let us be bold!
My friends, heirs to the future,
live your youth so that the sun,
refulgent with the Great Law,
rises ceaselessly, steadily,
in your hearts!

My young friends!
Youth is another name for the sun.
Embracing the sun of infinite possibilities,
may you make today
victorious in every way!

It is more than seven hundred years
since the Buddhism of the sun arose.
And now, in accordance with the teaching
"The farther the source, the longer the stream,"
a great, exuberant tide has flowed and spread
throughout the world.

A half-century has passed
since the founding, in 1951,
of the Soka Gakkai youth division,
committed to kosen-rufu—
people of courage and conviction
holding high the banner of
the Buddhism of the sun.
At that time,
some two hundred sixty youth
—gallant young men
and purehearted young women—
gathered with indomitable determination.

Over the course of five decades,
the flow to which they gave rise
has continued to gather strength.
At times its waters
have piled up on
massive rocks;
at times they have risen
in response to storms and downpours;
at times they have receded
beneath the scorching heat.
Yet today this flow has grown
into a grand and vibrant current
of five million young people,
a sustaining force for Japanese society.
Please remember—
the authentic successors to the
Soka Gakkai founding presidents
have all been members
of the youth division.

No one has the power to stop
this majestic and mighty flow!
It will continue to surge on
toward the ocean
growing ever deeper,
ever wider along the way.
It rushes to the forefront of the era,
unimpeded by whatever forces
of authority or sinister obstruction
are mustered against it.

Thanks to the brave and vigorous
efforts of youth,
Nichiren Daishonin's Buddhism of the sun
has come to shine beyond Japan
to illuminate the entire world.
This mighty current
of people practicing the Mystic Law
now flows in
one hundred twenty-eight countries.
As an unparalleled global expression
of the Buddha's Dharma,
it flows jubilantly and eternally
for peace, for the dignity of life,
imparting compassion
in every imaginable form.

It has always been young people
who have led the way in these efforts!
The Daishonin declares:
    If Nichiren's compassion
    is truly great and encompassing,
    Nam-myoho-renge-kyo will spread
    for ten thousand years and more,
    for all eternity.

Our well-ordered procession
of compassion and philosophy,
committed to protecting religious freedom,

has no class distinctions,
or national borders.
We advance so that
each individual may realize
the mission, rights and happiness
that are inalienably theirs.

We absolutely oppose violence!
We absolutely oppose war!
Grounded in these great Buddhist teachings,
gaining the support of advocates
of culture and peace,
we cause expanding circles
of empathy to flower—
beyond borders
across ideological differences.
Because everyone
has the right to become happy.

I eagerly await your growth.
I pray for it with all my heart.
For I know that this
is the only way that
kosen-rufu will advance.
Therefore I say to you:
Never forget that our daily practice
—reciting sutra passages and chanting daimoku—
is the force to propel your ascent
of the challenging mountain of
the twenty-first century
as it rises before you.

"If a person cannot manage
to cross a moat ten feet wide,
how can he cross one that is
a hundred or two hundred feet?"
True to this teaching
you must win, no matter what,
in the place where you find yourself

at this moment!
No one can fail to respect
and be moved by a person
who chants daimoku with all their might.
For daimoku is the very essence
of the Daishonin's Buddhism!
My young friends!
Always bear in mind
the spirit of this passage!
Put it into action,
courageously and wholeheartedly!

Never lose hope
no matter how painful your situation!
Hope is the source of
infinite strength.
To have hope is to have faith!

Human beings possess
unique dignity and value.
They alone have the ability
to generate hope from within.
Over the course of life,
you may at times
appear beaten down.
But never be defeated
in the realm of faith.
So long as your faith
remains unyielding,
convincing proof of victory
invariably awaits!
That proof will be made evident
to all in society.
For the Buddhism you uphold
embodies the principle that
the three thousand realms
of the phenomenal world
are encompassed in a single life-moment.

Young friends
who will live on in the new century!
Grow as leaders
of insight and understanding,
never forgetting to walk
alongside the people.
For the people are sovereign,
and the history of the world
has always borne out their wisdom.

As long as our efforts
enjoy the support of the people
and we maintain faith,
we will continue to advance
limitlessly, enduringly
into history.

Therefore, my young friends,
have pride in the many difficult labors
you have taken on,
become guides and examples
for a life as good citizens.
Consider it your highest honor
to be youthful philosophers of action!

We know that the new century
will require the emergence
of outstanding young leaders.
Those who have
neither faith nor philosophy
are like compassless ships!
The times are in motion,
steadily, inexorably shifting
from an era of materialism
to an age of abstract ideas,
from an age of ideas
to an era focused
on the inner reality of life.
People have begun to see

that the values that bring
authentic happiness
are only to be found within life itself.
Today what matters
is neither popularity, fame nor wealth.
In their wisdom,
the people extend their respect
and seek expectantly for leaders
of genuine human greatness.

In this age of the common people,
the real leaders are those
who have won the people's trust.
We are all equal,
no one is superior or inferior.
My young friends,
I hope each of you
as leaders for the new century
will remain engaged with the people
day in and day out,
living among them,
communicating warmly,
resonantly sharing their concerns,
always breathing
in rhythm with their lives.

I have faith in you!
I cherish high expectations for you!
Without you
kosen-rufu will not be realized!

Enduring every manner
of persecution,
I, too, as a disciple of Josei Toda,
whom I chose as my mentor in life,
have striven to advance
the cause of the people,
the cause of the Mystic Law.
This is the goal I pledged

with my mentor and fellow members
to achieve!
And I declare here
my utter confidence
that all baseless calumnies
will meet with the strict, just
judgment of history.

Where a single, determined individual
has stood up to all the harassment
that power and authority
can bring to bear,
there the triumphant banner
of human revolution
will ripple forever
high in the sky!

My friends,
I urge you—
Never give in to base instincts!
Never be cowardly!
Never betray the trust of others!
For the hearts of such people
are sordid and degenerate.
However high-sounding their rhetoric
they in fact dwell in the realms
of all-consuming desire
and blind animal instinct.

Young leaders!
Direct penetrating insight
to perceive the essential nature
of every issue and incident!
Clearly expose the vicious intent
at the root of the challenges
confronted as we strive
to spread the Mystic Law!

Young champions of the future!
Be people of wisdom!
Be a revolutionizing force!
Do not be foolish!
Never allow yourself to be deceived!
Develop discernment!
These are the requisites of faith—
as the Daishonin states:
"When the skies are clear,
the ground is illuminated."

At its essence
Buddhism is a struggle
between the forces of happiness and misery,
between justice and iniquity,
between the Buddha
and the demonic forces of destruction!
Please recognize this
deeply and firmly
as the reality of your own life.

My young friends,
pass victoriously
over those sad comrades
who abandoned our once-shared faith.
Associate with people who seek the truth
who actively embody
the Treasure Tower in their lives.
Time and again
turn the wheels,
revolve the spheres
of our great movement
grounded in Buddhism.

To lead a life richly meaningful
we require a profound philosophy
in which to place faith.
There is no greater glory
than to embrace this magnificent

Buddhism of the sun
as you live out your youth
with passion and joy!
Here is found
the very essence of youth!

The mountain of the twenty-first century
looms before us!
It is already within sight!
This new century belongs to you!
This is your dawn!
This is your time to shine!
This is the grand stage on which to realize
your fullest potential
and further solidify
all that you have achieved!

May 3, 2001—
Let us aim for that glorious day
when we together reach the summit!
Remember that our struggles
up to that moment
will determine the outcome
of the current phase of kosen-rufu.
My young friends
possessing profound mission!
Aiming for that day,
continue to exert yourselves
in your Buddhist practice
with light and cheerful step!
Give your all each day
in health and high spirits!

All of your exertions
are for your own benefit.
They are for the sake of the people,
for friends who struggle and suffer.
Know that this is the voyage of youth
dedicated to all that is good and just.

Write the magnificent history
of your own life
inscribing it in eternity!
Bold, sustained and energetic efforts
are the only way to do this!
When you confront suffering,
when the way forward seems blocked,
muster courage, dauntless courage!
Remember the many comrades
who believe in you
and in whom you can believe!
Seniors in faith everywhere
await your success!
Fellow members
eagerly follow your efforts!
These comrades are to be found
throughout the entire world!
More than anything, chant daimoku
in order to master
and triumph over yourself!
Do not spare your voice!
Speak out clearly
with the force of a lion's roar!

Remember also
that all of your actions and endeavors
are unmistakably witnessed
by the original Buddha
who surveys the three existences of
past, present and future,
the original Buddha who assures us
that all the benevolent forces
of nature and life
will extend their protection
to the heroes of kosen-rufu.
To have this confidence
is to have faith!

Never fear the slights, insults
or scornful criticism of others!
Such travails are nothing
compared to those of Shakyamuni,
much less the great persecutions
that beset Nichiren Daishonin!
It is only natural
that we should encounter
buffeting winds of opposition,
as proof that we are living
in full accord with the
Daishonin's teachings.
We should consider this
our defining honor.

Noble young successors!
Cherish your venerable parents,
treasure human society.
And realize with pride
that the Buddhist principle
of the white lotus blooming
in muddy waters
applies to the
demanding, swamp-like
realities of human society.
Life in the real world is complicated,
full of contradictions.
But I urge you, young successors,
to confidently fight your way
into the magnificent inner palace
of your life!
Know that limitless happiness and peace
are to be found within
your own heart!

Sometimes you may have to wait,
patiently enduring!
At times, strike out boldly
to secure a stunning victory!

This day will never come again.
Therefore advance undeterred
today and every day.
This is the life of a bodhisattva
emerging from the earth.

Faith means to fear nothing,
to make yourself an eternal victor!
It is found in actions that give rise
to persons of outstanding humanity
who manifest the underlying unity of
people, society and the Buddhist Law.
Society is harsh—
do not be complacent,
do not let yourself be swept away
by the world's ever-changing tides!
Remember that you are the protagonists,
proud authors of your own history!
Do not be misled by superficial appearances!
If you allow yourself to be swayed
by the "eight winds"
of others' praise or censure,
you will have led yourself to sad defeat.
My dear young friends!
You must be victorious in life!

Young disciples
whose growth is my incessant prayer!
Now once more
come together in united striving
as you press forward
on this great unending path!
Advance cheerfully and spiritedly
singing well-loved Gakkai songs—
"The Song of the Crimson Dawn"
"The Song of Indomitable Dignity"!
Countless young successors
follow in your footsteps.
Let us share the struggle

of ascending the adamantine peak
of the twenty-first century!

When you reach the summit,
all the world
that unfolds before you
will be yours.
There is no higher path in life
than this—of a youth devoted
to joyous and
infinitely satisfying struggle
on behalf of the Buddhist Law.
Knowing this,
I entrust everything to you!

Composed in Oita Prefecture, Kyushu, on December 10, 1981, and presented
to the members of the Soka Gakkai youth division. An excerpt has been set
to music. This English translation is based on the version with subsequent
revisions made by the author in 1999.

Great Law: indicates the Dharma.

Buddhism of the sun: indicates the Buddhism of Nichiren Daishonin,
established in 1253.

"The farther the source": Nichiren, *The Writings of Nichiren Daishonin*, vol. 1,
p. 736.

"If Nichiren's compassion": Ibid.

reciting sutra passages and chanting daimoku: the practice of gongyo, the
daily religious practice of members of the SGI.

"If a person cannot manage": Ibid., p. 766.

"When the skies are clear": Ibid., p. 376.

May 3: designated "Soka Gakkai Day," May 3 is the anniversary of the
inauguration of the Soka Gakkai's second and third presidents in 1951 and
1960, respectively. It is often used as a target date for advancing the move-
ment of kosen-rufu.

eight winds: eight conditions that prevent people from advancing along the
path to enlightenment. They are prosperity, decline, disgrace, honor, praise,
censure, suffering and pleasure.

Days of value

If spring is the symbol of vibrant energy,
    fall is the season of intellect.
If summer is the time
    of the passions' wild dance,
        winter is the season of disciplined training.
Thus I have decided
    to pursue my own path
        through each of the seasons
    to realize a life
        of limitless value.

Criticism and calumny
    almost never arise
        from the pursuit of truth,
    but rather from emotionalism, envy,
        calculation and preconceptions.
To see through to this truth
    requires genuine wisdom
        and perception.

Nothing is so magnificent
    so eternal and enduring
        as the power
            of the common people.
    This is because
        no emperor
            no figure of authority
        can avoid submitting to their will
            in the end.

Those who embrace
  a primordial dawn
    in the deepest recess of their heart
      can enjoy supreme happiness.
Even if there are days
  of overcast skies
  winds and snow,
    in this coming year,
  never forget that you
    can make the sun in your heart
      blaze bright.

To live may mean
  a lifetime of repeated struggles,
    cycles of winning and losing.
This is why, in meeting each situation,
  you must forge the capacity
    to courageously persist.
  For this is the material
    of an unfailing crown of glory.

While it is important to win
  it is even more important to forge a self
    that is never defeated.
One name for the Buddha is
  "one who endures."
Young people must never neglect
    to establish this kind of deep
      foundation and core.

A person who
	extols and shares
		the Great Law
	is a person of wisdom
		who offers eternal happiness
			to others.
Such a person has firmly grasped
	the deepest, most lasting source
		of fortune and goodness.

A person of action, practice
	and actual experience
		has made the highest
			human capacities
			their own.
A person swayed
	by theory alone
		has put down only shallow roots
			and will collapse
		with the first fierce wind.
Herein lies the importance
	of constructing one's character,
		one's humanity.

I am very fond of the expression:
	"There is no honor
		without the effort to learn."
When people everywhere
	learn to learn
		each in their own way,
	the world will be filled
		with the brilliant light
			of new vitality, new life.

A person of greatness is one
    who always offers courage and hope
        to others.
The foremost condition for leadership
    is seemingly simple:
        you must possess
            the confident conviction that
                inspires courage and hope,
            a soul burning with
                passionate flames.

The purpose of any organization
    is to enable order, harmony
        and improvement.
    It exists for the sake of people.
        It must arise in human concerns
            and culminate magnificently
                in the service
                    of human interests.

Buddhism is focused on
    the present and the future.
The daily brilliance
    of living powerfully
        from the present into the future
    never captive to a past
        that will not return—
Please know that it is this
    that constitutes a life
        of highest honor.

My mentor said that
  men's jealousy is embodied
    in the example of Devadatta,
    and women's in Kishimojin.
  So many of life's conflicts
    originate in envy.
  Envy ruins and destroys
    people's hearts.
A genuine faith
  lifts people's hearts
    and brings them to flower
      in warm breezes of happiness.

Youth are the future's hope,
  children are future jewels.
Our highest duty
  is to place our trust and expectations
    in youth,
  to cherish children and offer them
    our heartfelt love.
Only by doing this
  will humankind be able to
    bring into sight
      a world where flowers
      blossom fragrantly
        over fresh broad plains.

Amidst the realities
    of a disordered age
  the relation of mentor and disciple
    might be the only
  certain proof
    of a life lived
    —of a human path traveled—
      with profundity and eternity.

A person of humility
  is always calm and composed.
A person of arrogance
  is always tormented by a gnawing
    sense of panic.
A person of composure
  accurately perceives the nature of
    things and events.
A panicked person
  sees everything in a
    mean, distorted light.

Happiness is not something
  that is given to us.
It is found in our efforts
  to generate courage and hope
    from within
  to discover the treasured jewel
    and polish it with care.

There may be truth
    in the seemingly ordinary:
    To have eyes that see
        is happiness,
    to have ears that hear,
    to be able to speak and to walk
        is happiness.
We must each do something
    with these capacities
        and with our lives.
    I choose to do kosen-rufu.

In work, it is important
    to be proactive
        to the point of being criticized
            for doing too much.
Slyly doing just enough
    to avoid getting into trouble
        can end up snuffing out
            more magnificent possibilities.

How we choose
    to make fulfilling
        and free from regret
        the time that is accorded
            equally to us all—
    this will determine
        whether or not we construct
            a life of
                glory, victory and happiness.

A life in which the
　　enthusiasm of the novice
　　　　has been extinguished
　　destroys the foundations
　　　　built in the critical years of youth.
Without this foundation
　　it is impossible to construct
　　　　the joyous towers
　　　　　　of a life of greatness.

Daily, unassuming work
　　neither recognized nor praised—
　　　　this is what matters.
It is people and history
　　that will determine
　　　　when my ability and achievements
　　become apparent to the world—
　　　　and for me, that is enough.

Certainly young people need
　　to be able to think things through,
　　　　but the "go for broke" spirit
　　　　　　is also indispensable.
In the effort to scale and surmount the peaks
　　of a world of unknown realities,
　　　　calculation on its own may lead to
　　　　　　cowardice and inaction.

You, my friends!
   Make the timeless sun rise
      within your chest,
            let it fill your heart completely.
   And let us solemnly pledge
      to each other
         to continue to advance serenely
            along this perfect path
         eyes sparkling, dark hair streaming
            on this great and golden stage
               linking the realms of
                  past, present and future.

Conviction as immovable
   as a sheer rock cliff;
affection as warm
   as the gentle spring;
a clearly defined attitude toward life
   like the crisp and golden autumn.
A heart attentively considerate
   like the sparkling stars
      always seeks to share
         the news and music
         of magic lands
      constantly, without cease,
         even as others rest.

Culture is the flowering
    of an individual
        and of a people.
A movement for culture
    thus constitutes
        a movement for peace.
This movement for culture is,
    more than anything,
        evidence of the effort
            to bring happiness
                to full fruition.

Whatever the reason or justification
    people must never kill
        other people.
People must never kill
    themselves.
The wisdom of Buddhism
    starts from this one point
        and returns to it.

Youth is
    the most essential beauty.
Although people
    may exert themselves
        pursuing beauty
            in its various forms,
    it is folly to lack
        the confidence that
            your youth itself
        is the very pinnacle
            of beauty.

From the ashen complaints
    of youth,
        from the kind of nihilism
    that disgusts others,
        nothing fresh or novel
            will be born.
The true ideal of youth
    is found in a heart that is
        strong, clear and courageous—
    a person brimming with new life.
Such a heart
    will give rise
        to immeasurable meaning.

The happiness of a marriage
    is not determined by its timing.
Many marry early
    only to divorce
        and suffer.
There are many
    who married late in life
        and now enjoy days
            of happy satisfaction.
Never forget
    that marriage
        is not a dream
            but an exacting reality.

More than the top political leaders
   or men of power in
     any country,
the "politicians" who live
   with weed-like resilience
     and wisdom
   amidst the realities of society,
     who can acutely see through
       to the essence of any matter,
   are ordinary individuals,
     the people themselves.

It is fine to agree
   and fine to oppose.
It is fine to criticize
   or to be persuaded.
But for human beings
   the question of purpose
     —to what end?—
       is crucial.
My young friend!
   Never lose sight
     of this one point
   over the long course of life.

To have a mentor in life
   is happiness.
For this above all
   is proof of our humanity,
     and it is here, more than anywhere,
     that we find a life of fulfillment—
       the solid bonds and shared melodies
         of the heart.

Lincoln famously spoke of government
    of the people, by the people,
        for the people.
But today, if we are to keep
    those words from ringing hollow,
        we need a vital philosophy
            —a philosophy of life—
        that will enable human beings
            to live humanely for the sake
                of our fellow humans.

Only those
    who have suffered,
        who have grieved,
            who have been tormented,
    can fully know
        the true depth and brilliance
            of life's wonder.

The summer is newly arrived—
    season of bright sun
        time for training
            and tempering oneself.
If I am going to shed sweat
    I want it to be heartfelt sweat
        with meaningful purpose.

Awards and honors are fine,
　　but even more brilliant
　　　is the dazzling light
　　that issues from within the lives
　　　of those who exert themselves
　　　　at their places of work
　　　　　and in their homes
　　　earnestly, sincerely, true to themselves
　　　　day after day
　　　　　their hearts brimming
　　　　　　with goodwill.

If you lose today,
　　win tomorrow!
To struggle without cease
　　is to possess
　　　the heart of a victor.

In its original state,
　　our Earth is a green oasis
　　　with no need for
　　　　national borders.
　　It is the shared venue for
　　　human existence,
　　　　the embodiment of
　　　　　our common destiny.
The times demand
　　that we address again these questions:
　　　to what end national identity?
　　　for what purpose national borders?

Even if it is burdened
   by many difficult challenges
      I consider support
         for the United Nations
            to be essential.
   For I fear the setting back
      of human progress toward peace
         if there is any further loss
            of sites for dialogue.

              ⌒

If you desire a peaceful death
      as the final accounting
         of your life,
   live each and every day
      with enthusiasm—
Make everything that happens
   an opportunity
      to open and expand
         your state of life.
Exert yourself to the fullest
   in the place
      where you are
         right now.

These short poems appeared in the *Soka Shimpo*, a Soka Gakkai publication for its youth membership, between October 1985 and December 1987.

Devadatta: a cousin of Shakyamuni who, after Shakyamuni's enlightenment, first followed him as a disciple but later, driven by envy, became his enemy.

Kishimojin: a demoness said to have five hundred children. According to the Mother of Demon Children Sutra, she killed other people's babies to feed her own children.

My mentor, Josei Toda

He was a strict teacher.
He was a caring mentor in life.
He was an insightful and strong-willed teacher.
He was an open and embracing mentor.
He was an impassioned teacher.
He was a mentor of genuine intellect.
He was enraged by arrogance and evil intent.
He was easily moved to tears.
He saw through to the essential nature of events.
He was a mathematical genius.
He was a teacher of rock-like faith and conviction.
He was a mentor loyally dedicated to protecting the Dharma.
He had a character as severe as autumnal frosts.
He was always ready with a smile like a spring breeze.
He would pour you a drink with a gentle look.
He brimmed with the dignity of a monarch.
He was at all times a person of highest character.
He was a mentor always on the side of the average person,
    one who never forgot those who struggle with
    the problems of suffering and death.
He was a teacher always ready to share people's worries,
    a mentor capable of both optimism and pessimism.
He exerted himself to the last measure of strength
    when confronting evil.
He was a teacher who grasped a person's essential character,
    an outstanding mentor who brought out the very best
    in each person.
He was a teacher calling on humanity
    to adopt correct views and realize a peaceful society.
He was deeply grieved by the sight of families afflicted
    with poverty.
In one sense, his life was a series of painful struggles.
He took the highest pleasure in other people's happiness.
He hated being thought of as a kind of guru,
    and took pride in being an ordinary man of great faith.

He was a teacher who always cherished the people.
He was a mentor who could perceive
    the deepest wellsprings of a person's life.
He was precisely attentive to detail, careful and guarded.
He had an expansive character, courageous and bold.
In teaching his disciples, he was gravely exacting.
To protect his disciples, he would offer his life.
He was a teacher aflame with passion.
He was a mentor whose life was the embodiment
    of intelligence.

Introduced in a speech at a meeting held on December 25, 1986, in Tokyo.

Arise, the sun of the century

On the thirtieth anniversary of the kosen-rufu movement in America

America! Oh America!
Nurturing endless dreams
of myriads of people,
awakening their frontier spirit,
you are the New World of rainbows,
you are the great land of freedom.

America! Oh giant America!
As the century draws to a close
and the shadows of anxiety deepen,
you are the protagonist and producer
of the drama of world history—
the drama of incessant change.
Your powerful vigor will determine
the destiny of our precious oasis—
our spaceship Earth.

The limitlessness of freedom,
the rhythms of harmonious collaboration,
the richness of democratic experience
and the refreshing spirit of pioneering;
the conviction in autonomy,
the unbounded space,
and the vitality of the people united.

I see those varied and colorful images:
Songs in praise of America
—indeed, of all humanity—
revolve like a kaleidoscope,
deep in my mind.

Since my youth, years ago,
Emerson and Whitman have been

my constant companions.
We have talked together—a dialogue of the heart.
The land they so loved and took pride in,
the land I too longed for,
this haven of hope—America!

Although signs of malaise
can be seen here and there,
your latent energy
like bubbling magma
only awaits the moment of eruption.

Oh my beloved ones!
My precious friends!
Bound by some unfathomable connection
you have come together
a throng of champions, hundreds of thousands strong,
emerging from the earth in solemn dignity.
The curtain rises
announcing the long-awaited start
of a grand drama,
enacted under the banner of human dignity.
The morning bell sounds high and loud
heralding the arrival of a new renaissance.

Ah, some thirty years have passed
since one youth arrived
in this unfamiliar land
where so few embraced the Mystic Law.
Moved by a powerful karmic bond,
he burned with the mission
to cultivate and to accomplish
the noble task of kosen-rufu.

I also trained and encouraged another youth
to set off for those shores.

Together they cherished
the fervent pledge

to dedicate their lives to America
until they became its soil.
Along with many others,
they stood up and forged on
along the treacherous path
bravely opening the way for the Mystic Law.

Seeking to respond to the brave struggles
of my dear friends,
in the autumn of 1960
I took the first step in my travels for peace
in this great land of America—
where all the world's diverse races
are represented.
Twenty-seven years have passed since then.

So many friends were at a loss
in this vast and unfamiliar land,
sick with loneliness
and weeping at the harshness of their destiny.
I summoned the last reserves of my strength
in order to kindle
the flame of courage and happiness
in their dark and sunken hearts.

Time flies like an arrow.
In the intervening quarter-century
I have returned more than twenty times
to this American land.

My friends' faces blossomed in smiles
and small yet precious seeds of propagation
began to sprout;
it is the pioneering fathers and mothers
—the mothers above all—
who with sweat and tears and joy and hope
wrote the history of the early stages of kosen-rufu;
and now, in this land
hundreds of thousands of Treasure Towers stand tall.

In praise of the mothers who toiled so tirelessly
across the great land in the early days of propagation,
the Statue of SGI-USA Pioneers
stands on a scenic hill in Hawaii,
overlooking the Pacific under the brilliant sunshine.

Thus the great river of your glorious history has unfolded,
and waves of compassionate action
to spread the Mystic Law
throughout this land of America
continue to rise.

In order to create a new American history,
my dear friends,
resolve to be people of trustworthiness.

Descendants of the proud forebears
who transformed the pristine land
into a great continent of civilization,
you are bright with optimism.
With unswerving frontier spirit,
your minds are always open to the future.
From its inception, this country
has been a land of genuine freedom.
Filled with the spirit
of democracy and broad-mindedness,
the citizens are linked in comradeship,
and warm goodwill binds you all.

By drawing forth and illuminating
these characteristics of the American heart,
you, as believers of unwavering faith,
participate in the community as model citizens,
the rhythms of your lives unseparated from society.
My precious friends who are to open the road
into the future,
throughout your entire lifetime
always hold firm to this course
in which faith finds expression in daily life.

It is through the certain steps we take in daily life
that a magnificent future
of peace and kosen-rufu
is brought closer.
It is the light of your humanity
that gives it its brilliance.

Do not forget that Buddhism is reflected
in life, living and society.
Take compassionate action for others;
manifest proof as a person valued at work;
be the foundation for happiness and harmony at home
and the light of good sense in society.

Nothing is more persuasive than trust,
nothing more far-reaching in its effects;
the true meaning of our faith
is revealed
in our behavior as human beings.
Since this is so, strive to merit
the praise of others as trusted persons
and models of good citizenship.

Behold the soaring Rockies,
eternal and imposing,
ranged against the skies in dignity,
just as trustworthy individuals
remain unshaken in the midst of howling gales.

My friends,
construct mountain ranges of trust
that like the Rockies
will rise high into the sky and stay unshaken,
a majestic sweep of capable people.

Armed with a philosophy
that comports with the latest developments
of scientific civilization,
possessing a fresh perspective on the future,

resolve to write the new history of America
as people of persistence.

Only with the will, unyielding and indomitable,
to continue to make effort after painstaking effort
can we construct
a tranquil and illuminated realm
where peace and happiness prevail.

Be aware that without
the perseverance to continue,
past glories and achievements and labors
—no matter how great—
will all come to naught.
The greatest quantity
when multiplied by zero
results only in zero.
Buddhism is reason;
thus Nichiren Daishonin states,
"Fire can at once
reduce even a thousand-year-old field
of pampas grass to ashes."

Never succumb
to the merciless winds of tribulation
or to obstacles and adversity.
Advance along this road
with persistence, patience and perseverance,
for this is the path you yourselves have chosen.

Continue to advance
like the mighty Mississippi
flowing ceaselessly along its course
day and night—
in the biting cold of winter,
in the spring when the butterflies dance,
in the burning hot summer,
and in the autumn of the harvest,
always brimming with conviction and contentment.

There is faith like fire
that flares up violently
only to quickly fade and disappear.
And there is faith like flowing water
that continues with calm persistence.

Ours must be faith like flowing water,
ceaseless, knowing no end,
washing away the banks of stagnation and languor.
It must be a vast, eternal river
flowing on to reach the great sea
that is its one and only destination.

There is strength in persistence
and in the accumulation of efforts.
Never forget that it is only
through tireless, devoted exertion
that our faith shines with true brilliance
and a life of enduring happiness is realized.

You are the Minutemen of the Mystic Law,
the Whitmans of kosen-rufu,
shouldering the responsibility
to ensure the development
of the next chapter of worldwide kosen-rufu.

As the first step toward this,
resolve to write a new chapter
in the history of America, your home,
as people filled with a spirit of forward thinking.

It was forward-thinking people
who brought forth
from the immensity of the prairies,
from the boundless frontier,
the luster of culture
and the fresh breezes of civilization.

The minds of forward-thinking people
never stagnate,
for they single-mindedly seek
the radiance of truth and wisdom.
The eyes of forward-thinking people
are free from all shadows,
for they never lose sight
of the distant rainbow of hope.
The hearts of forward-thinking people
know no hesitation,
for taking the initiative to act
is our supreme honor.

The history of America
is one of ceaseless advance.
In search of a new world,
filled with hope for an abundant harvest,
people cultivated the land
never letting up.
The pioneer spirit that drove one advance after the next:
this is your eternal pride—
for the pioneer spirit is nothing other
than the spirit of forward thinking.

For years since my youth
I have cherished the maxim
"Renew yourself, day by day;
each new day, renew yourself."
Thus have I forged on with all my might.

Filled with satisfaction for this day
and determination for the next,
today and tomorrow, consistently,
let us climb the hill of progress and development.

The spirit of forward thinking
is another name for a seeking mind.
For this reason, my friends,
never neglect the source of energy

that nurtures and sustains progress.
Never neglect this source
—the essential practice of gongyo and daimoku—
morning and evening,
sitting upright, reciting and chanting sonorously.
Never neglect to call forth
boundless, endless joy.

Let trustworthiness, persistence and forward thinking
be the badges of honor you wear,
valiant ones fighting for the happiness of this vast land of
    America.
Embracing a clear and unfailing philosophy
of life and humanity,
deeply cultivate the frontiers of transience
to bring into being a land of enduring happiness
filled with blooming flowers and fruit-bearing trees.
For this is the magnificent crown
of courageous fighters for kosen-rufu.

I call on you, every one of you!
You who will water and enrich the arid earth
with the Mystic Law,
you who will determine the future of kosen-rufu,
it is you who hold the key to the future
of our faith as a world religion.
You are the true champions, who,
with deep and firm determination,
will shine forth in the splendid history
of worldwide kosen-rufu.

Walt Whitman writes:
    O soul, repressless, I with thee and thou with me,
    Thy circumnavigation of the world begin,
    Of man, the voyage of his mind's return,
    To reason's early paradise...

How profound and strong our karmic ties!
For we also are aware

of what the great poet sought:
the early paradise
is nothing but the Buddha land
that knows no decline;
it is nothing but the treasure land
that knows no dissolution.

For that cause we stand tall.
A single wave summons a second;
the second, a third;
and the third inevitably
brings countless waves to follow.
With this firm conviction we each rise up,
taking up the challenge
of transforming the tenets of the heart,
to realize a peaceful society.

Behold, at this moment,
the magnificent sun rises,
tinting the surface of the Rockies vermilion,
cherishing the great prairies of Colorado
in its golden embrace,
turning the waters of the Mississippi crimson,
and casting the morning rays of hope
through the windows of Manhattan high-rises.

My beloved friends
who cherish splendid dreams!
A new dawn of kosen-rufu in America has come.
The gateway to our journey
into a future filled with infinite possibility
has opened.

Gallant pioneers of the Mystic Law,
courageous fighters for peace!
It is time to set out!
It is time to embark!

Toll the bell high and loud, again and again!
It is the bell of departure!
It is the bell of daybreak!
It is the bell of happiness!

Let us aim for the summit of enduring happiness
in the new century
shining beyond the vast prairies.
This day, this very morning,
with lofty pride and profound conviction
we have set out on our voyage,
a fresh beginning.

Malibu Training Center

February 26, 1987

Written for SGI members in the United States and presented at a commemorative meeting in Los Angeles.

"Fire can at once": Nichiren, *The Writings of Nichiren Daishonin*, vol. 1, p. 636.

Minutemen: members of colonial partisan militia during the American Revolutionary War. The author often praised their rapid response to danger as a model to the Soka Gakkai youth.

"O soul, repressless": Whitman, "Passage to India" in *Leaves of Grass*, p. 537.

Toll the bell of the new renaissance

To my dear fellow members of Italy

Renaissance!
Renaissance!
How I love the pure
reverberations of this word.
In it we hear the sounds
of humanity, of liberation,
of freedom and energetic action.
From it wafts
the floral scents of art and literature,
the gleaming brilliance
of a fresh new day.

Centuries ago, the Renaissance
arose here in this land of Italy,
in magnificent Florence.
And today
the sun of a new renaissance,
—a renaissance of life—
is rising above
the floral tiled roofs of this city.
How wondrous this procession
of mission-entrusted youth
emerging as from the earth,
setting forth under the banner
of the Mystic Law!

Listen! The daybreak bells are ringing
and the songs of renewed life resound—
in the vibrant city of Milan,
in Rome, aflame with morning light,
on the beaches of Santa Lucia
and in the peaks of the Apennines.
Behold the primordial dawn!

The curtain lifts on a new
and truly human age!

Humanity,
the human being,
this vast mystery
has been variously described—
Man the enigma, the paradox,
the self-deceiver,
the creature of drama.

Humans are:
wise yet foolish, foolish yet wise,
noble and debased, vulgar yet lofty,
drawn to beauty yet mired in ugliness,
aspiring to good but perpetrating evil,
seemingly weak yet strong,
seemingly strong while actually weak…
Striving to become yet betraying ourselves,
questing for freedom yet ending in constraint,
talking of peace and yet ceaselessly
spawning violence and war.

The historical Renaissance
released the vast mystery of
human possibilities
from the fetters of God and Church,
urging a return to antiquity,
to the classics,
to humanity.
This was unquestionably
a moment of human triumph,
a paean to human freedom.
As one intellectual would describe it,
the history of the Renaissance
is the history of the attainment
of self-conscious freedom
by the human spirit.

And yet, dear friends,
I strongly encourage you
to remember that
the attainment of freedom
still lies before us.
For a renaissance
is not so much something
achieved or perfected,
but something that leads to
the further flowering of human potential—
not a conclusion but a beginning.

Without this awareness and vigilance,
the triumph of humanity,
the paean to freedom,
may end up opening
a Pandora's box,
unleashing horrors on the world.

Ask yourselves, my friends:
Has humanity,
seemingly finally free
of the constraints of God and Church,
won genuine freedom?
Have we truly taken our place
as history's protagonists?
No! Surely not!
Has humanity not found itself instead
in a miserable subservience
to systems and ideologies,
to science and machines?
Here lies the paradox of freedom,
the contradiction of history.

And so, my friends,
as standard-bearers of a new renaissance
—the renaissance of a century of life—
continue to advance the cause
first pioneered by the Italian Renaissance—

the attainment of freedom!
Grasp this spirit as a baton
that has been passed on to you
and run with it to the ends of the Earth—
restore humanity
to its rightful place within
history and society!

To this end, my friends
—in order to become truly yourself,
in order that all people may be truly human—
dedicate yourselves
to seeking out the ultimate principle,
the law of life that dwells within.

A Buddhist scripture instructs us
to be the masters of our minds
and not let our minds be our masters.

When people make their minds their masters
egotism runs rampant in the world.
The widespread failure of self-restraint
leads eventually to despotism
and the steely, demon hand of fascism.

When people become masters of their minds,
gardens of peace and happiness surely await.
By appreciating each other's strengths,
complementing our shortcomings,
we can ultimately reach
a concert of humanity
where harmony abounds.

This is why, my friends,
to truly master your minds,
you must never disconnect yourself
from the incomparable Law
that is our source of confidence and strength,
or slacken in its practice.

Be a person of pure and earnest faith
one who "rises every morning with the Buddha
and rests with the Buddha every evening."
Strive to better yourself without cease,
polishing the mirror
of your life both day and night.

Prevailing over the heart's
whims and weaknesses,
deftly take the reins
of the wild, unruly horse that is the mind,
and race ahead, straight and true,
along the grand course of kosen-rufu.
For this is the essence
of our movement of human revolution.

My dear friends,
standard-bearers of a new renaissance,
stand firmly on the side of the people!

The Renaissance
was led by aristocrats
and was thus estranged
from the people.
It was focused on classical learning
and thus unable to reach down
into the bedrock of daily life.
It was highly individualistic,
and thus failed to foster solidarity
with the masses.

Our new renaissance movement
must never be allowed to unfold in this way.

Truth is only found among the people,
in their joys and sorrows,
their pleasures and pains,
their happiness and grief.

Separated from this grounded foundation,
all becomes empty illusion and mirage.

This is why we cast ourselves
into the great sea of the people,
sharing the reality of their lives,
advancing through the swirling currents
of their sorrows and their joys,
striving to transform all
into a surging tide of happiness.

The universal genius
Leonardo da Vinci once reflected:
"Obstacles cannot crush me
Every obstacle yields to stern resolve."

Young pioneers, to blaze new trails
means to endure great hardship!
It is only from adversity
that spiritual greatness is born.
It is only after passing through obstacles
that we can leave
our clear and certain mark on history.

Indeed, intense and painstaking exertion
has been the constant pivot
propelling humankind's
dramatic transformations—
from darkness to dawn,
from chaos to order,
from tearing down to building up.

Think of Dante Alighieri!
One of the greatest minds of the Middle Ages,
he was forever banished from his native Florence
at the age of thirty-six.

And yet, and yet!
His love and longing for home,

his painful anguish,
gave birth to *The Divine Comedy*—
the poetic masterwork
to which he devoted a lifetime
and which continues
to cast its brilliance
across the ages.

I vividly recall the time,
six years ago, when I stood
on a street in Florence
a city I had longed to see since youth.
Gazing at the relief of Dante
that was set in the wall
of an old house,
I sensed the massive,
inexorable currents
of history and philosophy—
from *The Divine Comedy*
to Goethe's *Faust*
and to a century of life...

In May of 1981,
I arrived in this beloved southern land
after an absence of sixteen years.
Calling out:
"Benvenuto! Benvenuto!" (Welcome! Welcome!)
hundreds of young friends,
eyes as radiant as the Italian sun,
met me at the airport in Pisa,
and offered their raucous welcome!

My friends,
I will never forget
the six days of heart-to-heart exchange
we enjoyed in Florence—
to discuss and interact with these young lives
vigorous as young fish
darting through mountain streams,

untainted as freshly fallen snow,
was true happiness.

We stood together,
looking on the Arno
flowing serenely past,
and the ancient bridge where Dante once walked.
On that hill that holds the Piazzale Michelangelo,
I was reminded of my visit to Rome
twenty years earlier.

Standing for the first time
in the Roman Forum
on broken stone pavement
among crumbled columns,
I felt how the history of a millennium
is but a single night's dream
and directed the groundswell
of my emotions into this poem:
    Among the ruins of Rome,
    this thought occurs:
    The land of the Mystic Law
    will never decline or fall.

Knowing that those who
gathered on this hill,
these young men and women
bound in deep unity,
embody the pioneering energy
to build an eternally indestructible
land of happiness,
my heart swelled with joy.

Oh my dear friends of Italy,
I urge you, each of you—
forge overlapping bonds of friendship
with your fellow members,
just like Rossi and Bruno in *The Eternal City*,
a novel I read with intense pleasure

under my mentor's tutelage
in my youthful days.

Rossi was a brave young revolutionary
who lived to realize his ideal—The Republic of Man.
His sworn friend, Bruno,
embraced this cause as well.
Although imprisoned through
the machinations of the powerful,
Bruno's faith in Rossi, his belief in justice,
remained unwavering to his death.

The bonds of trust people forge
through shared belief
are more unyielding, more beautiful
than diamonds.
Let us never forget—
because the Law is supreme,
those who uphold it
are equally worthy of respect.
Because we live
for the noble goal of kosen-rufu,
we can create unequaled value in our lives
and make sublime flowers
of friendship bloom.

Oh, my young friends in Italy!
Strive to be "one in mind"
even as you remain "many in body"!
Let us instill this axiom of kosen-rufu
—one in mind—
deep in the bedrock of our lives
so that we may bring to full and brilliant flower
our unique personalities and distinctive gifts—
the true meaning of many in body.

Bruno continued to cry out,
"Long live Rossi!" to his last breath.
This was a proclamation of

trust's triumph over distrust,
a testament to human authenticity
in the face of powerful conspirators
who direct their oppressive contempt
against ordinary people.

"Long live humanity!"
This must be our cry
as we continue to live and live,
working with our whole being
to usher in an age
of the people's everlasting victory.

Italy! Verdant land
of olive-scented breezes!
Since ancient times,
the sparkling sun of southern Europe
has drawn such masters as Goethe
—so many artists and writers—
to this land basking in blissful light.

Italy! Heart of an empire
that held sway over the ancient world.
In ensuing ages, you experienced
repeated conquest and fragmentation,
and yet maintained
the passion and vitality
of the Latin people,
your proud tradition of
the rule of law.

Passing on the heritage of
Western learning and scholarship,
you have given rise
to towering genius in each era—
people whose prodigious gifts
render lavish bounties of culture!
Italy! The spirit of creativity

that has been nurtured
in your rich and fertile soil!

My love for this land
and her people
knows no bounds.

My heart resounds
with the echoing peal
of a new renaissance.
This is the bell
which you, my dear friends,
strike with steadfast force and will.

Today, the skies over southern Europe
are cloudless to the edge of sight.
The seas ripple and sparkle
a deep ultramarine blue.
Now is the time
to unleash the full force
of this vital spiral flow—
a renaissance of life!
Now is the time
to take unfettered flight
toward the majestic peaks
of a century of humanity!

Spread your young and mighty wings
my precious friends, for you carry
the boundless promise of a better future.
That is the mission
you bear within your heart.
You have emerged from the earth
to rise up and soar beyond
the furthest extremity
of the bright and unbound heavens!

Praying for the success and happiness of the youth
division members and my dear friends of Italy

Soka University European Language Training Center

May 30, 1987

Composed in France while the author was traveling in Europe to encourage
the SGI members there.

the history of the Renaissance: see Symonds, *A Short History of the Renais-
sance in Italy*, p. 3.

"rises every morning with the Buddha": trans. from Nichiren, *Nichiren
Daishonin gosho zenshu*, p. 737.

"Obstacles cannot crush me": Leonardo da Vinci, *The Notebooks of Leonardo
da Vinci*, vol. 1, p. 356.

The Eternal City: a novel by the English writer Hall Caine (1853–1931).

Dunhuang

For Chang Shuhong, director emeritus
of Dunhuang Research Institute

At the West Lake
the reflected lotus bloom
floats on waves of deepest blue.
A crimson plum tree clings
to the slope of Gu Hill,
striving with the autumn moon
to complete the landscape's beauty.

As a child, you grasped your brush
advanced along the path of beauty
your family poor, your aspirations vast.

Despite all difficulties
you reached Paris, metropolis of art.
For ten years of labor and study
you communed with the masterworks
of past and present.

Late one autumn,
in an open-air bookstall
on the banks of the Seine
you encountered a book
that would shape your destiny—
a pictorial record of the caves of Dunhuang
in your far-off homeland.

A beauty transcending
the vicissitudes of history—
chaos and order,
flourishing and decline.
Millennial murals convey
the distant brilliance
of their lights to the present moment.

You returned to a homeland
in upheaval.
After seven years of struggle
—an oppressive season of gray—
you set out in the teeth
of a freezing wind.

Westward, always westward,
into the vast and desolate highlands,
the bone-piercing fury of frigid winds,
the Gobi Desert that turns back all.

There in the midst of this barren
inhospitable ocean of sand—
a world separate, unto itself,
where apricots bloom
and white poplars see themselves
reflected in the waters
of mountain streams.

Your heart and mind
filled with uncontainable emotion—
at last you had arrived,
finally you could view
the Mogao Grotto of Dunhuang!
The towering face of Mount Mingsha
cliffs carved, sculpted into
a treasure-house of beauty.

In ancient times
people explored the Western Region
forging historical routes
from the Chinese heartland
into these endless plains.

Here, armies battled against the Xiongnu;
a general launched
a voyage of distant conquest

in search of the blood-sweating horses
beyond the Tian Shan Mountains.

Camel caravans laden with trade
bore the cultures of East and West;
Dharma-seeking monks
ventured to ancient India.

In the fourth century, as Buddhism
spread eastward from India,
these cave temples were founded,
elaborated and extended
for the next thousand years.

Over decades and centuries,
spanning ten dynasties
the flower of art blossomed
here in this oasis.

But now before your eyes
the sands flow down, heap high—
a scene of overwhelming
destruction and neglect.

Decades have passed
since you rose to the task
of preserving this priceless
cultural heritage.
Inspired by your selfless struggle
gifted youths have followed in your steps.

This trove of ancient treasures
now shines ever more brilliant,
its majesty known to all the world.

Forty-five thousand square meters
of frescoes—painted prayers for peace,
a prodigious desert gallery
of unsurpassed grandeur.

Thousands of clay figures
convey an enduring beauty,
bespeak the glory of nations
flourished and fallen.

Our first meeting was
in the brightness of a Beijing spring
when you were seventy-seven.
Your demeanor reflected
a life lived with singular purpose.
And the vernal light of your wife
who enabled your endeavors...

Five springs passed
before we met again
this time in autumnal Japan.
At the Saitama Peace Culture Festival
we witnessed together
the passionate energy of youth.

The tragic history of war
between China and Japan—
the flames of invasion
cruelly robbed young lives
of their future bounty of years.

Inscribed on the painting
you presented to me, the words:
"Remembering the past
as a teacher for the future,"
transmitting the enormity of your sentiment
to the youth who will succeed us.

Bonds of friendship deep and firm—
the Tokyo Fuji Art Museum,
an institution of value creation,
hosted the exhibition
"Treasures of Dunhuang"

affording a third opportunity
for us to meet and share thoughts.

That day you brought a gift of friendship
from the far-off Mogao Grotto:
The mysterious five-colored
sands of Crescent Moon Spring
and a pair of camel skins...

"The brown camel has
a golden saddle of friendship,
the silver white one
a saddle on which rides
the sincere aspiration for peace."

With this touching message arrived
two stuffed camels which you,
in the mid-autumn of your life
at age eighty-two, had named
"Golden Peak" and "Silver Crag."

Glorious hues blinding bright
adorn the canvas of a life
offered in all purity
to beauty's pursuit.

Ah, someday to traverse
the many-hued Silk Road!
To stand with you in the caves
where you have poured out
decades of unimaginable care,
there to discuss with you
beauty and the mind's adventure.

June 15, 1987

Written for Chang Shuhong (1904–94), a Chinese painter and custodian of the cultural and artistic treasures of Dunhuang, an ancient trading center on the Silk Road. The author and Mr. Chang first met in 1980 and published a volume of dialogues, *Tonko no kosai* (The Brilliance of Dunhuang), in 1990.

blood-sweating horses: a superior breed of horses native to the region of Dayuan or Ferghana in central Asia. Emperor Wu of the Han dynasty sought these horses for use in his campaigns against the Xiongnu nomads.

Like Mount Fuji

Recalling the late Eiji Yoshikawa

The green leaves brilliant,
the wind pure and refreshing.
At last, I have come
to the Hall of Grass and Thought
here to reflect on the noble path
of this lone and lofty literary master.

Here the book I pondered in youth.
There the book I studied with my mentor.
The visage of this man
whose writings have been nourishment
to my heart and mind
hovers and rustles in the stand of plum.

A wave-swept life,
destiny's harsh trials—
at age eleven
your family's fortune ruined,
you set out apprenticed
on an autumn morn.

Your passion to learn
unextinguishable,
you read books, wrote verse
beneath the moon,
the fever of creation
swelling your young heart.

Your ailing father
confined to bed,
the undivided labors of day and night
inadequate to keep your family fed,
you stood alone
gazing at a dawning sea.

Members of your family
scattered like petals
adrift on the waves of the world.
Your sister returned home stricken;
she expired, calling out
your mother's name.

Desiring to bring some ease
to your mother's gaunt and wasted face,
you sought out work.
At the dock where you were employed,
the scaffolding collapsed
nearly costing you your life.

Because of your mission
by some wonder you survived,
returned alive from
the abyssal border of life and death.
Embracing the desire to work and study
you trod the earth of the capital.

Having made your vow as a man
never to succumb to defeat,
you cared not if exhaustion reduced you to dust.
"Relentless exertion
in the face of suffering
polishes one's character like a jewel."

Your only concern your family's welfare—
how, how could they get by?
Apologizing to them in your heart
you persevered in your studies,
a letter from your beloved mother
carried with you at all times.

Changing jobs, time after time.
Studying through the night, year after year.
As a man of courage, seeking and learning,
you lived by the ideal:

"Everyone other than myself
is my teacher."

Pursuit of the path of humanity
deepens with humility;
humility polishes the spirit.
Your cloudless eyes reflected the vision:
"In the common people,
a great wisdom."

There is no night not followed by the dawn.
Bright beams of success
fell on a life of unlit struggle.
You gained fame,
your name finally known to the world—
a world from which your parents had departed.

Where in this life,
roiled by tempest waves,
is a true path to be found?
After four years, your anguished pen
produced *Musashi*,
a novel of seeking and self-mastery.

I, too, read this book
its memory treasured deeply in my heart,
the guide it offers to the young:
"Become a person
as unmoving
as Mount Fuji!"

With an inner vision
of warmth and compassion,
you penned a vivid portrait
of the young hero in history,
reflecting your love
for all that strives and grows.

The nation shattered,
the people grieve;
transient cycles of thriving and decline,
flourishing and ruin.
In Yoshino, the man of letters
sets down his pen, lost in thought.

How can one find happiness
in a world where each feeds on each,
gnawing the bones and flesh of others?
In tearful contemplation of the human folly
woven of ambition and desire,
you wrote *New Tale of Heike*.

Beneath the surge and ebb
of power and authority,
the people in their constancy.
How inestimable, how precious
the fulfillments of their
ordinary happiness!

Though humble and distant
from the palace gates,
the long voyage of husband and wife
—their lives honest and true—
concludes with the strains of victory
in a landscape bursting with cherry blossoms.

The tragedy of human nature,
men intoxicated
with the demonic taste of power...
The solitary figure
of one in meditation
by the banks of life's deep eddies.

All things scatter impermanent.
Is it only the flower of
the Dharma that remains?
Long is the journey of letters

for this seeker
of an eternally enduring path.

"The written word reveals
the person, his measure and his worth!"
My mentor had the highest praise
for your sure and penetrating
insights into history, your fine and vivid
portrayal of each age.

Ah, with what rich poetry
you breathed new life
into the classic of our neighbor, China—
depicting the timeless, majestic flow
of the Yellow River,
river of my youthful dreams!

Never could I forget the
Romance of the Three Kingdoms
read and studied with my mentor,
who taught us to be generals of generals,
who urged us to construct an eternal garden
of ease and happiness for the people.

My mentor shed tears
at the lonely anguish of Kongming,
ever loyal to the grand ideal.
Heart overflowing with emotion
he would raise his eyes to the moon
ensconced in the midnight sky.

Reading of Kongming, gravely ill,
anxious for the nation's fate
should his tenuous life lapse,
my mentor cried out words
that pierced my being's core:
"You! You must take charge!"

Wuzhang Plain, swept by mournful autumn winds.
When I take this book in hand, the paternal figure
of a strict and loving mentor
arises before me.
Romance of the Three Kingdoms—
vow of parent and child, mentor and disciple.

In the life of this great author,
father of deathless masterpieces,
the winds of illness likewise swirled.
But the flame of life blazed only higher
as you worked and worked
to pen your golden words.

At seventy, midway through
The Water Margin,
you completed nature's term,
sleeping with infant-like serenity,
surrounded by the love
of your wife and children.

I had hoped for the time
when we could meet and talk,
but now the admired master
is no longer of this world.
And yet he lives
eternally in my heart.

Standing on the banks
of the upper reaches of the Tama River
lit by falling beams of light,
an infinity of feelings
melt into the waters
and a gentle smile floats upon the waves.

Like the fragrant purity
of wild plums blossoming
in a desolate field,
you lived among the common people,

enriching and enlivening
their hearts and minds.

The soaring summit
of your literary achievement
rises and towers like Mount Fuji.
Ah, may you shine forever
in the burning progress
of the morning sun!

July 1, 1987

Written as a tribute to Eiji Yoshikawa (1892–1962), a Japanese writer
renowned for his historical novels and adaptations of Chinese classics. The
author visited Yoshikawa's former home in Yoshino in the western suburbs
of Tokyo (now known as the Eiji Yoshikawa Memorial Hall) on May 1, 1987,
where he met Yoshikawa's widow, Mrs. Fumiko Yoshikawa. The poem was
later written and presented to Mrs. Yoshikawa.

Hall of Grass and Thought: Yoshikawa's name for his home in Yoshino,
where he lived and wrote from 1944 to 1953.

"Relentless exertion": Yoshikawa's personal motto.

Musashi (Jpn *Miyamoto Musashi*): Yoshikawa's famous novel about the master
swordsman Miyamoto Musashi (c. 1584–1645), first published in serial form
between 1935 and 1939.

New Tale of Heike (Jpn *Shin Heike monogatari*): a historical novel depicting
the rise and fall of the Heike, one of the two mighty samurai clans in Japan
during the ninth to the twelfth centuries, first published in serial form
between 1950 and 1957.

Romance of the Three Kingdoms (Jpn *Sangokushi*): an adaptation of the Chinese
classic, first published in serial form between 1939 and 1943.

Kongming: style name of Zhuge Liang (181–234), chancellor of the state
of Shu Han during the Three Kingdoms period in China. Recognized
as a great military strategist and accomplished scholar and inventor. An
expedition to conquer a hostile neighboring state, Wei, reached a stalemate
at the Wuzhang Plain where Zhuge Liang became seriously ill. Knowing his
sickness was fatal, he was tormented by the prospects for the battle and the
future of his country.

The Water Margin (Jpn *Suikoden*): an adaptation of the Chinese classic on
which Yoshikawa was working at the time of his death, first published in
serial form starting in 1960.

The lion's land, Mother India

To the youthful prime minister of India, Rajiv Gandhi

Eternal rivers, the Ganges and the Indus,
twin primeval flows
changing, yet unchanged.
And India herself
existing magnificent and serene
from time without beginning.
Nature, at times benevolent,
at times punishing.
The works of man too,
confined by and rising above history.

India!
Land of variegated nature,
diverse peoples,
a great secret
hidden in your breast.

India!
Land of the spirit.
Since ancient Vedic days,
deep contemplation and broad faith
have flowed from some ceaseless inner source.

And living there, one family,
consecrating their constant toil
to the nation…

When Western imperialism was
at its height,
your grandfather, Jawaharlal Nehru,
in shared struggle
with the great mentor, Mahatma Gandhi,
led the people toward sovereignty,
completing the great work of independence.

Embodying the essence of East and West,
he devoted the energies of his intellect
—his life itself—
to the people.
In the prime of life
he willingly endured
arrest and imprisonment
countless times.

His spirit remained free
even in confinement.
He wrote letters
to his beloved only daughter—
later celebrated as the book
Glimpses of World History.
Profound historical insight,
an abiding trust in humanity
found expression in
these remarkable letters—
his literary bequest to mankind.

Daughter Indira grew
to be his inseparable aide and companion,
inheriting this legacy of leadership.

Cherishing in her heart
his will to realize
the peace of the Middle Way,
this decisive woman of action
set herself to the task
of creating India's future,
pressing forward through
trying and turbulent times.

But, tragically,
this great woman leader
fell prey to an assassin's bullet.

Hearing this,
my heart was rent with grief
and apprehension
for the people's future.

But mother Indira
had already raised
a young lion
from the rich Indian soil.

Rajiv Gandhi,
emerging from the depths
of an unendurable sorrow,
burning with great compassion
and sense of mission,
the young captain set out
among raging waves
into the starless night,
heading for the shores
of a new and dawning century.

On a late autumn evening in 1985,
one year after Indira's passing,
I met for the first time
this youthful prime minister
at the government guest house in Tokyo.
Intelligent face exuding courage
and bearing the signs of deep thought,
manners gentle and refined,
the composure born of modesty—
In your bright and piercing glance
I read the scale of your confidence
and the depth of your responsibility.

I exalted in the sight
of this young lion,
took pleasure in our quiet
yet animated discourse
on the themes of peace and youth

in the world at large
and in India in particular.

It concerns me even now—
that the diversity of race,
language, religion, the land itself
may erupt into storms of violent conflict,
that yours will be
the difficult task
of surmounting
the stubborn walls of regionalism,
that there may be times
when thick fogs slow the nation's progress
toward her plotted economic goals.

Yet I believe,
I continue to believe
that with a wise hand at the helm
—in tune with the times
and sensitive to the people's desires—
India will ply through
the angry waves
that rise before her,
that she will navigate
the maelstroms of confrontation
to make her way to broad sea plains
aglitter with the gold and silver waves
of true happiness.

In India's rich heritage
is the tradition of wisdom (*jnana*)
the great way of devotion (*bhakti*).

The Buddha, born in India,
perceived the eternity of life and
gave rise to a teaching of great compassion.

There is also the ancient example
of King Ashoka
whose enlightened rule,
illumined by the Buddha's mercy,
brought peace and prosperity
to the people's lives.

In Nalanda
was built a Buddhist university
where the mind's brilliant treasure
shed its light on lands many and afar.

This rich spiritual soil
also gave birth to
the master poet Tagore
who praised in song
nature's vastness and
the inner life of man.

Also nurtured by this
vital native force
was that great soul—
father of India, Mahatma Gandhi,
who advanced the cause
of nonviolence.

It was your grandfather,
following in the footsteps of Mahatma,
who won the respect and love
of the people.

Behold them now
seven hundred million strong—
where can they quench
their thirst for a life of true happiness?
What can call forth
harmony from the mutually opposing forces,
and the best from each form of diversity?
What can instill in all

respect for the inviolable
sanctity of life?

From a single droplet
deep in the Himalayas
flows the broad Ganges.
Likewise, the wellspring of a new
and united humanity,
bound by heart-to-heart dialogues,
is to be found in your country, India.

Rajiv—
I see you in the predawn dark
walking, lost in thought,
on the banks of the Ganges
so loved by Nehru,
on the paths of resolute action
forged by Indira.

The resonant melody of consensus—
this is the music
that is yours to make.
This is the art
that will be rejoiced
by man and nature alike.

Oh India—
Cradle of Buddhism!
I offer you
my deepest thanks,
my deepest prayers—
May all happiness be yours!

    Oh soil enfolding
    the stone on which
    I engraved my youthful pledge,
    Buddh Gaya!
    Since then
    throughout my travels

in many lands
you have never left my heart.
Namaste.

July 17, 1987

Written for Rajiv Gandhi (1944–91), prime minister of India (1984–89), and presented to him through the Indian Embassy in Tokyo. The author had met with Prime Minister Gandhi in November 1985 in Tokyo during the latter's official visit to Japan.

Ashoka (*c.* 304–232 BCE): the third ruler of the Indian Maurya dynasty and the first king to unify India.

Rabindranath Tagore (1861–1941): Indian poet, playwright and educator.

Buddh Gaya (Bodh Gaya): the site where Shakyamuni Buddha is said to have attained enlightenment. The author visited the site in 1961 during his first overseas trip in Asia.

Youthful country with a shining future

To my dear friends in Malaysia

Malaysia, Oh Malaysia!
Country of unbounded future,
youthful land brimming
with the spirit of construction.

The sun with its rays
of courage, righteousness and hope
rises again today
over the rich verdancy of
your proud capital, Kuala Lumpur,
with its tall ranks of skyscrapers.
The air is so pure and refreshing
under the piercing rays of the sun—
land of endless summer,
each new day is filled
with energy and vitality.

Multihued flowers
sway in the breeze
against a sea of green,
exchanging gentle floral smiles
with the *bunga raya*,
noble queen of flowers,
shining in scarlet
majesty and splendor.

The tropical sun
instantly embraces
the thick green forests
harboring unknown vital depths.
The leaves of rubber trees rustle
as they produce their traditional bounty
and palm trees rise straight and proud
on shores lapped by silver waves.

Asia was long derided as a region
of chaos and stagnation,
but here in Malaysia one finds
the will, the passion and the energy
of nation-building—
the stir of Asia rising.

Looking back on history,
for centuries Malaysia was a place
where diverse peoples and civilizations
encountered and mingled.

With enterprising spirit
youths set out on the ocean's vastness,
their boats laden with people,
laden with civilization.
Malaysia has been a bridge
transmitting the cultures of
continental Asia to the southern islands,
a maritime crossroads
linking East Asia, India and Europe.

Sadly, this strategic importance
of your sea lanes made you the target
of encroachments by the great powers.

In the fifteenth century,
the ancient capital of Malacca,
with its fine natural harbor,
was bustling with the ships of East–West trade,
reaching heights of prosperity.

Then the tentacles of
the imperial powers,
seeking control of Oriental trade,
reached out for this city.
At the beginning
of the sixteenth century, it fell,

changing hands again and again,
as fortunes twisted and shifted.

Foreign control extended to
the entire peninsula.
Monopolies of tin and rubber
based on the dominance of monoculture—
later this same colonial economy
would give rise
to a multiracial nation.

Freed finally from colonial control,
Malaysia took her fledgling steps
down the path of independence
three decades ago, in 1957.

A nation in the bloom of youth!
You kick the springboard with strength
as you leap toward the new century.

Abundant resources—
you boast the world's top production of tin,
as well as plentiful resources
of rubber, petroleum and palm oil.

The richness of culture—
a swirling mix of cultures,
East and West, Chinese and Thai,
Indian and Arabic
—even distant Europe—
were gathered to you
by the maritime trade routes.

Diversity of peoples, resources and cultures—
diversity holds unlimited possibilities,
and foretells a great future of unfolding plenty.

The sinuous twisting
of the dense, layered forest—

here nature's mysterious power
brings forth vegetative life
in hundreds, thousands of species.
Uncountable trees and flowers,
each in its own way
choosing its place, its time,
manifesting its unique self,
exchanging greetings,
together thriving and luxuriant.

Many diverse species,
coexisting, vying,
together form a wondrous organic whole.
The "harmony of diversity"—
this guideline of yours
is the source of creative energy,
whether in nature or in human society.

Imagine a child's top with seven colors
—red, blue, yellow, green... even purple—
spinning faster and faster.
The colors blend and merge,
approaching one single
yet infinitely beautiful tone.

The colors of this spinning top
are the diversity of nature and society,
and the final single tint
is the mystic beauty
of harmonized diversity.

And the top's rapid spin—
this, my dear Malaysian friends,
is your spirit of construction;
your resolve to win;
your unflagging, committed efforts,
continuous from yesterday to today,
from today toward tomorrow.

And now, throughout Kuala Lumpur,
the growling engines of cranes
and the song of hammers building
reverberate and echo.

So young and full of vigorous energy
is this rapidly transforming metropolis!
It is this that reminds me of a top that,
while throwing out its sharp whine,
stands firm and unmoving.

Malaysia, land of youth!
Malaysia, land of the future!
It is youth who will shoulder
your unbounded future;
more than anything,
their vigorous growth
contains the promise
of a flourishing tomorrow.

Youth, with little but its infinite promise,
is the earth in which lie hidden
unknowable prospects,
brilliant jewels of ability,
inexhaustible mines of golden creation,
and immeasurable sources of power.
It takes a hundred years to raise people;
indeed, my young friends,
a great tree does not become so overnight.

Extend your roots
deep into the unseen soil,
ceaselessly absorbing nutrients,
growing and learning without pause,
without giving up.
The long years of untiring effort
will shape you into a great tree
that soars into the sky,
stately and unmoving.

My young friends!
Advance with the sun in your hearts,
move forward with pride and dignity.
Young trees grow into great ones
when bathed in showers of sunlight.

The sun does not shine, though,
on those who resent their surroundings,
who are caught up in the past,
or who hide themselves in shades of sorrow.

Stride each day
down this broad and royal way,
smiling radiantly,
conversing with the sun.

The hardships of youth
are the nutrients of future growth;
no tree will grow to greatness
without adversity.
Hardships are another name
for training;
they are precious "treasures of the heart,"
as they make possible your future flight.
My young friends, be altruistic,
courageously taking on hardships,
sharing friends' pains and sorrows,
serving people and society.

My dear Malaysian friends,
our faith finds expression in daily living;
it does not mean chasing after phantoms
removed from the realities of life.
Nor does it mean having to fit yourselves
into a special mold
that is different from other people.
The brilliant light revealed
as your true self shines naturally from within,
in the home, the community,

the workplace;
as you are genuinely admired and trusted;
as you contribute to the peace and welfare
of society.
This is the true meaning of faith;
this is the path
of "faith manifests itself in daily life."

For this reason also
you should develop yourselves,
polishing your character
for the role you will play
in the twenty-first century—
the "rainbow century."

A person of character
is a person of compassion.
Maintain, as the Daishonin says,
"a smiling countenance at all times."
Real compassion does not depend
on the other person.
Just as the sun sheds its light
equally on all,
the compassionate person,
with a broad and open mind,
an unshakable state of life,
can love, comfort and embrace
any person.

Good character is an expression of good sense.
My mentor used to say,
"Be sincere and never use violent language;
always use reason in guiding people."
The world of faith is the world of willing consent.
People are not convinced
by the force of authority, nor by rank.
The unparalleled persuasiveness
of Buddhism, made manifest in your life,
in sensible words and conduct,

has a power that will leave
no person unmoved or unconvinced.

Character is the product of perseverance.
When I met last fall in friendly talks
with Vice-Chancellor Royal Professor Ungku Aziz
of the University of Malaya,
he shared with me his desire that the young sapling
of Malaysian culture will grow into a great tree.
He also spoke of the importance
of patience and of never giving up,
of carrying through to the very end.
His sagacity reminded me
that a profound knowledge
of the world's ways
is always consonant with Buddhism.
Never tiring, never fearing
persevering through all,
looking always for the light—
the true path of humanity
is also the true path of faith.

Ah, what mystic bonds we share!
What unfathomable mission
you possess!
My dear friends,
you have emerged in this land
of beautiful nature,
embracing in the depths of your lives
the mission to realize
its magnificent development.

On the magical island of Penang,
on Ipoh, land of tin,
on Kuantan, home of the green sea turtle,
in the state of Sabah, at the foot of Mount Kinabalu,
I see your smiling faces.

My friends,
true to your pledge
you have striven wholeheartedly
for the happiness of people,
for the peace of society,
for the sake of the country you love.

You gather joyfully
in the treasure castle
of a new culture
and proclaim your departure
on to the next stage.

Filled with emotion,
I offer my praise, my felicitations,
as you are about to embark—
May happiness, glory and victory
crown the future
of my courageous friends!

The mountains of the new century
are bathed in the radiant hues of dawn;
flowers tremble in the gentle breeze;
the roar of a silver waterfall
echoes through the trees,
announcing your departure.

Dear friends!
Baskets laden
with the fruit of happiness,
and a cheerful song of hope upon our lips,
let us commence our proud journey!

Unfold great wings of hope within your hearts
and soar into the future,
toward the new century,
like the beautiful bird of peace
crossing the boundless sky.

Like brightly colored butterflies
dancing gracefully through the air,
let us also dance in the floral pastures
of lives of good fortune,
creating an indestructible paradise of peace
here in Malaysia.

Across the blue ocean plains
resounds the crash of joyful waves,
playing a prelude
to Malaysia embarking.

Youthful country with a shining future,
Malaysia!
Land festooned with green,
paradise of culture,
beautiful Malaysia—
may eternal prosperity be yours!

Shangri-La Hotel, Kuala Lumpur, Malaysia

February 5, 1988

Presented to the members of the SGI in Malaysia on February 5, 1988, the
day the author arrived on his first visit to the country.

bunga raya: hibiscus, the national flower of Malaysia.

"faith manifests itself in daily life" (Jpn *shinjin soku seikatsu*): a Buddhist
principle emphasizing the importance of striving to manifest one's faith by
making a tangible difference in one's daily life and community.

"a smiling countenance": trans. from Nichiren, *Nichiren Daishonin gosho
zenshu*, p. 1107.

Be an eternal bastion of peace

To my dear friends of Okinawa

The sun burns passionately
in the blue skies,
coral-reefed oceans sparkle an emerald hue.
White and silver spray dances in the distance.
The bright red blossoms of the coral tree
adorn the seashore with their smiles.

Okinawa—
land of beautiful seas!
Waves gently washing white sand shores.
Sunbeams pierce waters utterly clear,
illuminating the deep seabed.
The darting dance of colorful fishes
invites us to visit the fabled palace
of the dragon god.

Mother sea—
giving birth to and nurturing
all forms of life,
blessing us with rich abundance.
Ocean paths—
transporting friendship and culture
from afar.

At times the ocean
rages and seethes.
But in the peaceful solemnity
of morning,
it becomes once more
a smooth and silvery mirror.
With cool sunset breezes,
it spreads bands of gold.
And with giant arms,
strong and gentle,

it wraps and braces
people's hearts.

The people of Okinawa
have their special term
—*kariyushi*—
to celebrate the ocean's plenty.
At all times, Okinawa has been one
with the beautiful ocean.

I sing of Okinawa,
am filled with love for Okinawa,
weep for Okinawa...
In Okinawa
I hear the tide-sung songs
of the people's joy and triumph.

Here the Ryukyu Kingdom flourished.
Since ancient times,
Okinawa has been redolent
with the blossoming of its
unique native culture.

The open and generous hearts
of a seafaring people
who rode the raging waves
with fierce courage
to reach the shores of
China and Southeast Asia
as Okinawa became
the vital crossroads
in a great era of trade.

Unflinching in your love of peace,
deeply loyal in friendship,
kindhearted,
you rescued and nourished
untold numbers of foreign friends

who came shipwrecked
to your shores.

But the muddy currents of history
swept down upon
these lovely coral islands,
and you were yoked
by oppressive rule.
Groaning under the cruelly exacted
burden of annual tribute,
when storms or drought
brought famine,
people endured by eating the
starchy extract
of the toxic cycad plant.

Time passed and flowed,
and now you faced
the scourge of global conflict
as Okinawa became a sacrificial pawn
in the defense of the Japanese mainland.
Green mountains and streams
were stained with blood,
the agonized cries
of an earthly hell
filled the air.

Innocent people fled in terror
through the flames of war.
The "Typhoon of Steel"
raged on without pity.
Artillery fire destroyed hills,
pounding and pulverizing the land.
Flames reached deep
into trenches and caves,
incinerating all within—
soldiers, mothers, students,
young girls, infants...
People were ordered

to commit mass suicide.
In all, some two hundred thousand
precious lives were lost.

Further suffering followed
in the wake of Japan's defeat,
as Okinawa became a land
administered by the United States,
a land of military bases.
Over these islands,
missile batteries
cast their black shadows.
From here bombers took off
for Vietnam.

Ah, Okinawa!
Islands of pain, subjugation and lament!
You who, more than anyone,
have endured in torment,
have the right, second to no one,
to live in happiness.
Indeed, until these islands
are peaceful and secure,
our world cannot be
truly at peace.
Until blossoms of joy open here,
the world will not know
genuine happiness.

We must turn the page
on the tragic history of the past,
transforming the destiny
of this place.
And we must
without fail
create here in this haven,
on these islands,
a noble community
where ordinary people

live lives of lasting
happiness and joy.

On July 16, 1960,
some two months after my inauguration
as president of the Soka Gakkai,
I set foot on Okinawa.
It was seven hundred years to the day
since Nichiren Daishonin presented
to the ruling authorities of Japan
his treatise—
"On Establishing the Correct Teaching
for the Peace of the Land."
I was filled
with deep and overwhelming emotion
as I engraved the will of the true Buddha
deeply in my heart.

The following day, July 17,
the first chapter
of the Soka Gakkai in Okinawa
was formed.
This was the date,
three years earlier,
when I was released from jail
having been arrested on spurious charges—
the machinations of authority
seeking to contain a rising
popular movement for peace.
What wondrous, unfathomable
karmic bonds I share
with this land of Okinawa!

At the celebration of
the chapter's launch,
more than ten thousand friends,
all Bodhisattvas of the Earth,
gathered at Naha Commercial High School—
their sunburned faces

suffused with broad smiles,
the deep black pupils of their eyes
burning with the determination
to fulfill their vow.

I called out,
voicing our mission
as Soka Gakkai members.
And I pledged deeply, deeply
in my heart:
I will give my all for Okinawa—
whatever the cost,
whatever the effort,
I will blaze the path of kosen-rufu
for the eternal happiness and peace
of my friends.
This I will accomplish without fail!

Here a new page in history was penned
as the burning morning sun
of Okinawa kosen-rufu
lifted into the sky.

On that occasion,
I visited the sites of battle,
the terrible tragedies of war.
At the Himeyuri Monument—
the Monument to Student Soldiers—
I pressed my palms together
in deepest prayer
and renewed my vow
for a world without war.
And I determined
that I would write the first words
of the novel *The Human Revolution*
here in Okinawa, the land that had
suffered most grievously
the horrors of war.

Striving to break the spell of fate,
you emerged
from the agonized caves
and tragic chains of the past.
Eyes fixed resolutely
on the star-filled skies of the future,
you rose up to build anew
your beloved homeland.

Proudly singing
"The Song of Okinawa Youth,"
raising the banner
of the true teachings
to realize the peace of the land,
you remained undeterred
by hurled stones of prejudice.
Your warm smiles and earnest discourse
brought down the walls
of attachment to custom
as you strode forth powerfully
to share the teachings
with others.

Ten months after this swelling tide
of kosen-rufu arose,
I again visited Okinawa.
Like a dragon
rising into the heavens,
the membership had expanded
to become a general chapter.
Waves of smiles and joy
washed the shores of these islands.

The following year
I traveled again to Okinawa,
ready to pierce and penetrate
the hardest bedrock—
to drive the pilings deep,

to lay an indestructible foundation
of eternal flourishing.

On this occasion
a castle of the Buddhist Law,
a base of peace, was opened,
becoming the pivot
around which the gears of kosen-rufu
began to turn,
with a great, rumbling roar.

The time was ripe,
the time had come,
and on December 2, 1964,
I took up my pen to begin writing
The Human Revolution
in a room in our Okinawa headquarters.

Scenes of war's atrocity
crowded my mind—
the unvoiced cries,
the unattended wails
of crimeless people,
consumed by the flames of war.

Entrusting to my pen
a vow for peace
in Okinawa and the world,
I wrote—
     Nothing is more barbarous than war.
     Nothing is more cruel.
This is the cry that Okinawa
—your fervent yearning for peace—
aroused in my heart.

     A great human revolution
     in just a single individual
     will help achieve a change
     in the destiny of a nation

and further, will enable a change
in the destiny of all humankind...
Manifesting this principle
here in Okinawa—
this is the mission and responsibility
that you and I share
in this world, in this lifetime.

Human revolution is a fierce battle
waged within,
between our Buddha nature
and our demonic aspect.
Thus we must struggle valiantly,
triumphing over our weaker selves.
To this end, I urge you—
make each irreplaceable day of faith
replete with unhesitating,
uncompromising courage!

Quietly ask yourself
if it isn't in fact true
that each of us,
before being defeated
by an external adversary,
is first defeated
by ourselves.

The weak in spirit,
the cowardly,
even before wandering reluctantly
at the foot of the wall
that towers in their path,
shrink first before the sight
of their own shadow.
Terrified of illusory figures
of our own creation,
we are defeated by the bandits
that infest our heart.

The strong-willed,
the courageous,
are always the conquering masters
of their own minds.
Thus, they fear nothing,
remain unbowed, unflinching.
Whatever occurs,
they live in perfect accord
with the Daishonin's counsel:
    The wise will rejoice while the foolish will retreat.
They know that they themselves
are like that brilliant monarch, the sun.
Shooting bright beams
through the clouds
of impermanence and change,
they advance, heads held high,
into the raging tempest.

Ah, dear friends!
The memories we share
of working together for kosen-rufu
sparkle like lapis lazuli!
Nothing will erase
the fond and treasured knowledge
of the days we have spent together.

That day when,
drenched with sweat
under a scorching sun,
we loaded blocks of ice
into a car and drove about
to meet and encourage friends.

That time when,
committing our eternal vow
to a commemorative photograph,
we marked a new departure
with courage and energy.

The visit that day
by friends from Kunigami,
the earnest sincerity
of the young girl
who presented me with a spray
of cherry blossoms.
The smiles of my Koza friends
determined to construct
the "defenses of peace"
in a town dominated by a military base.

On Ishigaki Island,
I visited the seashore of Yadopike…
With shouts of joy
we together tugged and pulled
the fishing net ashore.
Friends in Yaeyama
with whom I danced,
headbands wrapped above our brows.
The sea turtle that emerged
from amidst the waves
to offer a celebratory dance
to lasting prosperity.

The friends of Miyako who greeted me
having passed through fierce storms.
The dance of joy that erupted and spread
to welcome the arrival of spring
at the Hirara community center.

And the many times I enjoyed conversing
with my young friends,
bathed in clear moonlight—
young friends to whom I entrust
the ongoing work
of the rising generation.

Sharing thoughts
with members of the university group—
your sparkling eyes,
the purity of your hearts.
Our spirits leapt
to the adventure of life,
and we gazed together
at the soaring peaks of the new century.

Yes, it was in Okinawa
that the first high school group was formed
leading the way
for the whole country.
Cherishing hopes for youth,
pouring my entire being into youth,
I have embraced young people,
fostered and trained them.
I have done so
because it is my faith and prayer
that real leaders of the common people
will emerge one after the next
from this land of Okinawa.

And now, having triumphed
over all sorrow and self-pity,
you have transformed
the flames of outrage
smouldering in the rock holes
of the lesser self
into the unparalleled joy
of propagating the Mystic Law,
as you have opened
a broad new path of peace.

The Shattered Coral Islands
was the first volume of
the antiwar publication series
compiled by the youth division.
Your precious, painstaking efforts

revived the promise to eliminate war
that was fading from awareness
over the horizon of years.

Likewise, an exhibition
conveying the realities
of the Battle of Okinawa
and of the atomic bombings
of Hiroshima and Nagasaki
forged bonds among those
who had experienced
the most unspeakable horrors of war,
building new networks
of solidarity for peace.
Further, the exhibition of drawings
from the Battle of Okinawa
planted seeds of empathy
—the basis for humanity's peace—
deep in the hearts of all,
spanning generations
from infants to the elderly.

The stirring, powerful
peace culture festival
held at the Okinawa Athletic Stadium!
The rain,
which had started falling earlier that day,
grew heavier by the moment.
The sight of you performing
was at times obscured
by veils of mist and rain,
and yet you continued
without the slightest hesitation.

Friends who braved
cascading torrents of rain
as you ran out onto the muddy field.
You danced a widening dance of joy,
smiling unperturbed,

your faces wet—
with raindrops or with tears.
Yours was the *kuicha* dance
traditionally performed
as a prayer for rain!

That day I was moved
to offer this poem:
    The courageous cry
    of thirty thousand
    raised as a prayer for peace
    moves the heavens and
    brings down this silver rain.

Undaunted by the torrential rain
you danced.
Or rather, your indomitable spirits
turned this rain
into the stirring drama,
of nature's artistic production.
Here is the very essence
of the Okinawa spirit,
powerfully expressing
the robust energies
of the common people.

Today the missile base in Onna village
has been transformed
into a place of study and training
for the creation of peace,
a place where green leaves
rustle in the breezes
that cross the azure ocean
and red hibiscus flowers
exchange their quiet smiles.

Where once this launching pad
stood in a desolate field
pointing its hideous, threatening muzzle

at the Asian mainland,
now is a center
commemorating peace.
Before it stands
the World Peace Monument—
the pledge and prayer
of Okinawa's young people.
Bronze statues are ranged
against the sky
in a paean of praise
to the glories of youth…

Two hundred thousand people
have now visited this place.
Encountering the source
from which the light of peace emanates,
they have set out again
with renewed commitment,
filled with fresh courage and energy.
Truly this embodies the principle
of the threefold transformation of the lands.

Further, on Ishigaki Island
so dear to my heart
the Yaeyama Training Center
stands pure white and magnificent,
as if awaiting and watching over
our embarkation.

My friends of Okinawa!
As pioneers of peace
your mission is indeed profound!
Together let us
with these hands
create a citadel of peace
here in Okinawa,
a land of indestructible
happiness and joy!

And you, my dear friends
both young and old
please know
that this will be achieved
through sustained and steady efforts
continued day to day.

The magnificent spectacle
of the Gyokusendo Caves was created
by the uninterrupted coursing
of limestone-laden droplets
over unimaginable lengths of time,
shaping icicles of stone,
nurturing stalagmites
giving birth to a world
of mystic beauty.

As Nichiren Daishonin wrote:
    You cannot strike fire from flint
    if you stop halfway.
Advance today
and again tomorrow
taking even a single step,
or a portion of a step,
forward…
In all things,
not being defeated
or dispirited,
taking on each challenge
in turn,
persisting in your convictions—
here is found ultimate victory
in life and for kosen-rufu.
It is this that will bring a brilliant
crowning glory to your life.

My Okinawan friends,
let us come together
in solidarity, hearts pure
like the waters of the clear blue sea.

The banyan tree
luxuriant with green leaves
stands firm against the storms.
The strength that supports its lush crown
does not derive from a single trunk.
Rather, aerial roots
sprouting from trunk and limbs
drop down to sink deep into the earth,
protecting the trunk,
gathering and coming together
to uphold the great parasol of green
as it spreads into the sky.
The strength of this unity
at times overtakes established trees
or wraps huge boulders
in its embrace.

The era belongs
to the common people.
Each individual
must now play a leading role.
Thus the bonds that connect people,
that help them pool
their wisdom and strengths,
are more crucial than ever.

During the Russo-Japanese War
the Five Heroes of Hisamatsu
rowed a small skiff
a day and a night
over rough seas
to wire news of their sighting
of the Russian Baltic Fleet...
This is the power

of the common people,
their wisdom.
When this strength
flows together
swelling and surging
as a great movement
for the rejection of war,
the sun of a century of life
will rise over oceans of peace.

In Okinawa there is a deep tradition
that values courtesy.
Genuine courtesy is
the spontaneous expression
of a natural sincerity,
the unfeigned actions
born of forged character,
the strength of autonomy
and individuality.

As Nichiren writes,
    Never take questions of courtesy lightly.
We must always be people who uphold courtesy,
emulating the sun which,
with its warm rays,
persuades the traveler
to remove his cloak.

The power of courtesy
is the power of culture.
Ah, the magnanimous capacity
to absorb, to choose and select:
that is the mark
of Okinawan culture!
This is the assimilative strength
before which so many outsiders
—even conquerors—
have knelt in respect.

Without resort to force
or the threat of arms
the power of culture
transforms and inspires.

I once stated my view
that the social role and mission
of the Soka Gakkai
is to wage a spiritual struggle
—one that issues from within—
against the forces of violence,
authority and wealth.
Thus, my friends of Okinawa
who brim with such strengths,
you are pioneers
of a culture of value creation,
standard-bearers
in the forward ranks of our movement.

Ah, my friends of Okinawa,
children of the sun,
heroes of the sea!
On the great bell of Shuri Castle
is inscribed the determination
to act as a bridge
linking all the nations of Earth,
to use mastery of maritime skills
to span the roiling waves,
connecting all countries
through culture and trade.
These words resound
with the fresh, determined energy
of a renaissance dawn.

Once again it is time for Okinawa
to be the harbinger of a new era,
to be a bridge for
peaceful cultural interactions
among the world's peoples.

It has been the fate of these coral islands
to be a military and strategic pivot
in the Pacific.
Now, wrapped in brilliant, wondrous light,
may you be the mainstay and pivot
of a maritime Silk Road
for Asia and the entire world.

With unfurled banners streaming,
solemnly lead the way to peace!
Go forth confidently!
Know the justice of your cause
and fear neither angry storms
nor raging seas!
Continue to devote yourselves
to this voyage,
this quest for what is right!

Look!
The sun of the dawning
century rises!
A rainbow adorns the sky
with a celebratory smile.
The pure white waves
that grace the water's surface
offer their applause.
Raising high their hands
they pay tribute to you
bathed in the brilliance
of the morning sun.
With head held high,
advance along this path of peace,
across this sea of peace!

Okinawa!
Eternally enduring
bastion of peace!

February 17, 1988, at the Okinawa Training Center

Pressing my palms together,
I pray for the happiness and security
of my friends of Okinawa,
and offer deepest prayers
that Okinawa may always be
a land of peace.

Presented to the members of the Soka Gakkai in Okinawa during a visit
to the prefecture on February 17, 1988. From early April to mid-June 1945,
Okinawa was the site of fierce fighting between Japanese and Allied troops.
Following Japan's surrender in August that year, Okinawa remained under
United States administration until 1972.

Typhoon of Steel: refers to the ferocity and intensity of the Allied forces'
assault on Okinawa during World War II.

"On Establishing the Correct Teaching for the Peace of the Land": a treatise
Nichiren presented to the most powerful political figure in Japan arguing
that peace would prevail if the people adopted the correct teaching of the
Lotus Sutra.

Himeyuri Monument: a memorial dedicated to the Himeyuri nursing corps
made up of the students and staff of the local high schools for girls. The
majority of the corps were killed during the ground battle in Okinawa in
1945.

Monument to Student Soldiers: a memorial dedicated to male students aged
from thirteen to nineteen who were mobilized by the Imperial Japanese
Army during the Battle of Okinawa.

"Nothing is more barbarous than war": Ikeda, *The Human Revolution*, vol. 1,
p. 3.

"A great human revolution": Ibid., p. viii.

"The wise will rejoice": Nichiren, *The Writings of Nichiren Daishonin*, vol. 1,
p. 637.

Threefold transformation of the lands: the principle of transforming the
country, area or place where one is into a land of peace and security. It
derives from Shakyamuni's act of three times purifying countless lands
described in the eleventh chapter of the Lotus Sutra.

"You cannot strike fire from flint": Ibid., p. 319.

Russo-Japanese War: February 1904 to September 1905.

"Never take questions of courtesy lightly": trans. from Nichiren, *Nichiren
Daishonin gosho zenshu*, p. 1527.

Embracing the skies of Kirghiz

For Chingiz Aitmatov, standard-bearer of perestroika

A lone runner crosses the broad plain
amidst the falling snow.
The sun has yet to rise;
the frozen, pre-dawn air
torments his flesh like a blade.

Running, silently running...
He runs toward a new tomorrow.
A herald of culture,
he holds high the torch of perestroika.

Thick eyebrows bespeak
an indomitable will.
The unimpeded clarity of his gaze
sends forth bright beams of intellect.
The furnace of his robust breast
glows with a sensitive warmth;
the flames of a passionate concern
for all humankind
flare high.

Wherever he goes
he forges the path of new thinking—
the hopeful sun lifts into the sky,
the frozen earth of the masses
awakens from the long deep sleep of winter,
and gardens of new life open and bloom.

His name, Chingiz Aitmatov—
renowned editor of
Inostrannaya Literatura,
arising to carry the burden of
popular trust and hopes
in the Soviet Union,

standard-bearer of perestroika,
great pioneer cultivating
the untouched expanses of the spirit!

A golden autumn afternoon in 1988,
quite unforeseen,
our meeting at the Seikyo Shimbun building
in Shinanomachi, Tokyo.
What tugging of the strands of fate
brought about our encounter?
This man of action and of letters and myself
—born in the same year
contemporaries to the same era—
conversed with utter frankness.
Directing our thoughts toward
humanity's future,
we spoke of culture, literature,
of a philosophy of peace.

You said: we are friends who share
the same ideals, the same convictions.
I said: a man of courage will die
for the sake of one who truly knows him.
The rhythm and pulse
of our passions
resounded powerfully, violently
like a thunderclap
in the sounding-board of our hearts.

Soul and soul merged white-hot,
leapt to the distant horizon
where a new century
beckons beyond the torments
of human history.

No person, no power imaginable
can now shutter the light our souls emit.
For this is the destined meeting and fusion
of conscience, philosophy, conviction and faith

that, like a mighty river,
moves ceaselessly forward
pressing on in grappled contest
with the great earth
of the realities of humanity and society.

And there we promised
—that it might benefit future generations—
to continue, to record in print, our dialogue.

On that day, two poplars of belief
were planted on the hillock
of our friendship.
In some future day these saplings
will stretch up into the Earth's open skies,
fill with rays of comfort and repose,
grow thick with the green leaves
of humanism and culture.
They will be a landmark for those crossing
the desert waste of a desolate civilization.
They will heal in their shade
the traveler's fatigue.

We have lived through
an age of crazed and raging storms.
You were born
in Kirghiz, a land of blue skies
and waving green grasses,
in 1928, as a gray dawn
foretold the coming winter
of Stalinism.

Childhood days in Moscow,
nurtured by the love of your parents,
your knowledge-seeking father,
who studied at a teachers college,
the strength and tenderness of your mother.

But already the demonic hand of the Purge,
the consuming tempest of Stalinism,
was closing fast on this peaceful family.

Your father, sensing danger
fearing for his family's safety,
secretly put his wife and children
on the train at Ryazan Station.
You were eight, unable to grasp
the parting words your parents exchanged.
Yet you must have sensed
an unbearable tension;
your young heart was gripped
by dread foreboding.

The train pulled forward
cleaving a family bound by love.
Your father started running after
the ever-faster moving train,
waving desperately,
calling out with all his being...
An eternal leave-taking
painted on life's canvas
with scarlet tears.

Your father's death
followed soon after—
a man who deeply loved the people
liquidated as their enemy.
He died solely for being one of the intelligentsia,
earnestly seeking to discern truth.
You remained, haunted by the question,
what had robbed your father of life?

Lonely years in remote Kirghiz—
in a house without a proper roof
you grew, drawing nourishment
from the kindness and support

of the poor and simple people,
surrounded by the stern beauty of nature.

Then war began.
All the men were uprooted
and sent to the battlefield.
And you, just out of grammar school,
became a secretary
and spent your days working at
the village office.
Everywhere were shortages,
all went hungry,
in every home was illness
and mourning for the dead.
Yet you were charged with the cruel
and wrenching task
of collecting taxes from those
who hadn't even enough to eat.

The war ended,
and like shoots emerging
from a winter-withered field,
you took your first steps toward a new life.
At agricultural college,
you studied animal husbandry,
while continuing your literary endeavors,
with the single-minded devotion of youth.
Finding sustenance in your trials,
rising above personal tragedy
transcending private enmity
you focused your vision
—penetrating, self-honed—
on the universal springs of humanity.
Your philosophy has been forged
in tireless seeking and suffering
in pursuit of the ultimate theme—
humanity and the human being.

Even as you worked
in the field you had studied
your passion for creative expression
surfaced and burst forth like magma.
Setting your heart on a life of letters,
you left for studies
at a literary institute in Moscow…

At times, in ways,
the pattern and picture of your life
reminds me of my own,
distant, separated by vast stretches
of land and sea.
For I grew up in an impoverished family
who subsisted by harvesting seaweed.
My father was confined to bed by illness
and as a child I often
helped with the family business.
Setting out from the shores of
Tokyo Bay before dawn,
blowing warm breath onto frozen fingers
from which the blood had fled.

One after the other,
my four elder brothers were taken to the front.
We evacuated, only to be burnt out
again in air raids.
Employed at a munitions factory
my lungs ailing, I often coughed up blood.
Then my eldest brother was killed in battle.
The sight is always with me—
my mother, her back heaving
in grief at the loss
of her treasured child.

What is war? The nation? The human being?
Seeking the answers in books,
I read as one famished,
studied literature and philosophy,

searched for a constant
in this inconstant world.
My youth was spent among scorched ruins
committing to verse the cries of my heart.
Then I encountered Josei Toda—
my life's mentor.
Entering the way of practice and faith
I rose into the skies of new life.

Ah! With your pen you cultivate
the vast bleak stretches of the human heart.
You take the vivid portrait of all living things,
breathe life into voiceless nature.
From the depths of people's hearts
you bring forth limpid outpourings
to cleanse and rarefy our souls.

In your writings, we find
courage, tears and love.
We find nature and seasons,
the fragrant smell of the earth.
We find people and daily life,
humanity's song, philosophy,
a seeking for truth.
We find an elevated spiritual beauty.

The French author Louis Aragon
praised your work *Dzhamilya*
saying that it was the most beautiful
of modern love stories.
The words are the author;
it is the beauty of your noble heart
that gives birth to the jewels
of your creation.

In your works I see
your as yet unseen homeland,
Kirghiz, your native place—
where the wind stirs the green waves

of the steppes;
where mountain streams spray silver
as they fall weaving between boulders.
And above, the perfect blueness of the sky
free from all tentative clouds,
while the sun casts down
a gentle smile.

Unperturbed by frigid gusts
the sky's uncompromising purity...
limitless depths fraught
with the brilliant light
of hope and courage.
Pressing down softly upon mountains
it wraps the Earth;
reaching up
it embraces the cosmos.
As the sun sets
a picture of gilded poetry unfolds.
When night comes
the heavens fill
with the diamond shimmering
of stars.

Ah! The blue skies of Kirghiz!
They are always in your heart
broad, unbridled.
Neither thick and heavy clouds
nor fierce blizzards can obscure
the blue skies that spread above
this soaring upright giant.

You who embrace the sky's expanse!
Although we have journeyed differently
our paths have joined
in a new Silk Road of the spirit.

As the poet Tyutchev wrote:
    Russia's not fathomed by the mind,

Nor by some common standard known:
She is unique in all mankind;
Her fate, revealed through faith alone.
I place my faith in the common people
in all their splendor.

This lone path forged in their midst
is long and filled with obstacles.
But innumerable highways of peace
will surely spread from this single way.
Let us advance with courage.

Ah! Countless divisions
—of nation, race and ideology—
fissure the earth of humanity,
sundering all in opposition and hostility.
Sullen clouds of dark ambition block the sky,
and the sparkling springs of life run dry.
Our blue-green Earth loses its luster,
drifts aimless toward disaster.
Together with the wise and courageous
leader of a reborn Soviet Union, Mikhail Gorbachev
—as a pioneer of the new thinking—
Atlas-like you stand, offering your shoulders
to our beloved human oasis.
Searching to bring harmony to
the diversity of your vast country,
awakening the energies of the common people,
you traverse the world on wings of words.

I also arise—
hoisting the banner
of a philosophy of peace and humanity.
A philosophy that commands me thus:
If you have shivered in the cold
wrap a scarf around the shoulder of a friend.
If you have been beaten by frozen rains
advance offering shelter to all.
For such is only possible

to one who has known suffering.
For such is your mission.

We have traversed the
imbecile horror,
the miserable tempests of war.
As contemporaries,
it is our task and duty
to announce the arrival
of an enduring season of peace.

So let us share thoughts,
let us sink our picks into the soil
digging for the moist sources
of ideas for all humankind.
Time will not wait.
The sun already slants to the west—
moment by moment the nightfall
of our century approaches.

Let us set out!
Transcending the chaos
as we voyage to the distant reaches
of the inner life,
to the glimmering
gardens of life!

April 2, 1989

Written for Chingiz Aitmatov (1928–2008), Kirghiz writer, former member
of the Soviet Presidential Council and Soviet ambassador to Luxembourg.
The author and Mr. Aitmatov published a two-volume dialogue, *Oinaru
tamashii no uta* (Ode to the Grand Spirit), in 1991 and 1992.

Inostrannaya Literatura (Foreign Literature): a Russian monthly literary
magazine which has been published in Moscow since 1955 introducing
foreign literature in Russian translation.

Louis Aragon (1897–1982): French poet, novelist and editor.

Fyodor Ivanovich Tyutchev (1803–73): Russian poet in the Romantic
tradition.

"Russia's not fathomed": Tyutchev, "Russia" in *Poems of Night and Day*, p. 88.

Banner of humanism, path of justice

Dedicated to Nelson Mandela, sublime champion of humanism

The light of hope
crosses the dawning land;
the great straight path
of justice opens before us.

The banner of humanitarianism
unfurls in the glittering morning breeze
and the people's song of freedom
resounds in the crimson sky.

Behold the sun of hope
rising over the African earth!
Nelson Mandela—
father of human liberation
who has devoted his life
to the ideals of humanism!

On February 11, 1990
after twenty-eight years of confinement
you walked the soil of freedom
enveloped in the thunderous storm
of the people's joy and celebration.

The years of pain and endurance
etched your face and whitened your hair
and yet your eyes shone with soft compassion
and a firm fighting spirit.
Your tall body radiated a burning passion
for the cause of liberation.

February 11!
How mystic that this day
should be the day that Josei Toda,
my mentor in life, was born.

As I heard the news of your release
I recalled my late mentor
and his tireless struggles
for humanism,
for the dignity of man.

That day, at that moment,
I sensed the cogs of history
beginning a new revolution.

The surging tide of liberty and human rights
has begun to flow majestically
from the land of South Africa
toward the entire world
and toward the new century.

Ah! The Father of Africa—
living for the ideals of
liberty, equality, democracy.

Sentenced to life in prison
you spent ten thousand days
—from the age of forty-four
to the age of seventy-one—
in unspeakably cruel confinement,
while insidious persecutions rained
one after the next
on the family you could not protect.
Almost every visiting-day
brought more tragic news—
the death of your beloved mother,
and then of your child...
How many nights you must have spent
moaning, rent by sadness?

Yet this valiant champion of
humanity did not succumb.
Never fearing inhuman treatment or intimidation
spurning all temptations to compromise

carrying through dauntlessly
with the spiritual struggle,
you applied yourself to learning
even in prison.
You were victorious,
giving testament to
the humanity of man.

The clouds which gather and cover the sky
cannot conceal the rays of the brilliant sun.
Even with your body fettered
your unbending spirit
was beyond the power of any man
to subdue.

When a single seed of conviction
sinks its roots deeply into the soil
numberless young sprouts will
without fail spring forth
promising the arrival of the
season of rich fruition.

You became a living symbol
of human resistance to tyranny.
How many comrades
were enheartened by your words?
What spiritual nourishment and support
you gave to all who struggle
to abolish apartheid.

I raise both hands in praise!
For the great power of the spirit,
for the indomitable strength of your convictions.
With profoundest respect, I declare you
who walk the way of humanity
comrade in spirit and proud Conscience of Africa.

Ah! Nelson Mandela!
Sun of hope rising above the continent of the future!

I have been picturing within me
the sight of you treading the free earth
and of our eventual encounter.

My friend and standard-bearer of
perestroika, Chingiz Aitmatov,
has expressed his certainty
that in this age of transition
from conflict to construction
what are needed are constructive people.
He named you as just such a person.

You cried out:
"I have fought against white domination and
I have fought against black domination."
In your heart there are no national boundaries.
Your gaze is always directed
not at the differences of race or birth
but on that inner source of light
which makes us human.

You asserted that
your freedom could not be separated
from the freedom of all others.

Together sharing joys and sorrows,
together bearing the responsibility,
the pride and preciousness of being human,
you have set out on a long and glorious journey
in search of humanity and justice.

The great scale of your being
convinces and causes even your enemies
to respect you.
The depth of your life
embraces all people.

The brilliant light of your
love for humankind

gently yet strongly illuminates
and brings forth
the sublime essence
beating in the depths of all people's lives.

You are a champion of humanity
to be ranked with Mahatma Gandhi.

Viva Mandela!
Sun shedding light on the future of humanity!
The chains which bound you for so long
have been severed.
The giant has risen!

Viva Mandela!
The Century of Africa is at hand!
The vibrant rhythm of this
continent of the future
reverberates far and wide!

Behold!
The dazzling rainbow of hope
in the azure skies of the twenty-first century.

Listen!
To the song of victory issuing
from the heated depths of the human soul
seeking freedom, liberation and peace,
unbending before all persecution.

Shine eternally
   Mandela's sun!
Prosper always
   Mandela's Earth!

   The morning of October 31, 1990

Presented to Nelson Mandela (1918–2013), leader of the South African anti-apartheid movement, eight months after he had been released from incarceration and during his visit to Tokyo as head of an African National Congress (ANC) delegation. Mr. Mandela and the author met again in July 1995 in Tokyo when the former visited Japan as president of South Africa.

Mother of art, the sunlight of happiness

To Nataliya Sats with affection and respect

Mother!
Your smile, a spring breeze,
softly nurtures young buds
on the frozen tips of trees.

Mother!
Your arms, the warm earth,
gently caress and protect
the innocent sleep of children.

And mother,
your eyes are a shining blue sky,
always reflecting
in the fullness of its colors
a magnificent rainbow of hope
stretching into the future.

In my heart I hear
the Russian proverb:
"It is bright beneath the sun
and warm by mother's side."

Ah, Nataliya Sats!
As founder of the world's
first children's theater,
you send the bright light of art
into the hearts and minds
of the children who will carry tomorrow.
You before anyone
are an eternal mother
to the world,
a prodigious mother of art.

Art is the power to live.
Like the pulse of spring
reviving nature,
the irrepressible energy
of life itself, breaking through
suffering and pain,
to arrive finally at joy.

Art is the power to love.
A symphony of fraternity
that continually discovers
the brilliant jewel
existing in the heart
of each and all.

Art is the power
to believe in each other.
A multihued bridge
linking all people,
founded solidly
on the universally human
beyond all individual or national
differences.

Mother of art!
Children gather
from throughout the world.
The warbled songs
of tiny birds call out to you:
"Tyotya Natasha! Auntie Natasha!"
The appeal of their eager faces
a priceless gift to you,
the noblest crown of jewels
this world can offer.

Treasured memory
etched in my heart—
May 10, 1981,
our first meeting at the

children's theater you founded,
a palace of the arts crowned with
this beautiful emblem—
a harp of gold on which
a bluebird, symbolizing happiness,
alights.

Greeting me warmly,
you yourself were like a
guileless maiden.
Your unaffected speech, bright smile
touching all around
like a vernal breeze.

Exactly as in Tyutchev's poem:
    Spring is coming, spring is coming!
    And the redcheeked, lightfoot choral dancers
    Of quiet, mild, Maytime days
    Gayly press and throng behind it.
That was you, Auntie Natasha!

Casting a gentle eye over the children
joyously singing and performing,
you spoke of your dream of
musical exchange.
And I promised to bring
your performances to Japan.

Having lived through this
century of violent upheaval,
having battled cruel fate,
you now savor victory's spring.
The prayer you
offer with closed eyes
in your dream-extending heart,
resounds with heat within me:
May all children find happiness!
May the world's children live in peace!

This has been your prayer,
your desire for so long...
It was the year after
the Russian Revolution.
In each village, each town,
storms of fanaticism and agitation raged.
In the violent, swirling current
of those times,
children's lives were set to drift
like tiny, storm-tossed leaves.

One day,
the fifteen-year-old Natasha
called on the Moscow
bureau of theaters and music.
You took on the untried task
of creating a children's theater.
You were the section's
only and entire staff.
The way forward was sought
step by groping step.
Paying no heed
to certain condescending smiles,
you threw yourself into your work,
believing always in the future
of brilliant creation
shining in the depths of the young eyes
of these barefoot children,
these children without parents.

Children and theater—
a region left blank
on the map of art.

Art for children—
when these young buds of the future
are ignored, cruelly trampled,
in such an age, more than ever,
it is our duty to bring to them

the bright light
of a smile.

Since that time,
for more than seventy years,
Tyotya Natasha, you have
unswervingly pressed forward,
triumphing over an era
of wind-driven snows.
The beautiful flower of children's theater
that bloomed in your loving heart
has borne fruit, sending seeds
to Eastern Europe, to the world,
spreading wide its rich
and lovely bouquet.
Your heart is filled to overflowing
with love for art, for people,
with love for life.
The grand endeavor of
children's theater
is the glorious garden
that grew and blossomed
unrehearsed
in the fertile soil of your soul.

A theater director
from distant Japan
encountered you in youth.
Moved deeply, powerfully
by your devoted labors,
he described them as
a brilliant pioneering effort
transcending the confines
of borders or peoples.
To his praise I join
my applause.

Ah, Auntie Natasha!
Like the sun,

you shine most truly
when you pierce the
dark of seemingly endless night,
when you drive the bitter cold
of winter back to the far horizon.

One day, without warning,
fate came to deal its crushing blows.
Your husband arrested,
you yourself jailed,
the warm flames of the *pechka*
around which the family had gathered
utterly extinguished.

"Traitors to the fatherland? Us?"
You were investigated, then exiled,
for crimes of which you
had no knowledge.
The vast stretches of Siberia
engulfed you like a cave.

Life among the prisoners,
outrage at this injustice,
consumed your mind and body.
Your chestnut hair lost
all color overnight.
You were taken
to the sick ward
then, slow to recover,
to a ward for invalids.

The raging torrents of destiny too cruel...
But, you were saved
at the last moment
by your mother.
Having finally learned your whereabouts,
she intuitively sensed: my child is ill.
Walking the snowy steppes
a trunk in each hand,

braving danger to cross
frozen rivers, searching, always searching...
At last your mother
held you in her arms.
It was this deep maternal love
that revived hope within you.

I must be strong, stronger!
I must live. I must!
Rousing and spurring yourself
you initiated artistic activities
among the prisoners.
Like the sun, you dispelled
the dark clouds,
bringing to bloom roses and sunflowers
in a frozen Siberian wasteland.
Under your skilled direction
the inmates became actors, stars.
You traveled with your troupe
from one gulag to the next.

Anna, wife of Nikolai Bukharin,
imprisoned as a traitor's wife
in the same camp,
described you thus:
In the greatest adversity
you never lost your creative energy
or sense of humor,
and you never, ever, lost your
passion and love
for the children's theater.

Art is the pulse of life.
It is proof that we live!
At all times, in all places,
you wanted to sing,
to make the song of hope resound.
You refused to allow the

resonant chords of your heart
to be severed.

After enduring an endless
five-year winter,
you greeted the spring of freedom.
Freedom! Freedom is something
won by one's own hand.
The battle against fate
is a battle with oneself.

Amid intolerable oppression
you never ceased singing
the songs of your conviction.
The gleaming light
of high-spirited courage and wisdom—
marshaling the grand forces
of your will, you confronted fate.
This, truly, is freedom!

Beloved, respected Auntie Natasha!
The drama of your life,
shining victorious,
is a light of hope for all women,
a courageous paean for all
who confront and battle fate.

Whenever I think of you
my heart grows glad
with the memory of
our encounters, your lovely smile—
in Moscow, in Tokyo.
At each meeting, you were so youthful,
each conversation, so refreshing.
Tyotya Natasha!

The Moscow Children's Musical Theater
has performed repeatedly in Japan.
World-class actors, singers, dancers,

whose beautiful, comical,
heartwarming, passionate performances
bring forth cries of delight
from young audiences!

Then again this fall
your theater came to Japan
in a performance to commemorate
the hundredth anniversary of
Prokofiev's birth—
Prokofiev who wrote
Peter and the Wolf at your behest.
This truly was a rainbow bridge
of culture that will link the people
of the Soviet Union and Japan
far into the future.

At just this same time,
your autobiography
was published in Japanese as
The Bluebird I Found.
Difficulties are evidence of life;
suffering is the soil
from which real joy grows...
Your life's story
brightly permeated by
your determined hope,
is certain to awaken
immeasurable courage
in many lives.

Ah, mother of the world's first
children's theater.
Marvelous mother of art!
The joyful voices of children
resound on the grand stage
of the twenty-first century.
Bathed in the dazzling sunlight
that pours down on them

these fresh buds of future
sing, run and laugh.

Looking up at the blue sky
beyond the plains of wind-tossed grass
a beautiful, multihued symphony.
May your sunlight smile, your mother's smile,
shine brightly on forever!
Tyotya Natasha! Spasibo, Tyotya Natasha!
Auntie Natasha! Thank you, Auntie Natasha!

November 18, 1990

Presented to Nataliya Sats (1903–93), the founder of the Moscow State
Musical Theater for Children, during a meeting in Japan. Ms. Sats and the
author met several times in both Japan and the Soviet Union.

Fyodor Ivanovich Tyutchev (1803–73): Russian poet in the Romantic
tradition.

"Spring is coming": Tyutchev, "Spring Waters" in *Poems and Political Letters
of F. I. Tyutchev*, p. 42.

pechka: a Russian oven or stove used for both cooking and domestic heating.

Nikolai Ivanovich Bukharin (1888–1938): Russian Marxist, Bolshevik revolu-
tionary and Soviet politician. He was one of the most prominent victims of
the purges of the Old Bolsheviks in the late 1930s.

Sergei Sergeevich Prokofiev (1891–1953): Russian composer.

Shine brilliantly!
Crown of the Mother of the Philippines

Dedicated with profound respect to President Corazón Aquino

It was a grand drama of reversal
by the people's hand.
It was the triumph of
a husband and wife's beautiful love.

Riveted by the image
broadcast to the world,
I watched the gay procession of tens,
hundreds of thousands filling the EDSA
with their explosive enthusiasm.

As far as the eye could see
the scene was filled with the
shout of yellow and
wave upon wave of "L" (Laban) signs.
Cries of "Cory! Cory!"
joyously greeted the new leader
as she advanced to the podium to speak.

In every mouth was the shout—
Long live freedom!
People jubilantly declared—
Dictatorship is gone!

I can never forget this day,
February 25, 1986.
President Corazón Aquino,
you stood, with your refined smile
wrapped in the ecstatic call of the people.

You said then that the
long years of suffering were over,
that freedom and a new
hope-filled life had begun.

Ah! The years of unceasing betrayal!
Authoritarian rule. Opulent corruption.
Rampant deceit. The groans of the people.
But, finally, the time for renewal arrived.

The person who truly embraces ideals
will find that ideals are her ally.
The person who truly practices justice
will find that justice is her friend.
The person who truly protects the people
will find the people on her side.

You stood up.
The people stood up.
Against the oppression of authority
the people resisted bare-handed.
Against the threat of tanks
the people formed "human chains"
to turn them back.
Into the streets! they cried,
Let us show them the power of the people!

It was a magnificent victory for nonviolence.
You always said that violence
invites more violence
and that you would adhere to peaceful means.

Nothing can defeat the power of the spirit.
Nothing can overcome the power of the people.
Together with the people of the Philippines
you have proven this sublime truth.

I have heard that the red of
your nation's flag
symbolizes courage,
white, peace
and blue, lofty ideals.

In the stirring design of
your nation's flag
the visage of your beloved husband
can be clearly discerned.

Benigno Aquino!
His name will shine forever
in the history of the Philippines!

Born to a well-to-do family
had you desired it, you could have
married into comfort and ease
and spent peaceful, untroubled days.

But your husband was a man struggling
for democracy and for freedom.
What hand of fate brought you to choose
as your partner this man of struggle?

Time passed.
The insidious plots of authority
descended on the two of you.
Persecution followed persecution.
Convicted on trumped-up charges
your husband was sentenced to death.
He spent more than seven years jailed
until released due to illness.
He left then for the United States.
And you, a mother of five
an "ordinary housewife"
had also to endure
many unjust persecutions.

Unbending husband and wife!
Amidst the flames of suffering
your husband's ideals blazed even higher.
Through these burning trials
your sense of oneness of purpose
with your abused husband grew even deeper.

The Filipino revolutionary José Rizal wrote:
"The school of suffering tempers the spirit,
the fighting arena strengthens the soul."

A person struggling for a cause
does not seek comfort or ease.
A fighter dares to throw herself
into life's raging currents.

Your husband returned to the Philippines
disregarding those
who warned against the danger.
The people are suffering, he said,
and the future of our nation is in doubt.
He was determined to return
even though he knew
that death perhaps awaited.
The thought that democracy might fail
if he did not return was more
than he could bear.

Fateful day! August 21, 1983—
Moments after treading the earth
of his native land,
your husband was cut down by a
foul assassin's bullet.

Hearing the tragic news
you returned immediately.
Wiping away your tears,
you recalled your husband in life
as a man of nonviolence
a man of peace
a man of courage.
You also pledged to
uphold his beliefs
to the very end.

Could death become new life?
For in you was born a new warrior
for freedom and democracy.

Heir to your husband's ideals
    you stood up.
Comrade to your husband
    you fought.
Together with your husband
    you won.

Indomitable husband and wife!
Comrades in the struggle
for freedom and democracy!
History sends its
resounding applause
for the spiritual drama
of this noble pair.
I also offer my
deepest respects.

In the blue sky of your homeland
—often praised as the Pearl of the Orient Seas—
flutters the banner of democracy.
The radiant sun of nonviolence, peace and courage
rises over your beautiful green isles.

People Power
—the massive strength of the grassroots—
is the cry of humankind
which no authority can suppress.
It is the eddying soul of the common people
that cannot be stopped by any oppression.

People Power
is also the power of women
who stood proud and unflinching
—the flame of conviction burning fierce in their eyes—

before the thunderous approach of tanks,
protecting their children's future.

As the first woman president in Asia
your strong yet gentle gaze
is always directed at the common people
toward the impoverished who suffer
under the rule of the privileged few.
You have said that
you lean to neither left nor right
but align yourself always
with the common people.

The Philippines was the first nation
in Southeast Asia to gain independence,
an achievement realized through
unseen tears and tragedy.
The cruel domination of foreign powers
brought oppression, exile, torture...
and the execution of the hero José Rizal.
Although independence was won in 1898
the raging waves of imperialism
did not stop their onslaught.

A century later you
brought to a boil
the surging power of the people's energy
which had been flowing swiftly
through underground streams.
The magma of indignation
seething in the earth of the common people,
the signal fires of rebellion
became a swirling storm.
Tyranny collapsed
in the face of the people's determination.

The dawn of a new democracy!
The curtain rises on a
new era of the common person!

We must never forget, however,
that revolution is not
the realization of a goal
so much as a departure toward one.

The elimination of poverty.
The promotion of education.
Economic reconstruction.
The battle against corruption...
Mountain after mountain of
enormous challenge lie ahead.
The treacherous and thorny path
is certain to be long.

And still you rush forward!
Summoning every ounce of
energy and wisdom, you fight on!
Brushing off the sparks and embers of rebellion
based on rigid ideology;
reining in the forces of separatism
which would rend the bonds
between the hearts of citizens;
bearing up under the dark clouds
of attempted coups which
convulse the capital city;
you advance, embracing in your heart
the great hope for a new century
in which the common people will
raise their voices in songs of victory.

Looking one hundred years toward the future,
José Rizal declared:
"We shall never tire of repeating this
while a ray of hope is left us..."
Hope is the engine of the soul.
Hope is the wings on which to rise into
the unbounded skies of the future.
Rizal's hope is your hope.
Your hope is the hope of the world's people.

Whatever billowing waves may beset you
never forget that you have friends
throughout the world.

The great flow of the universal desire
for happiness and peace
in the hearts and minds of the people
will not dry up no matter how
dictators might scheme.
The solidarity of culture
transcending national borders
creating human links between peoples
will certainly bring about a great shift in
the currents of world history.

The performance in Japan of the
Ramon Obusan Folkloric Group
was a crowning jewel
in our Min-On Concert Association program
"A Musical Voyage Along the Marine Road."
The subtle and gorgeous performance
—a song in praise of humanity—
was like a beautiful screen unfolding,
moving the hearts of the Japanese people.

The educational exchange program between
the University of the Philippines
and Soka University—
the bonds of shared learning
between the hearts of youth
will surely grow into a great tree
that will bear the fruit of friendship
between our nations
into future centuries.

Ah! People of this beautiful southern nation!
The strong and cheerful spirit of your people!
To you we bear an ancient debt
for bringing to our distant land

a multitude of civilizations and cultures
borne upon the currents of the *kuroshio*
the "marine silk road."

It continues to pain me that
—forgetting all hint of gratitude—
the Japanese military trampled
your gem-like islands
stamping out the lives of
your mothers and fathers
in a history of tragedy and atrocity.

Broad and deep bonds
between the hearts of peoples
will heal the
illness of chronic conflict
between nations,
will build a strong
foundation of friendship.
In this way
the grand door upon the new century
will be opened.

You who make the heart of the
common people your own!
Mother of the Philippines
like the pure white *sampaguita* flower!

I pray that you will continue to advance
toward the triumphal arch
of the indestructible revolution
of the common people;
that your great nation will continue
its limitless progress
with joy and confidence.
May you enjoy prosperity forever
and future centuries of shining brilliance!

April 22, 1991

Presented to Corazón Aquino (1933–2009), president of the Philippines, when the two met at Malacañang Palace in Manila. Mrs. Aquino led the 1986 People Power Revolution, which restored democracy in the Philippines, becoming the first female president in Asia.

EDSA: The main boulevard in downtown Manila.

Laban: Tagalog word meaning "to fight."

José Rizal (1861–96): the hero of Philippine independence.

"The school of suffering": Rizal, *El Filibusterismo*, p. 297.

"We shall never tire": Rizal, *The Philippines a Century Hence*, p. 110.

May the laurels of kings adorn your lives

To my beloved young friends in Germany

That day,
a fine drizzle
had settled over Berlin.

The fresh bullet holes in the wall
were seared into my mind
and my heart was stricken
by the sight of wreaths laid down
for those fallen
in their flight for freedom.

Just over the wall,
within earshot if one called out,
must surely be family, friends and lovers!

Built just two months earlier, the wall
—the unfathomable design
of malicious minds—
tore apart people and their hearts,
shredding the happiness in their breasts.

To be denied the right
to share and partake of life,
to have such sharing
rendered criminal—
this was a command
forbidding people to be human.

Who could dare to claim that right?
Yet, the wall had been built
by human beings, people drunk
on the demonic draughts of power.

These were the thoughts
that arose within me
as I stood before the Brandenburg Gate:

Though human ingenuity may one day stem
the flow of the mighty Rhine,
the people's soulful cry
for human dignity
will never be suppressed.

Beware, imperious holders of power
who despise and manipulate people
as if they were puppets!
The day will come
when you must bear history's harsh verdict
and feel humanity's rebuke.

At some point the rain lifted,
and a glorious dusk bathed distant steeples.
A crimson cloak fringed with gold
settled over this tense, apprehensive city—
Berlin, it seemed, was blanketed
in a moment of peace.

"Of sunsets such as these,"
one Berliner told me, "we say that
the angels have come down from heaven."

Around that time thirty years ago
—perhaps before, perhaps after—
you, my young friends,
were born into this world!

Thus I am convinced that
you are angels of peace,
heavenly emissaries of happiness!

By what unfathomable promise of time,
through what profound connection,
have you come together here?

That day, I offered deep and fervent prayers
for the unification of this land, for peace;
I prayed that a people and a country
forced to endure utmost suffering
would one day revel in the light
of utmost happiness.

You then witnessed the moment
when your homeland was transformed
from the symbol of a world divided
to the symbol of a world united.
And you heard the footfalls of
Germany striding forward to lead
the unification of Europe and of all humanity.

As witnesses to this transformation,
I implore you:
Break down all the walls of brutality
remaining in the world,
and in their place, upon their ruins,
construct the broad and open
plazas of humanity!

My noble friends!
The old century has been stained
with blood and bitter remorse.
On the canvas of the new century,
paint masterworks of culture and joy!

To that end, I urge you:
Become the new people
of a new era;
become the humane leaders
of a century of humanity!

Nichiren Daishonin writes:
"The deeper the roots,
the more luxuriant the branches."
Germany is the land of forests
and the oak is the monarch of the forest.
These leafy giants bore with thick roots
deep into the earth, holding it tight.
They extend their sturdy arms
to clasp the high and open sky.

It is precisely because each individual
is autonomous and self-supporting that,
when united, their bonds remain
robust and unshakable.

My friends,
be like the king of the forest!
With august ideals,
reach stretching for the skies;
and through your real-life efforts,
delve deeply where you stand now,
until you pierce the Earth's very core!

Immanuel Kant,
Germany's towering giant, observed:
"Two things fill the mind
with ever new and increasing
wonder and awe, the more often
and the more seriously
reflection concentrates upon them:
the starry heavens above me
and the moral law within me."

How true this is!
The magnitude, depth and extent
of your being is far greater
than you imagine.
In order that you may
truly be you, sink deep roots into

the great earth of your inner life.
Taking in the awe-inspiring
precision and harmony
of the orbits of the stars,
pursue throughout your life
the mystic principle that
governs the cosmos.

The journey of the inner realm of life
and actions in the external world
are one and inseparable.

Therefore be
people of unquenchable seeking,
people of thoroughgoing action!

The Bible states:
"In the beginning was the Word."
In *Faust*, Goethe recast this as:
"In the beginning was the *Deed!*"

The trunks of oaks that
have grown for several decades
remain slim enough
to be encircled by one arm.
Yet when they have lived on
for two centuries or more,
they become giants of massive girth.
Some are said to still be flourishing
after one thousand years of life.

We, too, will be measured
by the gratitude of humankind
two hundred years from now,
by the flourishing
of the exquisite forest of life
a thousand or even ten thousand years
in the future.
This is why, my young friends,

you must never be impatient.
What you need to do
is to triumph today,
to make each day of life
more fulfilling than
the one that came before.

Young men and young women!
Develop yourselves
to command the same admiration
as the towering oak,
massive monarch of the woods!

Find freedom through reason!
Grow strong through principles!
Realize greatness through perseverance!
Make yourselves eternal through courage!

Master yourself!
Rise up unhesitating!
Lead your life
with proud and regal faces
turned toward the sky!

The world is contained within your heart;
your innermost resolve
can embrace and shape
your natural surroundings,
the land in which you live.

The sun and the moon
are your faithful companions.
Everything—
clumps of violets in spring,
red–gold foliage in fall,
the mountains of the Harz,
the peaks of Taunus,
the Alps and the North Sea—

all are partners
in the majestic symphony of life.

The essence of faith likewise
lies in the transformation
of our innermost awareness and resolve.
When this resolve
is honed like the arrow
of a battle-hardened warrior,
it has the power to change all things.
Facile compromise,
easy temptation,
complacency—
the whisperings of Mephistopheles
arise from within us,
not without.

Recognize and repulse
such seductions, my friends.
Nurture the forest of your life
until it is lush
with the fruit of victory.
And together let us
extend these green woods
of culture and philosophy
as a refuge of comfort and solace
for those grown weary in solitude,
who are stricken by aimless wandering.

Nichiren Daishonin also writes:
"The farther the source,
the longer the stream."

The Rhine has some
twelve thousand tributaries.
Along its banks have arisen
towns and cities.
Its waters have nourished
meadows and fields,

conveying people, hopes and ideas
as it makes its way
to the universal sea.
Mighty Father Rhine,
giving life to the great German nation!
The river and its source are one,
their connection is never broken.
This is the cause
of its immense, enduring power.

Kosen-rufu flows
like a vast, expansive river.
Its source is found in the example
of the original Buddha—
a life of triumph over
unimaginable adversity.

In more recent history,
it was Tsunesaburo Makiguchi
—upholding the Daishonin's teachings
with his very life—
and my own beloved mentor, Josei Toda,
who together defended and preserved
this pure and sacred current.
It was their struggle
that ensured that the river of kosen-rufu
will flow in perpetuity.
It is because we uphold
the correct heritage of the Daishonin
that we encounter obstacles—
a fact we embrace with pride.

The poet Victor Hugo
had an abiding love for the Rhine.
He described its various sources.
A brook that issues from Lake Toma,
a small stream originating
from the foot of Lukmanierberg,
an icy trickle

seeping from an ancient glacier—
these three converging
into a single riverhead.

We, too, have our three sources:
faith, practice and study.
It is through our unbroken
consistency and perseverance
that the great flow
of the correct teachings will be ensured.

The Rhine continues to forge on,
never stalling or retreating,
on clear and stormy days.
It remains true to the ancient sources
of its name, which means "to flow."

That which undergoes constant change
experiences constant renewal—
it is always new, yet keeps its identity.
A great river is always departing
always starting anew.

We practice the Buddhism of true cause,
the principle of forever making
a fresh start now, in the present moment.
This is a religious tradition
of perpetual hope, perpetual construction.
Thus we live entirely without fear.

This world we live in
delights in tarring that which shines,
in defiling the worthy.
But such murmuring waves
are but further proof
that the great river is alive
and continues its advance.

Life is inevitably a battle;
struggle cannot be avoided.
Our choice is simply this:
to fight as chivalrous champions
or as unscrupulous beasts.

People of noble soul
are nature's finest work!

Beloved young friends!
Be both the artist and art
of that masterwork!

And like the statues
of Schiller and Goethe
standing together in Weimar,
maintain the firm, unyielding bonds
of high-minded friendship
throughout your lives!

To have an authentic friend
is to encounter a second self.
To live without friendship
is to inhabit a world without sunlight.
One close and trusted friend can mean more
than innumerable blood relations.
Only human beings
can commit to friendship.

This is why Buddhism,
as a religion of humanity,
places greatest stress
on friendship and fraternity.
Shakyamuni Buddha
called out to those
who came to hear his teachings,
saying: "My friends!"
And he admonished them

against thinking of him
as somehow different or special.

"My friends"—
in this single phrase
the Buddhist spirit of
human equality shines,
as does the determination to eliminate
discrimination from the world.

"My friends"—
in this resides the soul of
human dignity, democracy,
refusing to look down on others,
maintaining mutual faith in
and praise for our own
and others' Buddha nature.

Herein also lies
the spirit of human revolution,
the determination to be
an eternal practitioner,
a person taking on new challenges
for all eternity.

Originally, *ji* of *jihi*
—Japanese for compassion—
connotes fraternity
while *hi* means
to share in the suffering of friends.

Indeed, it was Shakyamuni's wish
to create a growing confederation
of friends in free unity.
The noble undertaking of kosen-rufu
likewise seeks to build a fraternal society,
democratic and equal,
here on Earth.

History is moving toward
more open societies.
You must lead the way
by becoming people whose souls
are open and accepting.

Your growth is society's progress,
your call, an echo from the future.

The musical giant Beethoven declared:
"He who penetrates the meaning of my music
shall be freed from all the misery
which afflicts others."

My friends, you must also stand firm,
your hearts swelling with this conviction:
"When our humanistic symphony
is heard throughout the world,
humankind will prevail
over every wrong and wretchedness."

Sons and daughters of the sun!
When the white light of the sun
reaches the Earth, it splits into the
rainbow spectrum of colors,
each with its own purpose and mission.
How splendid! How lively!

Like the rainbow,
my young friends,
join together as one,
forging unity from among
your unique characteristics
and personalities—
many in body, one in mind.

And like the rainbow,
my young friends,
be a bridge of hope

by which society can cross over
into the new era!

How I long to behold
this resplendent rainbow,
formed by the free and vibrant
acts of youth in untold number—
to see this rainbow rise
in Germany's glorious skies!

   June 6, 1991

   Composed on the anniversary of first Soka Gakkai
   President Tsunesaburo Makiguchi's birth while gazing
   at the verdant splendor of Frankfurt's forests

Presented to the members of the SGI in Germany at a youth representatives' conference at the German Culture Center in the suburbs of Frankfurt.

"The deeper the roots": Nichiren, *The Writings of Nichiren Daishonin*, vol. 1, p. 940.

"Two things fill the mind": Kant, *Critique of Practical Reason*, p. 169.

"In the beginning was the *Deed!*": Goethe, *Faust: Part One*, p. 30.

"The farther the source": Nichiren, *The Writings of Nichiren Daishonin*, vol. 1, p. 940.

A brook that issues: see Hugo, *The Rhine*, p. 269.

"He who penetrates": Rolland, *Beethoven*, p. 101.

Like the sun rising

Offered to Walt Whitman, poet of the people, on the centenary of his passing, with affection and respect

Like the sun rising
shattering the dark
of old restraints—
with new words, new forms
the soul's liberator
lauds a new world, a new humanity;
sings out democracy's dawn.

Walt Whitman, poet of the people—
you raise your voice
in sonorous praise
of the common people, unknown and unnamed.

America in "the middle range
of the nineteenth century"—
echoing with hammers
pealing the song of construction.
Into the chaos and hope
emerges a man
in his hand a small quarto of poems—
the scant ninety-five pages
of *Leaves of Grass*.

Marking departure from
the civilizations of the Old World,
heart athrob at the thought
of a birthing New World,
prophet of a new age
prolocutor of new ideals.

In your own confident words you are
"Walt Whitman, an American, one of the roughs,
    a kosmos,

Disorderly fleshy and sensual ... eating drinking
    and breeding..."—
intensely human embodiment
of America's freedom,
you are buoyant and rustic,
filled with compassion.

Thick-chested with tempered steel-like arms,
sunburnt face framed
by wildly tousled white hair
and the untrammeled flow of your beard;
beneath thick rich eyebrows
in your clear bright eyes
burns a piercing untamed light—
intelligent and caring.

Your breast's crucible
overflows with the
bright red passion to build
a democratic future.
Your penetrating gaze takes in
the vast universe within
and the signs and promise
of a shining tomorrow.

Everything in the universe
is the subject matter for your poetry—
sky, ocean, mountain, river...
even a single grain of sand, even a solitary leaf
the stillness of the wild, the noisy bustling city...

You seek out your muse
in ships, in railroads, in tall buildings
in all things everywhere.

You applaud and praise all people—
the young, the old, men and women.
Those whose sweat builds the future,
the widowed wife,

the defeated revolutionary,
the prisoner in jail…

You sing the song of,
you sing in praise of
every person on our planet,
the unadorned,
the natural human being.

"Camerado, this is no book,
Who touches this touches a man."
Just so! Your poems flow from
your own overbrimming soul—
they are your very life!

But ah, the critical gales
that beset pathfinders, those who go first!

Because of their revolutionary newness
Leaves of Grass
the songs of your soul
are showered with ridicule and abuse—
"Nauseating drivel."
"As unacquainted with art as a hog
is with mathematics."
"Monster!"

The only words of support and praise
come from the philosopher Emerson
and a handful of people
of discernment and courage.

To you, however, soaring mountainous
the critics' clamorous attacks
are only the murmur of the wind
passing at your feet.
Unheeding of the animadversions
of literati clinging to vain authority
the poet spends his days

quiet and composed
conversing with nature on Long Island.

You do not sing to please the critics;
you sing for the common people
sinking their roots like weeds
into the rich American earth,
secret possessors
of vibrant powers
of birth and renewal;
the people, despised and trampled
driven from history's visible stage.

No one is another's master
no one another's slave—
politics, learning, religion, art
all exist for the human being
for the sake of the people.
To undo the prejudice of race
to break down the walls of class
to share freedom and equality with the people—
it is for this that you sing
to the last limits of your strength.

Your songs—
the Declaration of Humanity
for a new age.

You are the greatest lover
of the common people,
are yourself one
of the proud uncrowned mass
throughout your life.

Your elder brother ill in spirit,
at age eleven you went out
into the world, worked—
as a waiter, a printer, a teacher, reporter...
These arduous years

amidst the bitter realities of society
pushed out your bark and
swelled your timber-girth.
From those days of trial and enduring
you learned life's preciousness,
gained nutriment to grow
into a lofty tree of humanism.
Truly only he who has shivered in the cold
can know the sun's warmth.

Ah, your noble altruism!
In the agonized vortex
of the Civil War
you rushed from place to place
nursing the wounded
equally, without distinction between
the soldiers of the North
and those of the South.

Regal in your humanity,
august and proud
like the sky-traversing sun—
smiling, you walk the orbit
of your conviction.

Your verse is like
a clear and optimistic sky
without a single sentimental cloud,
like cresting billows dancing
across an ocean plain—
expansive, energetic, free...
Unfettered by the past
you move forward, always forward
toward a future
resounding with hope.

True cheer, true brightness
is the flash of an illumined spirit

resolved in its convictions
piercing the dark night of grief.

Behold Whitman after the war!
Forced to witness
corruption and decay
gnawing at the heart
of the young democracy;
listen to his maddened wail and lament
at the cruel betrayal of event.

But still you kept faith
with your ideals.
Still you sought out
the highest value of the human being.
Still you believed—
in the character of men and women
who would fill the world
with the brilliant glittering
of jewels and pearls;
that the floral gardens of democracy
would continue to spread.

You lived true to your words:
"Liberty, let others despair of you—
I never despair of you."

Fanfare of flight
performed by a soul erupting
from the abyss of pain!

The poet sets sail
on the journey home
across the spirit's great and fertile sea—
toward the eternal, the essential source
that extends behind all nature.

Living through turbulence
exuding the bright beams of your love

you never ceased your seeking
for the font of life's light.

Walt Whitman, explorer of the spirit—
you are the friend of my heart!

How can I describe the raptures
inspired in my mind
by this one book of poems
encountered in the midst
of the sufferings of youth!
Leaves of Grass—
the very title echoes with
freshness, beauty and strength.

On that day our dialogue began—
the sheer and solitary
nobility of your spirit
fanned within me flames of courage;
your vision of a light-filled future
brought up surging energy and hope.

The utter overflowing freedom
of your soul
struck me like a bolt
of empathetic lightning—
sundering the dark,
making bright the path of my progress,
inviting me toward the great way
of humanity.

Walt Whitman, giant star of freedom!
It is already one hundred years
since your passing—
but I have been with you.

Like a bird bathed in the sun's light
as it flies through the sky,
like a sailor on a night sea

addressing the stars,
I have spoken with you
of humanity's tomorrow,
sung songs of praise to life,
pondered the laws
that govern the infinite universe.

The curtain is falling
on the twentieth century;
the evening sky is shrouded
with perplexed fog.
But, look closer! Look harder!
In the depths of the thick haze
is the powerfully flowing
current of the age
toward a new dawning
of democracy.

This spiritual tide,
this thirst for freedom,
has borne the assaults
of raging militarism;
it has writhed in the spume;
its progress has been blocked
by stagnant reefs of decadence.

But time has grown to fullness
and the tide now rises;
with the joyous booming of waves
—the exult of ordinary citizens—
it washes all the world's shores.

The democratic ideal you espoused
has survived the trials and selections
of more than a century;
it has been passed on
in the conscience of the people
of countries everywhere;
it cracks open the door

on a new age of democracy,
brilliant and eternal in the night
of an uncharted era
bereft of all philosophy.

Walt Whitman, my friend—
it is just as you believed,
just as you proclaimed:
freedom has never betrayed you
humanity has never betrayed you.

The century's twilight
is prelude to the dawn,
the daybreak of the new age,
the beginning of new hope.

Look! My friend—
I will take up the banners
of democracy and freedom
which you held so proudly aloft;
I will fight on and will advance
along the path of the poet,
pioneer of the spirit's wilderness,
on a journey of infinite mission,
forging paths of friendship
to all corners of the Earth,
joining with people heart to heart
ringing out humanity's victory song.

You live within my breast—
like the sun brimming with
compassion and fight;
the rush of your blood's tide,
the thunderous pulse of your heart
courses hotly through my veins.
Walt Whitman, my sun!
Light my way, shine on forever!

March 26, 1992

Dedicated to the American poet Walt Whitman (1819–92) and read at a commemorative ceremony held by the Walt Whitman Association on March 26, 1992—the one-hundredth anniversary of his death—in Camden, New Jersey, where Whitman is buried.

"Walt Whitman, an American": Whitman, "Song of Myself" in *Leaves of Grass*, p. 50.

"Camerado, this is no book": Whitman, "So long!" in *Leaves of Grass*, p. 611.

"Liberty, let others despair of you": Whitman, "Europe, The 72d and 73d Years of These States" in *Leaves of Grass*, p. 407.

Cosmic traveler, our century's premier violinist

To Sir Yehudi Menuhin, with my profound respect

Music—
is a fountain of tranquillity,
a tossing to air of mystic sounds.
When one pauses on its banks
the burning heart is calmed and healed.
When washed in the seamless gush
of this profound rejoicing
the human being is revived and purified.
Ah, inexhaustible font of Life!

Music—
is a garden of happiness.
When one strolls among its flowers
and the waft of its noble rhythms,
sorrow yields to hope,
chaos transmutes to order,
hostility is channeled to empathy,
prostrate submission to fate changes
into the transcendent conquest of destiny,
and man—becomes human.

Music—
is an eternal climactic revelation.
The mysterious reverberations
of the stars' harp
transcend civilization and time,
shaking spirits East and West, North and South.
We shiver and awaken in its beauty
become true friends, true brethren...

Ah, the violin
—lustrous metaphysical object,
mysterious microcosm singing free—

it summons to itself all the universe's
purest, most gorgeous scales!

It is for this that you
—voyaging to lands of heterogeneous tonalities,
wrapped in the glow of universal humanity—
deserve the title of cosmic traveler.
Yehudi Menuhin!
Our century's premier violinist!

How is it that to play, to sing
can raise a man to such sublimity?
Now fast, now slow
the taut, the relaxed instant of your bow
captures the everlasting melody
of the cosmos; the moment passes, eternity remains...
Planets and stars whisper in tongues,
paving the earth with the
bloom of your *pizzicato*;
the sky is crossed by the gliding
rainbows of your *portamento*—
you weave for us a dazzling aurora of tones.

At times we hear—
the charmed songs of maidens,
then moonlight seeping into the earth,
then peal of evening bells
declaring the day's repose,
then waves colliding in the torrent...

Your violin—
is like a doctor persevering
in the effort to make men better;
like a philosopher ceaselessly
pursuing truth, pointing the way
to a life of wisdom;
like a religious deep in prayer
for the salvation of people's hearts and minds.

In that moment you are complete,
and issue to the world
your message of universality.
The depth of the artist
is the depth of the art, its loftiness his.
People the world over
lend their ears to your humanity.

Your "unfinished journey"
in the pursuit of beauty
began in childhood.
That day you stretched out into the world
the fledgling wings of your creativity.

People laud you saying
you are a man for all music
living in unending youth;
even more than to the rarity
of your natural gifts,
these laurel praises are offered
to the ceaseless devotion
and effort of your days.
For you played on through the long
tempestuous night of tribulations
which all great talents are fated to cross;
you continued to perform your quartet
of passion, propriety, sincerity and humility.

All the decorations and titles
bestowed on you
are inadequate to your greatness.
Nor has kudos global and numberless
dulled in any way
the luster of your path-seeking spirit,
modesty and sobriety.

Making of all sufferings
the unparalleled drama
of a life lived to completeness,

you further unfold the dreams of youth;
your wings continue their flight—
you have compounded
the sitar music of Indian tradition
with the refined essence of your strings,
become a great linking bridge
between music East and West;
you have also joined your voice
to the progressive enthusiasm of American jazz.

The wake you have plowed
—remarkable navigator of
this century's musical history—
is a guiding star for all lovers of music.
Your life as a master of the art of living
continues to carry
incomparable inspiration
to the depths of the hearts
of your young successors.

Ah! Maestro of humanism!
Your gaze has never drifted
from goodness and beauty—
the divine dignity of the human being.

There is no schism or divide
—as between races, states and dogmas—
unembraced by your cosmic magnanimity.
The innate light of your humanity
is backed by courage strong as steel,
unflinching before the poised archers
of the powers that be.

Furtwängler in isolation and despair,
Rostropovich and Oistrakh encircled
by the iron chains of authority...
The greatness of your humanism,
the scale of your generosity
could not remain indifferent to their plight;

the *cri de cœur* you could not repress
melted even the ice-mass
of authority and prejudice.

September 1951—
You set down in Japan,
a land bearing deep fresh scars
from war's ravages.
The mystic tones,
the passion of your unimaginable technique
emanating from the Stradivarius...
In thronged halls hearts trembled
and lives long starved
for true timbres danced
to pleasure-giving tones.
As if by heaven's revelation
the weary Japanese spirit
was roused and set upright
by the music's echo and sweep...

For untold numbers
you have thrown open
wide and with vigor
the window on the soul that is music—
by organizing music festivals,
by establishing
the Yehudi Menuhin School of Music,
through imaginative
performance projects for the needy...
Using art's resonant appeal
you have sought to create a forum
of human fellowship.
Your unpausing labor of love has opened the way
for youth, women, our elders
to know unbounded blue skies
of freedom and human liberation;
and, like you, they have come
to stand at the door of the eternal.

The path of your lifetime of pioneering
stretches to the sparkling horizon
of a century of peace, a century of humanity.
It is a path linking the hearts
of all humanity—world citizens
in a garden of harmony and solidarity,
florid with the clustered blossoms
of freedom and individuality.

Yehudi Menuhin!
Yours is a rare fusion
of goodness and beauty!

You whom I deeply respect—
you have lived through this century
of conflict and upheaval
always spinning your hope-filled melodies
far into the future.
The Indian poet-sage Tagore wrote:
    The true universal
    finds its manifestation
    in the individuality which is true.
And indeed you manifest
the pulse and beat of the universal
in the luxuriant flowering
of your astonishing gifts,
your liberated individuality.

The wails and conflagrations
of the twentieth century—
you have faced head-on
the belligerent contention of arms
that time upon time
has sotted history with blood.
And you have lived, progressed,
performed the harmonies of love and courage,
the symphonies of humanity's unification
amidst aromatic bouquets of amity and peace.

The flower gardens of beauty,
the palaces of goodness
that bloom and rise resistant
to misery on Earth.
The glorious kingdom of the spirit
you build will adorn the distant future.
Like the butterflies and birds
that fluttering flock
to the sweet fragrance of honey
and the heavy fruit of happiness,
people will gather
in the allure and restfulness
of the palaces of art.

In the Lotus Sutra
Shakyamuni Buddha,
whom I respect and venerate,
has taught us as follows:
   When men witness the end of an aeon
   and all is consumed in a great fire,
   this, my land, remains safe and unharmed,
   constantly filled with gods and men.
   The halls and palaces in its gardens and groves
   are adorned with all kinds of gems.
   Precious trees bear plentiful flowers and fruit,
   and the people there are happy and at ease.
   The gods strike heavenly drums,
   making a ceaseless symphony of sound.
   A rain of white *mandara* blossoms
   scatters over the Buddha and the people.

What a glorious merging
of the artistic and the religious!
What a rare reunion
of goodness and beauty,
the particular and the universal!
Against all atrocities
this republic of the spirit
remains indestructible.

No schemes or plots can obscure
its eternal, brilliant and human lights.
It is indeed a fitting place for your residence,
for your citizenship.

Most respect-worthy Yehudi Menuhin—
with harmonic cosmic rhythms,
brought to us from the far side
of distant constellations,
you warmly, ever so warmly
embrace and bring together
man and man
nature and man
the universe within
and the universe without.
Ah, noble master of the spirit!

From where do you come?
Where do you proceed?
Your heart hears clearly
the mystic symphony,
the ineluctable unity
of Cosmos and Self.
Your eyes and your melodies
are quietly fixed
on an endless procession
to the inner life of man.

Kant's words swell in my breast:
    Two things fill the mind
    with ever new and increasing
    wonder and awe...
    the starry heavens above me
    and the moral law within me.
My heart spills over with
magnificent melodies of the human spirit
that fill an eternally blue and unfettered sky.

I raise my voice in praise—
May you reign forever
in the palaces of goodness and beauty!
I offer my prayer
for your happy voyage to the distant reaches
of the Milky Way!
Glory to you, Yehudi Menuhin!

April 5, 1992

Presented to Sir Yehudi Menuhin (1916–99), the world-renowned violinist, when they met in Tokyo.

Gustav Heinrich Ernst Martin Wilhelm Furtwängler (1886–1954): German conductor and composer.

Mstislav Rostropovich (1927–2007): Russian cellist and conductor.

David Oistrakh (1908–74): Russian classical violinist.

Rabindranath Tagore (1861–1941): Indian poet, playwright and educator.

"The true universal": Tagore, *The English Writings of Rabindranath Tagore*, vol. 3, pp. 492–93.

"When men witness": see Lotus Sutra ch. 16, quoted in *Lectures on the Sutra: The Hoben and Juryo Chapters*, p. 125.

"Two things fill the mind": Kant, *Critique of Practical Reason*, p. 169.

The sun of jiyu over a new land

To my treasured friends of Los Angeles, the city of my dreams

A brilliant, burning sun
rises above the newborn land,
aiming toward a new century,
raising the curtain on a new stage
of humanity's history.
Shedding its light equally on all things,
it seeks the sky's distant midpoint.

In this land wrapped
in the limitless light
of the morning sun,
my splendid American friends
make their appearance,
bearing the world's hopes;
with power and vigor they commence
their progress anew.
To my beloved and treasured friends I say:
"Long live America renewed!
Long live SGI-USA reborn!"

Ah! This enchanting city, Los Angeles!
Land of freedom and pioneering spirit!

From jagged mountain ranges
to the Pacific Ocean,
variegated nature changes ceaselessly—
rich agricultural lands
nurtured by the sun's dazzling rays,
and the groundbreaking efforts
of those who came before.
Downtown, clusters of buildings soar skyward.

To think that this vast metropolis
could grow from a single aqueduct

stretched across the barren desert
from beyond the distant mountains!

It is said that in America
new winds blow from the west.
And indeed, the fresh breezes
of new ways of thinking,
new styles of living,
have arisen in California
and spread to the entire United States.
So many stories of the silver screen,
created here in Hollywood,
have delivered bountiful gifts
of romance and dreams
to the world's people.

This rich spiritual soil,
this great earth alive with the diversity
of peoples and traditions—
giving rise to new culture,
a new humanity.

Los Angeles is a city pregnant with future,
a city where, in the words of one writer,
you can set new precedents
with your own energy and creativity.

And more, Los Angeles is a bridge
linking East and West,
a land of merging and fusion
where cultures of the Pacific
encounter traditions of the West.

Ah, the Pacific that opens before our eyes!
The boundless, free and untamed sea
for which the great Melville
voiced his respect and praise:
"It rolls the midmost waters of the world ...
the tide-beating heart of earth."

Once, the Mediterranean
was inland sea and mother
to the civilizations of the surrounding regions—
Europe, the Middle East and Africa.

In like manner, the Pacific's depths
must not divide—
but be the cradle of a new civilization,
an enormous "inland sea" connecting
the Americas North and South,
the continents of Asia and Australia.

This is my firm conviction—
California will be the energy source
for the Pacific region
in the twenty-first century,
and Los Angeles its eastern capital.

In October 1960, I took my first steps on
the American continent
in California, the Golden State.
The honor and glory of becoming
the first chapter established in North America
belongs to the Los Angeles Chapter.

Since then, this city has been
the core and center of kosen-rufu
in the United States, the starting point
for world kosen-rufu.
My dear friends, never forget
this mission which you
so decidedly possess.

In the thirty-three years since that time,
I have visited Los Angeles seventeen times.
Kansai is the heart
whose beating drives the movement
for kosen-rufu in Japan;
Los Angeles plays this selfsame role

for the entire world.
For this reason, on each visit,
staking all, I drove in deep
and deeper
the pilings of construction.

In 1980,
the first SGI General Meeting was held,
and in 1987, SULA,
Soka University's first campus outside Japan,
opened its doors.

Ah, February 1990!
I postponed my visit
to South America and for seventeen days
gave myself heart and soul
to the work of encouraging
my beloved fellow members
here in Los Angeles!
Those impassioned, consuming days
of unceasing toil and action
are the collaborative
golden poems of shared struggle.

Nor can I ever forget
the spring of 1992—
even now my heart is rent with pain
when I recall how the
tragic news of the civil unrest in Los Angeles
raced around the world.

Heartrending images
of the evening sky shrouded in black smoke,
buildings collapsing in flames,
once peaceful streets shattered by riot,
the entire city gripped
by a battlefield tension.
People standing lost in confusion,
a woman holding an infant cried out:

What has become of the ideals of this country?
What are we supposed to teach our children?
Her woe-filled words tore
like talons at my heart.

I received continual reports,
extended prompt relief.
And, putting everything aside,
I sat before the Gohonzon and
single-mindedly prayed—
for the safety of my treasured friends,
for the immediate restoration of order,
for a world without violence and discrimination.

Ah, America, land bringing together
so many different peoples!
A republic of ideals
born beneath the lofty banners,
the uniting principles of
freedom and equality.
As this century draws to its close,
the soul of your idealism
grieves at the stark realities of racial strife.

What is to become of the
spirit of your nation
fostered by so many people of
wisdom and philosophy?

My treasured friends.
There is no question that
your multiracial nation, America,
represents humanity's future.
Your land holds secret stores
of unbounded possibility, transforming
the energy of different cultures
into the unity of construction,
the flames of conflict
into the light of solidarity,

the eroding rivulets of mistrust
into a great broad flow of confidence.
On what can we ground our efforts
to open the horizons
of such a renaissance?

It is for just this reason,
my precious, treasured friends,
that you must develop within yourselves
the life-condition of jiyu—
Bodhisattva of the Earth.

As each group seeks their separate
roots and origins,
society fractures along a thousand fissure lines.
When neighbors distance themselves
from neighbors,
continue your uncompromising quest
for your truer roots
in the deepest regions of your lives.
Seek out the primordial "roots" of humankind.
Then you will without fail discover
the stately expanse of jiyu
unfolding in the depths of your life.

Here is the home, the dwelling place
to which humankind traces
its original existence—
beyond all borders,
beyond all differences of gender and race.
Here is a world offering true proof
of our humanity.

If one reaches back to these fundamental roots,
all become friends and comrades.
To realize this is to "emerge from the earth."

Past, present, future...
The causes and effects of the three existences

flow ceaselessly as the reality of life;
interlinked, they give rise to all
differences and distinctions.
Trapped in those differences
human society is wracked
by unending contention.

But the Buddhism of true cause,
expounded by the Daishonin
whose teachings we embrace,
enables us to break the spell
of past karma, past causes and effects,
and to awaken to the grand humanity
—the life of jiyu—
that had lain dormant in our hearts.

My mentor, President Toda,
taught us that when one embraces
the Mystic Law,
all intervening causes and effects
ebb and retreat, and there emerges
the "common mortal of kuon ganjo."
This, another name for Bodhisattva of the Earth,
is the greatness and splendor
of the human being writ large,
after all false distinctions and adornments
have been removed. .

Awaken to the life of jiyu within!
When the bright sun of "true cause" rises
the stars and planets
of past cause and effect grow dim
and the supreme world
of harmonious unity emerges—
the unity of friends and comrades
each manifesting the life-condition
of Bodhisattva of the Earth,
offering timeless proof that, indeed,
"The assembly on Eagle Peak has not yet dispersed."

Ah, my treasured friends,
whom I so deeply love and respect!
It is critical for you now
to directly perceive
the web of life that binds all people!

Buddhism describes
the connective threads of
"dependent origination."
Nothing in this world exists alone;
everything comes into being and continues
in response to causes and conditions.
Parent and child.
Husband and wife.
Friends. Races.
Humanity and nature.
This profound understanding
of coexistence, of symbiosis—
here is the source of resolution
for the most pressing and fundamental issues
that confront humankind
in the chaotic last years of this century.

The Buddhist scriptures include
the parable of "Two Bundles of Reeds"
aptly demonstrating this relation
of dependent origination.
Only by supporting each other
can the two bundles stand straight—
if one is removed, the other must fall.
Because this exists, so does that;
because that exists, so does this.

For several brilliant centuries
Western civilization has encouraged
the independence of the individual,
but now appears to be facing
a turbulent twilight.
The waves of egoism

eat away at the shores
of contemporary society.
The tragedy of division
wraps the world in a thick fog.
Individuals are becoming
mere scraps, mere fragments,
competing reed bundles of lesser self
threatened with mutual collapse.

My friends!
Please realize that you already possess
the solution to this quandary.
First you must break the hard shell
of the lesser self.
This you must absolutely do.
Then direct your lucid gaze
toward your friends, fellow members.

People can only live fully
by helping others to live.
When you give life to friends
you truly live.
Cultures can only realize
their further richness
by honoring other traditions.
And only by respecting natural life
can humanity continue to exist.

Now is the time for you to realize
that through relations
mutually inspiring and harmonious,
the "greater self" is awakened to dynamic action,
the bonds of life are restored and healed.
And blossoms in delightful multitude
exude the unique fragrance
of each person, of each ethnicity,
in precise accord with the principle of
"cherry, plum, peach and damson."

Our goal—
the Second American Renaissance.
Holding high the standard of humanity
we advance—
from divisiveness to union,
from conflict to coexistence,
from hatred to fraternity.
In our struggle, in our fight,
there cannot be
even a moment's pause or stagnation.
My beloved friends,
Bodhisattvas of the Earth
readying yourselves
for the new century's dawn!
With your own efforts
bring about a renaissance here,
in this "magnetic land"!

The certain signs of America reborn,
Los Angeles rejuvenated,
are to be found within your hearts.
With this pride and conviction,
be victorious in your daily life,
overcome your own weaknesses every day.
Never forget that it is only through
relentless challenge
—one step following another—
that you can steadily transform
your ideals into reality.

Buddhism is reason.
Therefore always maintain self-control.
Be the master of your actions.
Exercise common sense in society.
Keep a smiling countenance at home.
Be courteous to your friends and fellow members,
like a warm spring breeze to the suffering.
Reason exhaustively with the confused.

But, when you deal with the arrogant ones,
be bold and fearless like the lion king!

Look!
Seen from the Malibu Training Center
the Pacific Ocean's unbounded expanse
is bathed in radiant California sun.
An ocean of peace across whose surface
innumerable waves murmur and dance.

Beloved Los Angelenos!
I want you each to be
like the California sunshine
showering on all people
the bright light and warmth
of your compassion.
Be people who extend hope and courage,
who inspire respect and gratitude
wherever you go.

Buddhism teaches us the means
to overcome life's fundamental pain
—the sufferings of birth, aging, illness and death—
which none can escape,
and which no degree of wealth and fame
can relieve in the slightest.

Everyone, anyone
when returned to
their solitary human existence
is but a karma-laden "reed,"
trembling before the onslaught
of the four sufferings.

Seeking eternity within impermanence,
crossing over delusion to nurture confidence,
building happiness from anguish,
rush forward from today
toward tomorrow

in the prodigious battle that is
our human revolution!
For you are the Buddha's emissaries
upholding the ultimate philosophy of life!

Comrades!
Fellow Bodhisattvas of the Earth!
Born here, gathered together here in Los Angeles
that you might fulfill your mission—
Raise your voices in songs of praise
for freedom, democracy and humanity!
Wave the banners of culture and peace!

Ah, Los Angeles!
Here is to be found SULA,
a palace of intellect
for the pan-Pacific era
of the twenty-first century.
Here is located the World Culture Center,
dynamo of American kosen-rufu.
And here rises the splendid form
of the future site of the SGI Headquarters—
which will become the mainstay
of the grand endeavor of world kosen-rufu.
Truly a new wind will blow from the West!
Los Angeles, the stage on which you act
with such freedom and vigor
is the launching site for world kosen-rufu,
the cornerstone that links East and West.

Walt Whitman
giant of the American Renaissance
penned these words:
"Come, I will make the continent indissoluble,
I will make the most splendid race
    the sun ever shone upon,
I will make divine magnetic lands,
        With the love of comrades,
            With the life-long love of comrades."

Ah, Los Angeles!
The sun rises beyond the Rockies,
spreading its light over the wide Pacific.
Now! In its luminous beams,
let friend and friend pull together
in perfect unity, rowing into the seas—
embarking on a new leg
of our journey of kosen-rufu!

Grip the rudder,
hold firm to your course—
the Stars and Stripes,
the tricolor flag of the SGI,
ripple as a hopeful breeze fills our sails.
The lapping waves beat out their message
of congratulations upon our ship's bow!
Our destination—
America's distant future,
the lights and colors
of a century of life,
the brilliant glory of human harmony.

Commemorating the
Second SGI-USA General Meeting

January 27, 1993

Presented at a meeting held in Santa Monica, California, on January 27, 1993.

jiyu: literally, "to emerge from the earth." See Bodhisattvas of the Earth.

Herman Melville (1819–91): American novelist and poet best known for *Moby Dick; or, The Whale.*

"It rolls the midmost waters": Melville, *Moby Dick*, p. 355.

Kansai: a region spanning the south-central area of Japan's main island. In his youth, the author led the Soka Gakkai's activities in the region, and since then it has always served as the driving force of major organizational endeavors.

Buddhism of true cause: a Buddhist term that indicates Nichiren Daishonin's teachings.

kuon ganjo: a Buddhist term indicating the fundamental state of freedom and purity inherent in all life.

Eagle Peak (Skt Gridhrakūta): a mountain near the city of Rājagriha in Magadha in ancient India. It is also sometimes called Vulture Peak. It is said to be the place where Shakyamuni preached the Lotus Sutra.

"The assembly on Eagle Peak": trans. from Nichiren, *Nichiren Daishonin gosho zenshu*, p. 757.

cherry, plum, peach and damson: a Buddhist principle that likens each individual to a beautiful flower that has its own unique mission and potential.

"Come, I will make": Whitman, "For You O Democracy" in *Leaves of Grass*, p. 272.

Salute to mothers

Mother
you are sublime
noble, indomitable.

You are gentle
yet stronger than anyone.
Always smiling,
you are engaging and
intimidating.

And while you
may appear childlike,
you are a perceptive student of life
with a doctoral degree
in daily living.

The world without you
would be darkness.
With you, the world is warm
throughout the four seasons;
fragrant breezes blow
and harmonious gardens bloom.

Your soul is like that of a Buddha,
your heart, a Bodhisattva.
Your leadership and direction
are masterful, artistic.

Through suffering, joy or sadness
you always create a realm
of ease and comfort.

You are a brilliant physician
healing the heart's wounds.

Your own heart
is deeper than the ocean.
Your open truth-seeing eyes
your warm, familiar smile.

Day after day
at dawn, at midnight,
your wordless words convey
"I'm not letting you go, not yet."

Your prodigious soul
burns red like the sun.
You nourish us with
your bright beams.

Flooding us with
love-filled light,
you abhor dark and gloom.
Day in, day out,
you point the way,
guiding people
toward the towering
landmarks of peace.

Forging bonds of joy
with everyone you meet,
you engage in the compassionate
fight for human rights, for peace,
always advancing
one further step
toward a better world.

No one can match or better you—
not the famous,
not the politically powerful.

In your grandeur,
you create a limitless store
of profound and precious memories.

Completely unconcerned
by your lack of wealth,
you smile, serene and unperturbed.

You prepare your simple fare
laughing, praising yourself—
"Better than the best restaurant!"
You celebrate cramped quarters as
"More efficient and easier to clean!"
You rise above all groundless
criticism and slander.

You are reality's actor,
with more wisdom
than the most renowned.
For on a grand stage
on a higher plane
you dance with Buddhas
of the three existences,
amidst the applause
of Buddhist gods.
Such popularity!

No matter the slander
or criticism, you know
who is a liar,
who a hypocrite,
who is driven by jealousy.
Your powers of perception
are unrivaled by
any prosecuting attorney.

Never submitting
to the power of authority
or malicious lies,
you are a mother
of truth and justice.

To you, my gratitude.
To you, my most
profound respect.

January 2, 1995

Presented to members of the Soka Gakkai women's division.

Unfurl the banner of youth

Ode to my young successors, our treasures of Soka

Let the intemperate winds
gust and rave!
Let the implacable waves
roil and rage!

I am young,
my youth a crimson banner
I unfurl against the wind.
I fear nothing,
succumb to nothing.

Here is the promontory
from which I depart,
today is my first campaign.
Gazing into my future
I feel ever-greater strength and courage
well forth from within!

Oh, wind and wave!
I will brave each harsh test unfazed
as a youth worthy of greatness!
My friend, set out on open oceans!
I will seek out vast new lands.

I will rise, come what may,
to take on a lifetime of struggles
of my own choosing.
With certainty I embark
knowing I possess
great purpose.

I am youth
eagerly flying
into the teeth of the storm.

Soaring—
on incandescent wings of freedom
to heights beyond those imagined
by any head of state, decrepit with age,
with more wisdom
than any cunning politician.

This is what it means
to occupy the imperishable
throne of youth.
Bearing in our hearts
the never-dimming star of destiny,
we shine.
To make the entire world our stage—
this is what it means
to be young.

Young people are humanity's treasure,
the great earth
from which peace springs.
When we come together in unity,
the thunder clap resounds
with an explosive roar,
admonishing
the arrogance of power.

Your sparkling eyes,
the vibrancy and dignity
that issues from your lives,
your limitless vitality
racing and running without end—
all this is the mark
of your hallowed, hope-filled soul.

No sorrow, anguish or impediment
can slow you as you set out
for life's triumphal arch,
raising a cheerful toast
beneath the proudly fluttering

banner of victory,
new and crimson.

I will forge on, come what may!
For this is clear proof
of youthful years
supremely spent.
To what end? For what purpose?
In pursuit of those answers,
I will battle on forever.

The night tormented by the storm's rage
—the night of billows that froth and spew—
inevitably yields to the day
as it breaks through eastern skies.
Confidently anticipating
that dawn, I forge on
again today.

I call upon youth,
I urge each of you:
with firmly grounded acumen,
be vigilant! raise your voice! charge forth!
Never forget:
Beyond the distant horizon
are those who will follow after,
who await the arrival of a light
whose source is as old and deep
as time itself.

Go now, my young friends,
set off on white steeds!
Gallop majestically, brilliantly!
Stand tall
in the front ranks of the people,
embracing your life's purpose
as the Buddha instructed.

Ascend mountains
traverse valleys;
ascend them with pleasure,
traverse them in wonder
together with a multitude
of kindred spirits.

Push on bravely
through the deepest dark.
Your prized labors, sweat and toil
will lead you to the golden stage
of a new era
long dreamed of, yearned for.

My young friends!
Lift your sights, stand proud.
Take the lead in all things,
issue the loud clear call
of your very being and worth!

Young people
need never concede defeat—
for the refusal to give in
is in itself victory.

Young people need never kneel—
if your heart remains unbowed
in the face of any circumstance,
you will find
a glorious crown awaiting you.

Observe! Behold!
When I, a youth,
awaken and arise,
summoning forth my innermost strength,
a new era is invariably born,
and the dawn of revolution breaks!

A youth is one who can declare:
I am the eyes that reflect the future!
I am the fierce, eloquent flash of light
that reveals all truth
and exposes all lies,
the knife-edge of incisive justice
eternally stirring and rousing
human society...

May the gaze of the young gleam with hope!
May your hearts swell with energy and strength!

The waning century passes brutally.
Souls struggle in grief and dread,
writhe in heavy remorse.
Dark recoiling of the century's end,
glowering clouds of chaos,
trembling before demonic weaponry.

The fracturing blasts of gunshot and bombs,
the screams of mothers and children
fleeing in desperation—
such are the notes and sounds
the decaying century
has splattered on its score.

To quote Beethoven:
"Oh friends, not these tones!"

It is the potent voices of youth in song
that will heal and restore
humanity's wounded history.

For this to be a truly new era
a truly new generation
must conduct the performance
of a magnificent music
that resounds through the cosmos.

Join me in song, my friend!
Share these solemn steps!
Let us dance together!

This sublime symphony
of young champions!
The grand prelude has already begun.

The bell has been struck!
Hoist sail!
Weigh anchor!
It is time for youth,
wrapped in stars of glory,
to set out upon
this vast, unending journey!

My eternal comrades!
Are you fully prepared to win?
Pay meticulous heed to each detail,
for once you leave this rocky,
sheltering shore,
there is no turning back.

Leap like orcas breaching
upon the vast, expansive seas.
Feel the rolling of each massive wave
as the rocking of a cradle.
Never forget the inner fortitude
that brings triumph and success!

Each and every one of you!
Strive so that the many
—ally and adversary alike—
may all without exception
reach the far shores
of happiness and peace.

Step forward to become
the bow that slices

through wind and wave!
Serve as roaring engine
and driving propeller!
Work around the clock,
toiling in the engine room
though soot and grease
clog your every pore!

With joy and enthusiasm,
explore and pioneer your self.
Cross the tempest seas
in search of the untrod soil
of a new continent
dense with thick forests.
Reach those lands,
go boldly ashore!

Life is a struggle,
a battle lasting a lifetime.
This is a fact
we can neither deny nor avoid.

A proud and independent champion,
I wait for no one.
My heart is the site of ceaseless struggle,
a battlefield where fierce contests are waged—
the advance and retreat
of hope and despair,
courage and cowardice,
progress and stagnation.

No matter how bitter or deadening,
how harrowing or strained
my days may be,
I will advance one step
and then another,
until I break through
and open the path for all.

May you always heed these words:
"Nichiren's disciples cannot accomplish anything
if they are cowardly."
"Until kosen-rufu is achieved,
propagate the Law to the full extent of your ability,
without begrudging your life."

Upholding these admonitions,
fight on with the noble spirit
of fearless heroes.

Young friends!
Because you are thoroughly versed
in profound philosophical truths,
you must never be fooled by impostors,
never mesmerized by their sorcery.
Unsheathe the blade of justice
until the last vicious oppressor
is brought low.

Let the winds of courage blow!
Daily strike this brazen bell!
Let the cry of our solidarity
reverberate in triumph!

Do not fear the howl of wolves!
Let them hear in turn the roar of lions!

In the midst of a defiled society
throw open the angry gates
and advance against those
who would upend what is right!
Let them know the strict severity
of endless regret!

Together let us win,
together spill tears of joy.
Never submit to those
who would bind our hearts with hypocrisy.

The pitched battles
in which youth engage
will invariably bring down
every last adversary of the Buddha.
Thus become
the effulgent sun
liberating people from fear!

In Hall Caine's masterwork,
Rossi and Bruno, two young comrades,
join each other's strengths in trust.
Undeterred by threat of execution
they struggle inseparably in order to build
"The Eternal City."

My young friends—
with an even greater comradeship
and unity of purpose,
succeed in constructing
an eternal city enduring over
the three realms of past, present and future!
This is the meaning of kosen-rufu.

Until that day,
lock arms on shoulders
and advance!

There are thousands, tens of thousands,
of young people who embrace
the same ideals of peace
awaiting you in the United States!
Thousands, ten thousands more
great comrades await
in Latin and Central America;
in Europe as well!
In Africa, Asia and Oceania!

Join hands
—freely, fully—

with all the world's youth!
Set your feet and move as one.
Build the Eternal City of the Twenty-first Century,
adamantine and indestructible!

In commemoration of July 3,
the day Josei Toda was released from prison,
the day I was imprisoned

Written in 1998 to commemorate July 3, the day the author was detained
on false charges in 1957. On the same day in 1945, his mentor Josei Toda was
released from prison where he had been incarcerated by Japan's wartime
military government.

"Oh friends, not these tones!": trans. from Beethoven, "An die Freude" (Ode
to Joy) in *Symphonien Nr 6–9*, p. 195.

"Nichiren's disciples": Nichiren, *The Writings of Nichiren Daishonin*, vol. 1,
p. 481.

"Until kosen-rufu is achieved": trans. from Nichiren, *Nichiren Daishonin
gosho zenshu*, p. 1618.

Hall Caine's masterwork: Caine, *The Eternal City*.

The poet—warrior of the spirit

Dedicated to Dr. Mbuyiseni Oswald Mtshali,
a great poet fighting for human rights

Truly great poetry
is born in the midst of struggle.

Just as the light of dawn
is born from pitched battle
between night and day.
Or the giant tree
soaring skyward
grows from a tiny
storm-battered sapling.

Just as the hammer
of hardship tempers
the treasure-sword of the soul.
Or the clash of stone against stone
sends a brilliant flash
through the dark.

The true poet
is born of the fight for justice.
He awakens and arises
from amongst a
people in struggle.

He writes poems
with his own blood,
recording the people's
crimson cries for truth—
preserving them eternal and indelible
against the erasing sands of oblivion.

He fashions a pen
from his own bones,

so that none may forget
the tormented groans
of a people whose backs have bent
beneath the crushing burden
of oppression.

He engraves his poems
in his own skin,
vowing to transform
the brands of discrimination
and contempt
into the glorious crown
of human greatness.

He offers his own life
to heal the wounded soul
of the people.
And the poet,
knowing the full brilliance of
life encountering life,
makes of himself a flame.

To warm the hearts
of those who shiver
in the hopeless desolation of winter.
To raze the strongholds
of malicious falsehood
and groundless rumor.

To become a beacon
that brightly lights
the way forward for those
who cross uncharted seas.
To offer himself
on the altar of ideals—
and send a sacred spark
leaping into people's hearts.

This is his joy.
Just as the sun
consumes itself
as it illuminates the world.

My dear friend,
great poet in the struggle
for human rights!
Dr. Mbuyiseni Oswald Mtshali!

The great earth of the people rumbles,
pulling down the wall of injustice,
hardened by suspicion and terror.

The thunderous call of the spirit
reverberates across the sky
joining and celebrating
the hammer blows of construction—
an eternal citadel of peace!

To the sound of your drum
a new humanity arose!
By your sword
the chains of resignation and despair
were sundered!
In your flame
the pride of a people
once laid prostrate
arose again and flared
toward the heavens.

And even now
the seeds and sparks
of hope you've sown
continue to spread
beneath the rainbows
of your motherland
across the fields
under the Earth's blue skies.

Ah, the true poet is born
in the midst of great struggle.

Together let us sow these seeds
in the vast expanse
of the hearts of youth
as they advance boldly
onto the brilliant stage
of the twenty-first century.

Together let us spread
flame-seeds of passion and vigor!
Sparks of freedom and justice!
Of courage and hope!
The soul-flames of humanism
that will brightly illuminate
our world.

> The memory of our first encounter, seven years ago,
> in early summer, is still vividly present in the depths
> of my life. I have written this poem to express my
> gratitude for the impassioned poem that you sent
> on the occasion of the anniversary of the founding of
> the Soka Gakkai. I have tried to express, just as they
> are, my deepest sentiments, of flame meeting flame,
> and rising ever higher.

> November 23, 1998

Presented to Mbuyiseni Oswald Mtshali, a South African poet and cam-
paigner against apartheid. Mr. Mtshali and the author met for the first time
in May 1991 in Tokyo.

May the fragrant laurels of happiness adorn your life

Dedicated to my beloved young women's division members

How beautiful is the sun,
its limitless, multihued lights revealing
the inherent dignity of humankind!
This undeniable force,
this unfaltering existence dedicated
to fulfilling its vow,
to illuminating all things for all time!

In the presence of the sun
there is no darkness.
In the presence of the sun
there is no discrimination.
In the presence of the sun
the same rights are shared by all
and a world of peace shines brightly.

Today once more
I will walk my chosen path
pursue my chosen work
bring my history to new luster.
Undeterred by deceitful rains,
I will walk a path of bright smiles
true to myself, as only I can,
undefeated by anything!
For I understand this path
to be my treasured way.

Youth—
this time in life that comes but once,
dignified and precious
like a glittering gem.
I will live vivaciously, with all my might.
Because to do so is to lay the foundations

of a lifetime,
and from here is born a new happiness
arising from the very core of my being.

I will never stop advancing!
Even in the face of great difficulties
I will not turn back.
Life must be lived—
strongly, honestly, cheerfully!

Of course there will be bad times
along with the good.
But I will never hurl insults at life.

The growing vital force that is youth—
in each joyous stride
there is so much to read and learn
so much wisdom to seek.

Whatever the blizzards of this life
you can emerge triumphant
by the strengths residing
within your heart.

What a joyful prospect—
to live each day of youth
with wisdom, savoring happiness
and meaningful hope
in a world peopled with beautiful hearts!

In such a life,
everything you undergo
forms a fragrant crown
of woven flowers
that adorns your brow.

Daughter of unfathomable mission!
You transform the ashen winter landscape

into a vivid dance of spring
bathed in soft sunlight.

I will not lose my footing
in the morass of society.
I feel no envy for the illusory shadows
of glamour and fame.
Nor am I shaken by heartless criticism.

For I embrace principles
that are eternal
and merit my complete faith.
I have my SGI family—
sisters who share my aspirations,
who are trustworthy
and with whom I can share anything.

The inner vitality of youth
bright as the morning sun
holds all the world's wealth of gold.
To be young, in itself,
is to inhabit a castle of jewels.

The palace of your life sparkles
with the light of gems more numerous
than the stars filling the heavens.

Nothing could be more sublime
than this treasure possessed by all.
No one in this world is better than others.
We are all equally, ordinarily human.

In his later years
the world-acclaimed violinist
Yehudi Menuhin declared:
God resides within our hearts.
Likewise, the Buddha is found
within our lives,
not in temples or monasteries.

This treasure is something
that no one can take from you
for it *is* you, you yourself.
To awaken to this fact
is happiness.

Just as the lamp you light for another
will illuminate your own way,
the heart that desires the happiness of others
will be filled with the bright starlight
of happiness.

My joy is not confined
within a narrow room.
There is space for all to enter,
for this friend and that.

The forces of selfish ego
work to drive others out,
to gain sole possession
of the jeweled chamber.
Such people end up
banished from their own palace,
left to wander in hellish solitude.

The warm camaraderie
of friends joined hand in hand,
like endless vistas of floral garlands,
multiplies my joy many times over.

"Kindness is the flower of strength,"
said José Martí, hero of Cuban independence.

As a flower that blooms proudly
despite the pelting rains,
I will share this smile
with my friends and companions!

If you are cowardly or weak
you cannot offer others protection.
In the end, you'll be left facing
your most pitiable, compassionless self.

Only by triumphing over your own sorrow
can you fully feel the dark misery
afflicting a friend.
Only when you win over your own weakness
can you ease the troubles of others.

Be strong! Ever strong!
These are the crucial watchwords
that open the doors
to the palace of happiness.
Bid farewell to songs of sadness.
Triumph over inner weakness.
Reject self-deception
and come to know yourself
as someone who never betrays
what is true and just!

Faith is not emotionalism or self-pity;
it is about winning in your life!

Daughter with sparkling eyes!
Your youth alone makes you
a princess of happiness!
Soar high above the
sinister anguished clouds!
Stretch wide the wings of freedom
propelled by the vibrant force
of your spirit!
Gaze down from those heights
on festering swamps of envy!

You must never submit
to forlornly swaying emotions.
Maintain your pride and dignity!

Direct your heart with
firmness and certainty!

Always remember
you are a monarch of humanity!
Maintain regal focus
on a treasured throne
enveloped in a world
of rich colors and varied lights!

Nichiren Daishonin instructs us
to be the masters of our minds
and not let our minds be our masters.
These words are an eternal beacon
to light your life's journey.

In my heart—
the flame of an imperishable philosophy burns
the light of lifetime purpose shines
magnificent goals reside.

Those whose hearts are set
on profound and focused prayer
are freed from hesitancy.
They do not fear
the aimless drifting into darkness.
In the depths of their being
a bright, untrammeled path
of peace and contentment
unfolds without end.

I will not drown in the
illusory images of renown
as they shimmer fleetingly
on the water's surface!

Make companions
of the sun and the moon
as they shine with undying light!

Take joy in quiet striving
on the ground of daily living.
Live out your life in its actuality
—in the midst of reality—
advancing always toward happiness!

Noble young women!
Do not cling to trivial things!
For the foolish find themselves living
far from the realm of heavenly beings.
They will be carried off by angry, roaring waves.

Never be deceived or taken in!
There is not the slightest need
to be jealous
of anyone else!

Only you know the reality
of your own life.
The scorn of others
based on their personal perception
is nothing more than that.
Live true to yourself—
those who do
are happy.

If you are wise and clear-sighted
you have already attained
a life of magnificent victory.

I possess the mirror
of pristine life
that reflects with unsparing clarity
the evil of this world—
a life that, like the pure white lotus,
remains unsullied
amidst the dirt and dust
of a squalid age!
I possess the jewel-encrusted

sword of an idealism that makes
the corrupt and unscrupulous
tremble in shame!

Fresh new flower of revolution!
Joan of Arc for the coming era!
With your silvery voice
you reinvigorate
the sleepy veterans
of past campaigns;
you inspire courage in the hearts
of a fatigued generation
spurring them
to rise and fight again.

History recounts
that Joan of Arc
was just an ordinary girl.
But the people of the village
where she lived described her
as a young woman of initiative.

She willingly worked,
she readily spun,
she gladly pulled the plow…
And when the time came,
she took the lead
to fight and rescue
France from peril!

The curtain is now rising
on the grand stage
of the twenty-first century!
The time has come
for the daughters of the sun
crowned with laurels
to take the lead
to move with vibrant
grace and courage! ·

A fresh breeze blows
and the pure blue sky
stretches into eternity.
So let us spread our wings!
Rise dancing bravely into the sky,
fly with flaming hope
into the future that awaits
in the vast new century
that is yours.

Daughters of the sun!
Always remember
the noble mothers and fathers
who worked selflessly
braving wind and rain
to build this Soka castle
of value creation!

March 24, 1999

Written for the members of the Soka Gakkai young women's division.

"Kindness is the flower of strength": trans. from Martí, *Amistad Funesta* (Fatal Friendship) in *Obras Completas*, vol. 18, p. 198.

José Martí (1853–95): Cuban poet, journalist and revolutionary philosopher known as the "Apostle of Cuban Independence."

The noble voyage of life

Dedicated to my respected and esteemed friends
in the SGI men's division

He was an elementary school principal,
lacking any particular renown,
and he was a geographer of vision.
He was further a hero of kosen-rufu
practicing precisely as the Buddha taught.
He was founder of the Soka Gakkai
and its tradition of refuting erroneous teachings,
the practice of the Lotus Sutra.

He became a towering practitioner
of the ultimate principle of life
—the Mystic Law expounded by Nichiren—
and died a martyr to his beliefs.

At the age of fifty-seven, in 1928,
Makiguchi Sensei
—my mentor's mentor—
initiated the struggle to spread the teachings
without regard to personal well-being.
Later, he declared to his disciples:
    With a joy that is beyond the power of words to express,
    I completely renewed the basis of
    the life I had led for almost sixty years!

At the age of fifty-nine,
on the eve of his sixtieth birthday
—highly significant in East Asian tradition
as the completion of one cycle of life—
Makiguchi Sensei
founded the Soka Kyoiku Gakkai—
Society for Value-creating Education.

Battling treacherous political authorities
and corrupt priests filled with
contempt for ordinary people,
he stood as firm as a sheer cliff.
Overcoming countless onslaughts,
he forged on with powerful conviction,
offering his crimson lifeblood to the struggle.

There were times
when family and followers
looked at him beseechingly,
fearful for their noble father.
There were times when the sight
of their stern father clad in the armor
of indescribable suffering
drained the color from their faces.

Ahead of him lay the harassments
of unbridled authority;
in his path loomed persecutions
at the hands of militarists.
Without thought of retreat he strode on,
bold as a lion—forward, ever forward.

When his disciples
were laid prostrate and confounded
in a desert wasteland of oppression,
he alone, a lion of lofty ideals,
traversed the deep ravines,
continuing his ceaseless quest,
his clear gaze trained always on the future.

Having sustained the fight for justice
until the final moment of his life,
with the banner of peace in view,
Makiguchi Sensei died in prison,
martyred to his convictions
at the age of seventy-three,

thus engraving the mark
of his struggle indelibly in history.

The membership of three thousand
who had followed him
were brutally suppressed and scattered
by the relentless persecutions
of the government.
But there was one disciple, Josei Toda,
who fully shared his sense of purpose—
a disciple determined to serve
his true and eternal mentor.
Toda shook with rage and wept bitter tears
in his own dark, cramped cell,
driven to paroxysms of grief
at the news of his mentor's death.

Moved by sorrow, outrage and pain
and a burning thirst for vengeance,
his heart began its pilgrimage—
he would triumph over the dark powers
that had made his just, beloved teacher
end his days in prison.

Josei Toda emerged
from the prison gates,
bearing within him a heart and spirit
of massive proportion.
A movement to rebuke and rectify
for all eternity
the insidious, violent abuses of power
had begun.
This was the bold, new start
of a battle against falsehood
and arrogance.

His intense efforts ignited a flame
of continuous struggle

that leapt from heart to heart.
He forged on
with unstoppable energy,
living each moment
of this never-to-be-repeated life
as if it were his last,
entrusting everything
to his disciples
as his will and testament.

It is now more than forty years
since the great Josei Toda passed away
like the tide withdrawing
and returning to the ocean.
Sensing the reality
of his eternal presence among us
we resolved to carry on his work
as his disciples, as comrades of like mind.
Determined to act as a direct disciple,
I stood in the vanguard
amid the gathering storm,
and many other disciples stood with me.

Makiguchi Sensei and Toda Sensei
were both active at ages
that would have made them members
of today's proud men's division.

They had no crown, no fame…
Enduring criticism and abuse,
they pressed on from one struggle
for the sake of the Law to the next,
in perfect accord
with the teachings of Nichiren.

My mentor, Toda Sensei, often said:
    Let cowards depart!
    Those who will leave should go!
    Let critics say what they will!

The impassioned core of our beings
connects directly to the Daishonin
and to the spirit of kosen-rufu.

We have tears of compassion
and the strength of the noonday sun.
In dark times of hardship
we maintain beautiful, noble hearts.
More than anything
we are surrounded by the most precious
jewel in the entire universe—
the treasure of our faith.

Both Makiguchi Sensei and Toda Sensei
raised their voices to call forth
heroic youth, youth who will
advance bravely into the teeth of the storm!
Disciples who will not weep
at approaching persecution,
but will fight on
brimming with calm confidence!
Youth who will pursue
this glorious advance
to the ends of the Earth
and into the endless future!

No one can help but pause for thought
when faced with the solemn
life-to-life bond
of mentor and disciple,
this most sublime of human ties.
Traitors will inevitably
be defeated and disappear;
cowards will unquestionably
incur karmic retribution.

With resounding music,
the heavenly deities
of future, present and past

aid this noble progress
of mentor and disciple.
Those who, out of envy,
criticize and attack this procession
of kosen-rufu, of mentor and disciple,
are nothing, devoid of all
substance or significance.

How joyous are our poems of glory,
how exuberant our melodious lives!
How magnificent to stroll
the gardens of our eternal destiny!

Above us, the celebratory skies
that encompass all things:
stars, moon, forests, clouds…
This path is true!
It is the path to realizing
our self's authentic purpose,
a path without regret!

Victor Hugo, poet and fighter,
proclaimed that life is a voyage.
Declaring himself an invincible lion,
he advanced fiercely,
turning aside the angry surge!

He lived a regal drama,
surmounting persecution,
plots and exile:
    Thunder, roar as you will!
    For I will roar back even louder!

Premier Zhou Enlai,
who dedicated his life to revolution
and to the construction of a new China,
declared:
    Victory cannot be achieved
    by sitting and waiting for it to happen;

it must be won through struggle.
His heart remained ever youthful
even as he advanced in years.
Always standing at the forefront,
he propelled the drive for success.

We who champion kosen-rufu,
the noblest of humanity's endeavors,
must never be afraid,
must never be defeated!

If we cease in our efforts,
the Daishonin will grieve,
humanity will sink into barbarism,
falling under a dark and endless pall,
adrift in interminable suffering
and unbroken cycles of misery.

The Daishonin proclaimed:
    Now when Nichiren and his followers chant
    Nam-myoho-renge-kyo,
    they are like the blowing of a great wind.
And:
    Nam-myoho-renge-kyo is like the roar of a lion.
Such serenely confident words!

It may be that
the fainthearted will despair
and the weak-willed will flee.

But we will inscribe a magnificent
history in the depths of our being
day after day, year after year.
In the Latter Day of the Law
—an age ruled by dark destiny—
our hearts burn ever brighter
as we journey across eternity,
laughing off the world's frenzied criticisms,

seeing, appreciating and extolling
all that is beautiful in this world.

Enjoying heart-to-heart ties
with so many treasured friends—
our lives will continue,
joyful and vigorous, beyond death,
across the full spectrum of time!
What an exquisite achievement
and indestructible honor
to share this voyage of life with comrades,
celebrating victory together,
bathed in the moon's beautiful light!

How sad and vain are the lives
of those who choose to stay behind!
The Daishonin rebukes those who,
refusing to think seriously about life,
abandon their humanity.
Never allow yourself to become alienated
from the harmonious community
of believers dedicated to kosen-rufu
and descend into the pit of isolation!
To choose solitude
may seem free of constraint,
but it is like a spirit
that has lost its weighted center
and flown into fragments.

Buddhism is win or lose,
the Daishonin declared.
The most intense persecutions
that he endured for the sake of Buddhism
all arose from false accusations.
The human heart can be frightening,
sinister and dark.
The persecutions that befell
followers like Shijo Kingo

were likewise the result
of base betrayal.

Why did the Nichiren Shoshu priesthood decline?
Because of arrogance and envy!
Because of their laziness and negligence!
Because of their idleness and chatter!
Because of smugness and conceit!
Because of greed and ignorance!
Because of their slander and lies!
Because they sought to destroy
    the harmonious unity of believers!

Why has the Gakkai flourished?
Because of our selfless dedication!
Because of our unceasing devotion!
Because we treasure the Law even above our lives!
Because of brave and diligent exertion!
Because of perseverance and fortitude!
Because of the spirit of oneness of mentor and disciple!
Because we enjoy the unity
    of many in body, one in mind!

My friends in the men's division,
it is crucial that you win in society
and in the workplace,
that you form bonds
of trust and friendship with many others,
that you be a citadel serving as
a happy haven to your family,
and that, in vigorous health,
you triumph over the
demanding challenges of daily life!

Your life, your being,
is yours for all time.
Thus everything depends on
how you forge yourself,
how you improve yourself,

how you develop a happy life—
this is the aim of human revolution.

Buddhism teaches reason,
the universal law of causality
by which we can realize
the eternity of our lives.

Buddhism elucidates
the essence of life's causal law.
This law is strict. It teaches:
the three thousand realms
—the entirety of being—
are ultimately a reflection
of our innermost life.
Buddhism surpasses
other philosophies
in keenly clarifying
this reality.

The truth does not exist
apart from our lives.
The law of cause and effect
is the reality of all phenomena.
Cause and effect exist simultaneously.
Causes and effects shape each moment
in the inexorable flow of time
as it carries us forward.

There is a profound continuity
of good and evil,
happiness and unhappiness,
hellish suffering and enlightenment.

My dear friends, my comrades!
Please enjoy good health and longevity!
For that is the first, essential step
toward happiness and victory.

Be big-hearted!
Be deep-hearted!
Be warm-hearted!
Be strong-hearted!
For this is the mark
of a victorious Buddhist practice!

Wherever you go,
be a pillar of strength
who brings peace of mind to all!
Be a person of expansive,
magnanimous character
who enables all to harbor hope!

Be a monarch of humanity
shining like the Treasure Tower
where you are in this moment!

March 26, 1999

Written for the members of the Soka Gakkai men's division.

"With a joy that is beyond": trans. from Makiguchi, *Soka kyoikugaku taikei kogai* (Overview of the System of Value-Creating Pedagogy) in *Makiguchi Tsunesaburo zenshu*, vol. 8, p. 406.

Soka Kyoiku Gakkai: forerunner of the Soka Gakkai, founded in 1930. Makiguchi formed this group of educators to promote the teachings of Nichiren based on his original theory of value-creating education.

"Thunder, roar as you will!" trans. from Hugo, "Ibo" in *Les Contemplations*, vol. 2, p. 177.

Victory cannot be achieved: see Zhou Enlai, *Shuonrai senshu*, vol. 2, p. 390 (in Japanese).

"Now when Nichiren": Nichiren, *The Record of the Orally Transmitted Teachings*, p. 96.

"Nam-myoho-renge-kyo is like": Nichiren, *The Writings of Nichiren Daishonin*, vol. 1, p. 412.

the Latter Day of the Law: a Buddhist term indicating the last of the three periods following Shakyamuni's death, when Buddhism is predicted to fall into confusion and his teachings lose the power to lead people to happiness.

Shijo Kingo (*c.* 1230–1300): a samurai and devoted follower of Nichiren.

Nichiren Shoshu (Orthodox Nichiren sect): a sect of Buddhism which regards Nichiren as its founder. It parted company with the Soka Gakkai, its lay organization, in 1991.

Standing among the ruins of Takiyama Castle

To my beloved Soka students
and members of the student division nationwide

In the far distance,
rising into the azure sky,
Mount Fuji clothed in white.

Oh, Hachioji!
Place of music,
of poetic artistry.

One winter's morning
when the world was bright
with the sun's embrace
I stood with my wife
among the castle ruins.

Beyond the old Takiyama Highway
which runs beneath
we could see Soka University
—flourishing sanctuary of wisdom—
sparkling in the morning sun.
Soka Women's College,
graceful and elegant as a flower,
glistened on an adjacent hill.

This historic place
nestled in tranquillity
is remote from the bustling world.

Coming here,
one enters a peaceful, verdant realm
filled with life and beauty.
Gazing up at magnificent white clouds
one is in a world apart,
wrapped in transparent stillness.

Nowadays, the old water wheels
and thatched houses
are rarely seen
on Musashino Plain.
Yet here remains, through untold ages,
this treasure house of nature's poetry—
the ruins of Takiyama Castle.

In the still, clear air,
a path strewn with fallen leaves
forms a tunnel through the trees,
and calls to the woods
with the loneliness of an orphan.

Along this narrow trail
which countless warriors
once traversed,
where soldiers once drank
in victory celebrations,
my wife and I approached the peak.

On both sides of the path
bordered by fresh, translucent green,
the unforgettable sight of towering trees.
Proud and composed,
roots steadfastly clutching rock,
they seem to proclaim a state
of calm, undaunted being.

A magnificent brocade,
woven of an infinite variety
of ever-changing flora,
blankets the slope of the rising hill.

The path, silent and resigned,
is strewn with blighted leaves.
Stirred by a gentle wind,
those still on the branches
flutter into a crimson blizzard.

The wood is silent and undisturbed
save for the occasional
purifying singing of wild birds.

Their shadows flash past
and the song of their joy of living
fades into the depths of the grove.

The bright sun
filtering through the treetops
shines upon each life,
caressing even the tips of leaves,
and a warm compassionate light
permeates the wood.

We reach the crest of the hill;
in the distance,
the clear waters of the Tama River
twined together like
silver threads.
A lone streak of cloud
stretches across the vast sky.

In bygone days the air was filled
with the raised voices of warriors
who marched along this path.

At times singing
loudly their victory songs.
At times exhausted
but filled with fresh resolve—
to fight once more today,
to defend again tomorrow.

The sound of a thousand suits of armor
gleaming in the morning sun—
together, my beloved comrade in arms,
let us adorn our undefeated lives!

There were times when
all that remained were
deep sighs and silent footsteps,
when there were neither tears nor words.

There were also times
in this history woven
of life and struggle,
when comrades endured parting
on this very path,
one wrapping another
in homespun cloth,
carefully shielding
his head from above.

Here in these ruins
I envision the ghostly
figures of warriors
laughing, bustling, milling about...

In my mind's eye I see
the brilliant students of Soka University
frequenting this place through the seasons.
In spring
a drift of blossoms from
a thousand cherry trees.
In summer
the rows of tall green trees
unyielding and staunch.
In autumn
the rich symphony
of the insects' cheerful song.
In winter
contemplating life and truth,
the sturdy wood
a silver world mantled in snow.

Sometimes it is a jogging track,
the "Takiyama Castle course"—

where mind and body are forged
strong as steel.

Sometimes a studio
where young da Vincis
cultivate their artistic skills—
their works, already exhibited abroad,
winning the praise of their peers.

Sometimes this place
is a natural plaza where,
engrossed in dialogue and
oblivious to the passage of time,
friends forge lifelong bonds.

At times, this is a place
where young students
from around the world
gather joyfully,
linking hearts across the globe.

Sometimes it is a path
of contemplation and philosophy
imbued with the personal memories
of a troubled heart.

From the window
of Soka University's newly built
Central Tower
the ruins of the castle,
surrounded by lush green,
are visible as well.

In my heart I am always
together with the students of Soka University,
walking where they walk,
pausing where they pause,
breathing the air they breathe.

And I offer words of respect
to the long-gone lord of the castle
for magnanimously embracing
protecting and nurturing
the Soka students:
"Thank you for taking care
of my beloved sons,
my precious daughters!"

In times past,
this is a place where
countless battles raged.
Always the castle remained undefeated,
defiantly defended to the last
though often destruction loomed.
The Kanto region's foremost mountain castle—
without keep or cut-stone walls
but fashioned of natural valleys and cliffs.

In 1569—the twelfth year of Eiroku,
Takeda Shingen, marching on Odawara
to attack the Hojo clan,
made camp in Haijima forest.
From there he sent twenty thousand of his men
exhorting them to hold
a "festival of blood"
in Takiyama Castle.

Although those who defended Takiyama
numbered a mere two thousand,
Shingen's expectations were betrayed:
"Why don't they give in…"
"What's taking so long…"

The lord of Takiyama Castle, Hojo Ujiteru,
gave this command:
"Fight or die with this castle
as your pillow.

Do not allow the enemy to take
even a single step inside these walls!"

The general Ujiteru
was the first to rush forward
to meet the attacking foe.

A single force, two thousand strong,
rose in a high-spirited,
indomitable response:
"We'll protect this, our castle, at any cost!"
"We'll fight until the very last moment of life!"

The outer defenses were breached,
yet the soldiers held their ground
and launched a fresh attack
which thoroughly unnerved Katsuyori,
the famous Shingen's son.
Shingen, once thought to be invincible,
finally sounded the retreat.

Oh, the glorious
ruins of Takiyama Castle,
which the soldiers resolutely
protected as their very own!

Later, Ujiteru moved
to Hachioji Castle
and Takiyama, now deserted,
was swallowed by weeds and wood.

Centuries of seasons have passed…
the deep trenches
seem even now to hide soldiers
and the level courtyards
are untouched since that time.

It is just as it was
in those ancient days

when generals saw the moon reflected
in their *sake* cups,
and the skies resounded
with the beat of battle drums.

Those several hundred years
seem like a single day in this place
where history's churning has ceased
and turned all to a tranquil paradise
of flowers and green
breathing life, the future, peace.

These ruins of Takiyama Castle
and Soka University
are like friends, brothers.
The enduring bond
of the two adjacent green hills
will remain in history for all time.

On mornings
when the same sun smiled on our waking,
through evenings when we slept
watched over by the same constellations…
The same wind and snow we braved
and on sunny days
the same view of distant Mount Fuji
we shared.

The fortress of past wars
has quietly watched over
a newborn fortress of peace.

Thirty years have passed
since Soka University's founding.
The ruins of Takiyama Castle
have listened quietly
to the hammering sounds of construction
as the school steadily grew.
You have watched

the noble sight of youth,
of students tempering
mind and spirit,
making their way
out into the world.

Whenever they came to you,
you enfolded them in your gentle embrace
just as they are
—all their worries, sorrow and sufferings,
their joys, excitement and hopes—
giving a long, deep nod of assurance.

I once told the students:
We are one
in body and spirit.
No one can break our bond.

On another occasion I wrote:
I shall protect you with all my life.
Because that is for me
the greatest joy.

To open a path for you—
that is everything to me.

I wish to spend the closing years of my life
here in Hachioji
watching over and fostering the Soka students...
These are my true sentiments
which I have expressed again and again,
and I wish to spend
ever more time with you
here on the campus of Soka University.

I want to do anything
I possibly can for you.
Soka University is my life

and you are my eternal comrades,
through the three existences of past, present and future.

A giant tree begins
as a tiny seed buried in the dirt.
With all its might it draws
nourishment and develops a robust shoot.
With all its strength it pushes through the soil
and expands myriad roots
to bind it firmly with the earth.

This precisely is the way
for you to grow.
Break through the hard ground,
face the wind and frost,
dauntless, unwavering,
dignified and unrestrained,
always true to yourself,
higher, taller.

My cherished friends,
students of Soka University,
I urge you:
Be strong in the days
of your youth!
Be strong throughout your life!
Be unyielding, decisive in your strength!
For herein lies the key
to victory in all things!

Relentlessly study and learn!
Single-mindedly, determinedly
study and learn!
For herein lies victory
amid the harsh realities of life!

Never be defeated,
never wallow in self-pity.
Conquer your own mind!

A struggle with yourself—
that is the reality of your life
for the entirety of your life.

In all things,
bravely challenge the
task that lies before you
heroic in your quest
for wisdom and intellect.

Do not be impatient!
Do not retreat or fall behind!
Advance, simply continue
to advance! This is the way
of victorious youth.
All you need do
is advance on your own unique path
true always to yourself!

Each of you give form
to the founding spirit
in a way that is true to you;
let it shine from your life—
this precisely
is your mission,
which I trust you to fulfill.

When I envision you,
together and in solidarity
with my beloved members
of the student division
throughout the nation and the world,
actively engaged, dynamically contributing
on the grand stage of the new century,
further faith and conviction well up,
my hopes and dreams expand
without limit.

The Japanese cedar soaring into the heavens,
the beautiful ash with its shining trunk,
oak, beech, cherry...
On the hill of Takiyama Castle
hundreds, thousands of trees quietly stand,
each with its own rich uniqueness,
connected, moreover,
within the unseen web of life.

Your elder brothers and sisters,
with whom you share such deep bonds,
are struggling to their utmost!
Even as they are tossed about
by the rough seas of reality,
with love and pride they earnestly strive
to eternalize their alma mater!

More than anything,
it is this robust and brilliant spirit
that brings me, as founder, joy.

How my heart leaps with delight
when I learn
of the successes and achievements
of Soka Alumni.
How it pains me
to hear their sad news.
These are feelings known only
by the founder of a university.

My friends,
for all eternity
I will be together with you!
For all eternity
I will be your ally!

Time has passed,
clouds have drifted westward

and the shadow of the wood
has grown darker by degrees.

Beneath the dry leaves
where we tread
young seeds are sprouting
from the earth.
Young buds, small and firm,
enduring the coldness of the wind
and eagerly awaiting the arrival of spring,
peer from the branches of the trees.

Beyond the dignified trees
which form a triumphant arch
I see, bathed in the crimson sunset,
the Central Tower of Soka University
rising majestically into the sky.

Spring—
In spring of the year 2000
again, the hills of Musashino
will be radiant with beautiful light,
a fresh abundance of green
colored by the drifting
petals of cherry blossoms
breathing new life to the world.

I wait for spring,
for the time when
my cherished Soka students
will soar into the skies
of the twenty-first century!
When we will celebrate joyously
our thirtieth anniversary,
and welcome fresh young scholars
to the campus of the third millennium!
And that is the time
when we send out into the world
a brilliant light of hope!

I wait,
in happy anticipation
I will continue
to await
your growth!
your victory!
your glory!

> Looking into the shining eyes of my Soka students
> bravely embarking into the twenty-first century

> January 2000

Written for students and alumni of the Soka Schools and Soka University as well as for members of the student division in Japan. The ruins of Takiyama Castle are located near Soka University in Hachioji, Tokyo, which was founded by the author in 1971.

Takiyama Castle: a mountain castle built in 1521; its ruins stand near the campus of Soka University and Soka Women's College.

Hachioji: a city located about 40 kilometers west of central Tokyo.

Kanto: the central region of Japan's largest island, which included the domains of both Takeda and Hojo. Today, it refers to Tokyo and its neighboring six prefectures.

Eiroku (1558–70): Japan has a unique system of era names. In medieval times, in addition to marking a new imperial reign, the era name was frequently changed following a natural disaster or major historical event.

Takeda Shingen (1521–73): a preeminent daimyo in feudal Japan with exceptional military prestige. He was the lord of the domain located west of Hachioji.

Odawara: a coastal city in present-day Kanagawa Prefecture. Hachioji is located en route from the domain of Takeda to Odawara Castle.

Hojo clan: one of the most powerful feudal lords during the warring states period (late fifteenth to sixteenth centuries) in Japan. Its core castle was at Odawara.

The path to a peaceful world, a garden for humankind

What is the conclusion arrived at
by the workings of humanity's
most essential wisdom?
It is the imperative to rid
the world of misery.

People are happy
when they are free.
They enjoy security
when there is peace.

Peace and freedom are
the blessed treasures
that humanity has long sought
with its very lifeblood.

Rich and stately
cities the world over
bustle with people
actively living their lives.
With the onset of war
those cities
are instantly transformed
into enormous dungeons.

Acute and vibrant will
to build a new society
in the twenty-first century,
bringing together
different peoples
in the passionate, palpable
interaction of life with life!

A single gunshot
can bring asphyxiating torment
to people yearning to live
in peace and happiness;
can plunge them into
a hellish world of blinding pain
and anguished cries.

Frightening is the human heart.
So, too, are human deeds.
In the depths of that heart
we can always find
a vicious precipice,
envious, arrogant and cruel.

Untold times humanity
has been stirred and troubled
by premonitions of catastrophe.
Thus we have lived,
one year giving way
to the next.

Hoping to avoid the worst,
for a better, more certain route,
the people, the human race,
have faithfully followed
the progress of those reverberations.

Is it impossible that we should find
some new way of thinking,
a path forward
more expansive and profound?

Violence is absolutely evil.
War is absolute, ultimate evil.

In the face of forces
that would make us despair
of our dreams

—our desire for happiness
and peace—
we must summon up
an unconquerable spirit.
We must work to
permanently restrain
those who hold others
in contemptuous scorn.

"Do what thou dost, be strong, be brave;
    and, like the Star, nor rest nor haste."
These are the words
of the great British explorer and Orientalist
Sir Richard Francis Burton.

Master of languages, erudite scholar,
he is widely renowned for his translation
of *The Arabian Nights*.

Traversing the globe on an odyssey of exploration,
he left us tomes of learning
to open doors on unknown worlds.

He did not seek luxury,
the comforts of easy position or fame.
Unafraid of envious attacks,
in the quest for humanity's future
he realized triumphant achievements
time and time again.

In Africa, he risked his life
to seek the source of the Nile.
Treading deep into the remotest regions
of South America,
he was able to witness new and unknown vistas.

His uncompromising commitment to exploration
is justly renowned and worthy of praise.

On another occasion
he walked the treacherous highlands of India.
He battled harsh conditions
and survived nature's fiercest blows
to share with us the invaluable lessons
of his experiences.

Further, he raised a critical voice
against imperial policies
and lambasted the clergy's role
in the slave trade...

It is an undeniable fact
of human history
that those who fight
for what is right
may end up denounced
as criminals, imprisoned.

The extremities
of contradiction and conflict
that mark human affairs!
Right may be defeated by wrong,
the unjust may triumph over the just.
Vicious individuals may bring
the decent and good to ruin.
Such things can be seen
in every age.

This formula applies always;
it reflects truth
as clearly as the surface
of a bright mirror.

Today again
under the cover of obscurity
unknown forces are in motion.
The rustling in the underbrush
suggests the ill intent

of those who plot and plan
for tomorrow.

Secret talks conducted
behind closed doors
hidden in darkness
are a dreadful, toxic
and bottomless abyss.

How deplorable
is the violence of words,
this perversion and abuse
of the ideal of free speech!
How lowly is the culture
of a land great only in envy,
this pathetic island country
whose people are slyly manipulated
by hacks who will write anything
—trampling the rights and dignity
of others—
so long as it sells
so long as it makes money.

One eminent thinker has argued
that a fundamental barbarity
lives on unchanged
from primitive times to this day.

The various attempts
to bring us down
through concocted accusations
lacked all truth;
these devious plots
all failed to hit their mark.

Only the vicious
fraudulent words remain.
The justice that is truth
has calmly and confidently won.

This also has been the history,
the shared experience
of people of greatness
the world over,
past and present,
East and West.

My mentor's words:
"The achievements of the first three presidents
will form the eternal foundation for our movement."

The first, second and third presidents—
all were imprisoned,
all endured the persecution of innocence.

We experienced exactly the kind
of severe persecution
described in the Daishonin's writings
and have, I believe,
laid the foundations for growth
that will persist for all time.

Do not base your happiness
on the suffering of others!
Forge a sense of self
that will not be swayed
by changing circumstances!

The criticism,
jealousy and slander of the world
are nothing more than volleys launched
in envy of the target's greatness.

Focus your thoughts
on the higher dimensions
as you live out your life.
It is foolishness
to pay the slightest heed
to small-minded critiques

arising from a narrow
insular mentality.

Abebe Bikila, the legendary athlete
whose marathon victory
in the 1964 Tokyo Olympics
earned him world renown, declared:
I am not competing
against the other sixty-seven runners.
I am competing against myself.

These words echoed like a clarion call
urging us to a life
of profound and excellent triumph.
I was among those moved by his words.

My friend!
Direct your anger
to the task of putting
those who spread
malicious falsehood
firmly in their place!
Strike the great drum
of truth and justice
with all your strength!

Make all your thoughts
and all your actions
a resounding shout
of justice!
Beat the great drum
until its skin splits!
Pummel the great drum
laughing raucously
at those whose hearts
have become absorbed
in evil!

Join with me
as I raise my voice
to urge people
never to be deceived
by the corrupt ones,
who scurry and caterwaul,
whose lies lead only
to bitterest regret!

Never fear
those skeletal wraiths
ceaselessly pierced
by demonic gunfire.
For they are forever slinking
through the darkness,
never able to see
the breathtaking
constellations above them.

My friend!
Become strong,
astonishingly strong!
My friend!
Live your life
in expansive greatness!

Reject the torment
of having to down
the bitter, hateful broth.
Those who would force this on you
are destined to walk
a pitiful path
a miserable road
of groans and lamentation.

Humankind!
Humanity!
Do not be taken in

by the deceptions
of hypocrites!

Never forget
that the road to absolute peace
is found in the hearts
of the people.

The experience of power
kindles demonic desire.
The powerful have
at their disposal
the means to terrorize
people's hearts
and harshly mete out harm.
But we are all equally human,
all equally alive.

We cannot merely sigh,
be driven to exhaustion or despair
by forms of authority
at once stifling
and illusory.

Stand up!
Advance
with unflagging courage!
Battle on
with righteous anger!

We must expose
the inner lives
of those who wield power
as heroes of twisted
and sinister intent.
Their essential depravity
is revealed
in the pleasure they take

gleefully demeaning
ordinary people.

The crown of happiness
is not something
we wait for them to bestow.
It is something
we seize triumphantly!

Humanity!
Rise up with joy!

Proudly wear
the valorous ideals
to which you are committed!
Reject and rebuke
all that is false and spurious!
Strike back, and triumph!

Confronted with
the massive, well-ordered
energy of the people,
the powerful will become
permanently incapable
of looking down disparagingly
on others.

Humanity!
Live each day
brimming with enthusiasm!
For we all have the right
to live out our lives
true to ourselves!
Everyone is equal.

My friends!
Advance energetically
toward the realization
of your highest aspirations.

Uphold the banner of
righteous anger's triumph
as you advance with
impassioned joy!

We must never be defeated
by the luxuriant madness of power.
We must not be dazzled
by the deceptions of appearance.

The despotic are fundamentally
incapable of understanding
ordinary people's pain.
Describe to them
the best and truest way of life,
and still their response will be
a sneer of chilly disdain.

We know
that the only thing worse
than such baseness
is to fall prey
to its manipulations.

Though dark, gusty storms
may blow,
though dust-filled whirlwinds
toss the air,
nothing can sever the ties
of our brightly shining spirits.

Our foes
are foolishly treading
a path of destruction, slander and lies.

Their sole conviction
is the rejection of faith,
a commitment
to criticize and harass.

They are unaware
that they are destined
to end up drowned
in a life of pitiful folly.

They obstinately confine themselves
to their inner darkness,
their woefully frozen hearts
consumed by constant
uncertainty and dread.

Advance, my friends!

We march to fulfill a mission
of unimaginably profound meaning
in this troubled world
of seemingly endless conflict.
Our progress will carry us
over savage mountain peaks.
It will take us to the triumphant citadel
where we will live in joy
forever enfolded
in the embrace
of justice's blue skies.

Their lives, their citadel,
will crumble into
the twilight oblivion,
the reality of ruin,
the sad sacrifices of destruction
that culminate in self-exile.

Whatever melancholy events occur,
we will remain
invincible creators, pioneers.
We must never cease to tread
this great path
of enduring triumph.

Whether the road underfoot
is difficult or gentle,
whether it is solid
or gives way beneath our feet,
we will advance holding true
to the noble convictions and spirit
we have cherished throughout our lives.
We will make our way
through this ever-changing world
faithful in our souls
to our ultimate ideals.

We will walk on, unbowed before all!
We will walk on, dismissing fear!
We will walk on, never dwelling
on the fact of this life's end.
And we will rush forward
breaking into a run!

We possess
eternally enduring hope.
Our proud city
is no place for fear, regret or endings.
It is a city forged by the solidarity
of people rejoicing together,
supporting each other
in our shared humanity!

And from that city
we will construct
the paths to a peaceful world,
a garden for all of humankind!

This is meaning of worldwide kosen-rufu
—the broad acceptance
of Buddhist ideals on a global scale—
just as the Daishonin foresaw.

"The Buddhist Law will spread for
ten thousand years and more, for all eternity."
This is the profound teaching of the Daishonin
which we must never forget.
For this is our mission.

August 1, 2000

"Do what thou dost": Burton, *The Kasidah of Haji Abdu El-Yezdi*, p. 37.

Sir Richard Francis Burton (1821–90): British geographer, explorer and translator known for his expeditions in Asia, Africa and the Americas.

Abebe Bikila (1932–73): Ethiopian athlete, winner of two Olympic gold medals for the marathon.

"The Buddhist Law will spread": Nichiren, *The Writings of Nichiren Daishonin*, vol. 1, p. 736.

Together holding aloft laurels
of the people's poetry

Dedicated to Dr. Esther Gress, Poet Laureate,
with affection and respect

The transparent Scandinavian skies
tinged with the rose of the morning sun.
Lovely city of Copenhagen!
Where rippling waves of silver and gold
seek the company
of the seaside mermaid.

It was forty years ago,
on a day lit by the rays
of a brilliant sun,
that a youth of thirty-three,
his heart filled
with a yearning for peace,
first set foot on the European continent.
Copenhagen!
City of dazzling memories.
Port city where I offered this vow
to the memory of my mentor:
    From this site I will commence
    my actions for peace.

The setting for *Hamlet*,
rich with the poetry of
Grundtvig and Andersen,
a land everywhere adorned
by flowers, greenery and water,
offering haven and relief
to distant-voyaging travelers.
With an open monarchy
loved and respected by the citizenry,
your country is a glistening palace
of the purest imagination.

Now from this evocative land
so dear to my heart,
come the sounds of a bell,
ringing in the dawn.
Your message, sent off by Gefion,
took flight amidst the morn's first rays,
it crossed aurora-lit night skies,
chased an endlessly receding horizon
to settle gently down before me.

Resonant tones,
deep with meaning,
strike my heartstrings!
The cheering timbres
that resound from the lofty bell tower
of Dr. Esther Gress,
world cultural figure,
Denmark's poet laureate!

Ah! The warm spirit of friendship
that emanates from each line
of this long and wondrous poem,
which you declared was to commemorate
the seventieth anniversary
of Soka Gakkai's founding.

On November 18, 2000,
the day of our founding,
at the Askov Højskole
a center of humanistic education
open to the people,
whose importance was noted
by Tsunesaburo Makiguchi.
On that day, at that site,
three cherry trees were planted
for the first three presidents
of the Soka Gakkai.
You honored us there
with your presence,

reciting your full
and deeply moving poem!

Your character, your poetic spirit,
are like the crisp clarity
of the Nordic skies and waters.
You direct your unclouded vision,
your penetrating perception,
at the history and ideals
of the Soka Gakkai.

And with the very greatest care
you have translated my verses into Danish
sending them, this past June,
forth into the world
from the soaring tower of your poetry.
"A Twenty-first Century of Hope and Courage"—
This is the very first occasion
for my poetry to be translated
into a Scandinavian language.

No words can therefore convey
my gratitude for your willingness
to undertake the many challenges involved
in the translation and publication
of my poems.
I understand that you were
moved by the sincere wish
to disseminate my ideas
within your country,
stating that the great ocean
starts from a single drop.
It is indeed impossible
to thank you!

The poem which you offered
as a preface is filled with
an impassioned belief
in peace and in ordinary people!

What courage I derive
from those gentle yet powerful words!

Within the collection also
you included poems
whose keen brevity
is imbued with the lofty dignity
of a flower.
The richness of your imagery!
A deep humanism
dances through the full meter
of your cosmology!

"A Twenty-first Century of Hope and Courage"
is the dialogue of our poems,
a lasting shared effort.

Your work has been translated
into twenty-seven tongues,
included in the anthologies
of sixteen countries.
Poet laureate of the West!

Inspired by you
this poet laureate of the East pledges
for the sake of peace in the world,
and for the happiness
of ordinary citizens,
to peal his own bells
with ever-increasing vigor.

Jean-Jacques Rousseau
lamented human inequality
stating that society shows us
the violence of the strong
and the oppression of the weak;
that what exists in surplus for some
is fatally lacking for others.

He also stated that superficial progress
in fact speeds our species toward decline;
that disaster for some
almost always means
flourishing prosperity for others.

The words of this wise philosopher
precisely describe the realities
of our contemporary world,
a new century in which
light and dark compete and cross
with increasing intensity.
Are the final grains of sand
about to slip through
humanity's hourglass?

Both the Earth and its people
are searching for the light of hope.
They await a healing hand.

You speak to people:
  Know that whatever you do to others
  is what you do to yourself.

You call out to them:
  If you want to change the world,
  you must transform humanity.

I deeply concur.
However far and distant
a route it may seem,
the development of humanity
is the fundamental solution.

Ah, the human being.
What a vast enigma!

The object of the sustained thought
of all philosophy,

the lights and colors
of all civilization,
the consistent theme
of all religion: humanity!

Genuine Buddhists,
those dedicated to
the happiness of the many,
have always discovered
the greatest brilliance
within the human being.

And I believe:
that the twenty-first-century challenge
of building bridges
between civilizations
must be founded in the lives
of individual human beings.

The poet addresses
the intelligent minds
of each civilization.
The poet poses questions
to humans,
about humans,
questions whose scope
transcends humanity.

"Whence do we come?"
"Where are we going?"
"Who are you?"
"For what purpose
do people live in this world?"
"What is the nature
of human happiness?"

It is from this search for answers
that the treasure of our humanity
derives its deepest luster.

It is this, above all,
that constitutes
the very essence of civilization.
If we link together
these treasures, these jewels,
we will certainly
refine and clarify
universal human values.

The poet's voyage
in search of peace
is a dialogue with the soul
of each civilization.
It is the work of binding humanity
at its deepest roots.

Your clear eyes
sparkle with a rich love
for humanity.
They peer into the profound reaches,
the font and source of our humanity.
You connect people to people,
engage people and nature,
commingle with people and the cosmos.

Your poetry enjoys
an infinite intimacy
with the people.
You sing with a clear voice
of the happiness of the people,
of daily life,
of engagement with others,
of the struggle against injustice.

On your brow
the laurels of the people's poet
shine with magnificent brightness.

To whom does the poet sing?
To the people!
On what does the poet stand?
On the great earth of the people!

What are the words of a true poet?
Amidst torrential flows
of false and empty language,
the poet offers people
words worthy of their heartfelt trust.
Words with the power
to make the impossible possible.
Words of true direction
illuminating the future.

Are the people without
the means to write?
"Then I shall write
the beautiful songs you sing!"
Do the people lack
a place to voice their needs?
"Then I shall shout
those things you wish to express,
the things you desire to know,
the corruption you want exposed!"
The words of the people
have been estranged
from them, suppressed.
The poet strives to set them down,
to engrave them in history
—forever—
as people's poems.

I wish, together with you,
always to be the voice of the people,
to speak on their behalf.
I wish always to be a poet
who fights for the people.
I wish to continue to sing

in a loud, clear voice
the grand epic poem
of the people's triumph.

The great humanist educator
Nikolai Grundtvig
aroused and awakened
the people through his poems.
He dedicated his entire life
to the people.

Hans Christian Andersen
was a poet laureate
redolent with a world
of fantasy and imagination.
His one hundred fifty-six tales,
his one hundred twenty-five poems,
are loved by the people
throughout the world.

You have lived a life of the pen
on the fertile poetic earth of Denmark,
which has fostered so many poets.
And now you are the muse
who warmly watches over
the drama of human revival
that is our SGI movement.

Poet laureate!
The words of your superlative poems
make shine the cheeks
of young men and women,
they bring a bright smile
to those whose hearts
have sunk into despair,
they ripen the buds
of various flowers
in barren fields!
They send white doves

conveying messages of peace
winging out into the world!

I wish, together with you,
to usher in a century of life.
Let us continue to ring
with the last measure of our strength
these chiming tones,
these poems of peace.

A century of life!
This is a world of universal
human community,
a world in which
the dignity of each single person
is respected to the utmost.
This is humanity's global civilization,
a world in which each culture
shines with vitality and energy.
It is a world in which
humanity and nature
find a richly creative coexistence
based on a new global ethic.
It is a century of women
cherishing peace and life
from the heart.

Toward a century of life!
Our poetic spirits have
resounded together
since the distant past,
since long before we
encountered each other
through the Indian poet-sage
Dr. Krishna Srinivas.

You call out:
    The poet is the conscience of humanity.
    The world needs poets.

Since that is exactly the case,
poet laureate of the West,
continue to ring your poetic bells
ever more true to yourself
setting the tones of your humanist songs
aloft on fresh Nordic breezes!

We will never cease our advance.
As the philosopher Kierkegaard
described his famous determination
on the day he launched
his philosophical efforts:
    Let the lot be cast—
    I cross the Rubicon!
    Although the way leads to strife,
    I will not forbear.

Let us bring together
the toning chimes of peace
rung from bell towers
of the world's poets!
Let us make the skies
of the twenty-first century
bright with the exhilarating
energy of our poems.
So that in those perfectly clear skies
we may look up to a rainbow,
the rainbow of
a century of life!

I deeply desire:
That the three young cherries
planted on the Askov Højskole campus
will sink their roots deep into the earth,
and spread wide their branches.
That the gorgeous abundance
of their blossoms
will eternally offer to those

who gather beneath them
the light of hope, courage and friendship.

And I truly hope:
That some day,
beneath the fullness of their bloom,
we may meet and speak,
my sister poet laureate
my comrade in the struggles of the pen.

December 20, 2000

Written for Esther Gress (1921–2002), Danish poet laureate. She came to know about the author through being involved in the translation of his poetry. Ms. Gress and the author never met but exchanged correspondence and poetry.

Nikolaj Frederik Severin Grundtvig (1783–1872): Danish poet and educator who advocated the idea of a national popular school.

Hans Christian Andersen (1805–75): Danish author and poet.

Gefion Fountain: a large fountain on the harbor front in Copenhagen.

Askov Højskole: a folk high school in Askov. It provides education of traditional Danish values for grown-ups.

Krishna Srinivas (1913–2007): Indian poet and founder of the World Poetry Society International.

"Let the lot be cast": trans. from Kierkegaard, *Søren Kierkegaards skrifter*, vol. 17, p. 30.

Eternally radiant champion of humanity

You and I agree:
The names of the uncelebrated
are the most beautiful
names of all.

The more famous one becomes
the more likely one is
to chase after vain pursuits
and puff up with conceit.
These winds darken the very sky
with shadowed clouds.

This I ask of you:
Always enjoy life!
Take unshakable delight!
Let our contact with others
liberate snared hearts,
igniting the flame of purpose
in even the glinting eyes
of expressionless men.

I have never seen you
defeated by grief.
Morning, noon and night
you have trod
the broad and glorious path,
your steps always soft yet certain.
Your gait is light
as you surge forward
like the flow of crystal waters.

The goal you seek
is a life of indestructible
justice and victory.
Undistracted by the

whispered rumors of miscreants,
your heart basks always
in the high praise
of a golden light,
a platinum glow.

No matter how deep
your physical fatigue,
you ply ahead
enthusiastically
proclaiming truth
for the sake of your friends,
for kosen-rufu.
I marvel at the sight of you—
for you know
the unmatched pride that arises
from living life fully
holding nothing back.

Propelled by your convictions,
your principles,
your spirit continues
to dance with joy
on the golden field
of the Buddha's land—
heedless of the abuse
others heap upon you.

Oh! We are privy
to rich melodies,
grand and sweeping.
We hear them clearly.

Watching the sun set,
our hearts bathed
in magnificent solemnity,
in lively delight,
we breathe deep
the lustrous air of happiness

and dance in celebration
of victory!

Those who would obstruct
your progress
are like lost and raving souls
of the netherworld,
moaning through
bitter, vindictive tears.

That man is like
a soul wending its way
toward the entrance of hell—
how pitiful to choose
a desperate future,
shorn of hope.

His dark and anguished stare
marks him as prey
for those of vicious intent
who gleefully await.

How wretched is
a life spent playing in the mud,
repeating petty crimes,
neglecting life's real and
crucial lessons.

Never be lured
into a world of
joyless stragglers!

My mentor
often admonished us:
Never look down on others,
or undermine them.
Never grow arrogant
or treat people with contempt.
The moment you do,

your life
and mind
begin to decline—
until all that awaits
is the murky, tormented
sleep of the defeated.

My friend,
never forget those days
when you took flight,
lifting yourself with
the mighty wing-strokes of youth!

You dashed, time after time,
freely, determinedly,
from one place to another
for the sake of kosen-rufu.
Never allow those bonds
of genuine friendship
to be severed.

Even if all regard
for what is true and just
should perish—
whatever ruthless tempests rage—
no matter how this may
provoke your fury—
you who know
the fierce, unstoppable energy
that issues from
the very depths of life,
you must never fail
to rally and respond!
Declare the cause of justice
with a voice that resounds,
that echoes and booms!

Laugh heartily
as the undeniable victory

wrought by your
perseverance and strength
makes smugly cunning faces
contort in twisted scowls!

Those who can sense
the nobility of a life
devoted to struggle
are certain to join with you
as allies.

Despite lies and fabrications,
brutal scorn and slander,
you stand tall,
a tireless champion
mustering primal passion
to counter all falsehood
and proclaim
an authentic way of life.

There will be times
when you are derided
as too simple, too honest,
too ignorant of the world.
But these are the voices
of those transfixed
by the flow of
dark and brackish waters.

Pay no heed, my friend,
to those shallow, eddying currents.
The jealous are encrusted
in the hard shell of their own vanity,
their turbid, tasteless words and deeds
do not deserve a second thought.
Distance yourself from those
who are full of themselves,
slurping the muck
as they boast and bluster.

When such base creatures
are consumed with bitter remorse,
how bright will be your future!
What brilliant promise lies ahead!
You will ascend the tallest peaks,
scale the highest principles,
master the loftiest realms of philosophy,
gain treasures of unmatched value.

You already shine
as a human being,
soaring proudly, freely,
dancing victoriously
on humanity's most exalted plane,
embraced by all
the forces of nature
and their delight.

You have prevailed!
Springing over hideous affronts
and all crude invective,
sidestepping the snares of intrigue,
you have secured victory—
a poised and confident
hero of humanity.

My friend,
may your breast and brain
forever remain those
of a sublime champion of life—
as you draw in new breath,
advancing onward, ever onward,
with easy composure,
unperturbed by bitter north winds,
blustering storms, dark paths
swept by evil spirits...

Wisely aware
of the calamities of life and death,

the nature of human destiny,
you proceed upwards
toward ever higher triumph.

Your heart's wisdom
takes in all eternity,
your spirit expands
to cosmic scale,
indestructible,
enabling you to prevail
as a grand champion of humanity,
brilliant with victory.

My friend, your earnestness
has propelled you to triumph.
Your sincerity shines
like an inextinguishable sun.
No matter how harshly
or how often people may scorn you,
in the final chapter of your life
you will be conferred
with the crown that marks
a true human hero.
This alone is certain!

Your innermost being
walks an eternal well-lit path—
the dedicated pursuit
of justice and happiness.
This, indeed, is the path
you have, in your wisdom,
chosen for yourself.

How foolish are those who,
wrapped in the vestments
of squalid arrogance,
live with rent and tattered souls.
Their flawed spirits

invariably lead them
to wreckage and ruin.

You, however,
direct the great stream of joy
that arises in hope
into your heart and breast!
You have decisively abandoned
the quagmire of regret
to embrace the path of justice,
as your destiny and fate!

My friend,
your truth
will surely be celebrated
in lifetime after lifetime,
for generation upon generation.
My friend,
let us live out this life
burning with fierce
and youthful intensity!

Every edifice here
sparkles with gem-like light;
the people here are all dressed
in floral armor.

The dirge of those
who loathed and envied us
can now only be heard
in the receding distance.
The path once traveled
by those savage beasts
now leads to happiness.

Time is short
yet life is long,
as are our struggles.

And now,
now we have prevailed.

You are the one
who determines
your own destiny.
There is no need
to mask or disguise yourself.
Openly share your story
as one who has mastered happiness
with flourish and aplomb.

Those who direct their thoughts
toward a bright future
are strong.
Those who abide in darkness
face a future that is desperate,
unsalvageable.

My friend,
make a stand,
never leaving behind
expressions of regret!
Unswayed by those
who would hurt and hinder you,
ascend and adorn
each day of life
with clock-like precision,
while strictly, forcefully
spurring and admonishing
yourself.

You are yourself;
you are no other.
Never let others
drive you from your course.
Hold fast to yourself.
Know that the key to victory
is that instant of joy

felt by, within and true to you.
Thus you can prevail
against madness
and rise above all vice.

Never permit your spirit
to be destroyed!
Never let your convictions falter!
Never allow your soul
to grow corrupt and foul!

Philosophers have long maintained
that it is the practice of the tedious
to raise a raucous clamor,
while truth and justice
speak in calm and quiet tones.

We must succeed.
By virtue of our humanity
we must triumph.
Without victory
happiness is out of reach.

Buddhism is about winning;
life, also, is defined by
failure or success;
that is why we must win!
Those who win
enjoy happiness.
Those who are defeated
suffer hellish anguish.
And the wellspring
of enduring victory
is faith.

My friend,
my friends,
you must go on to win!
Bequeath to generations

the example of your acts,
a grand stage
lit by timeless light
where champions of humanity
continue to perform
far into the future.

Your real victory
is the tenacity and perseverance
you have forged within.
Tenacity maintained!
Perseverance sustained!
You know full well
that this is the deepest source
of every victory!

You have consistently
given your best effort,
always your very best.
Underlying your efforts,
as their foundation and base,
is an even deeper force—
that of relentless perseverance,
and dogged tenaciousness.

Tenacity produces victory!
Perseverance generates glory!
You have never lost sight
of this key principle.

From this day forward
let us renew our courageous struggle
against tyranny and oppression!
Today, once more,
let us engage to the fullest
those adversaries whose malice
has poisoned so many minds!

Let us always be a friend
to those whose days
are darkened by grief,
whose wings quiver with fear.

Let us defend without fail
the countless people
who live shuddering
on the precipice of destruction,
staggered by a series
of heavy crushing blows.

You, and you!
My friends!
Unfurl the banner of glory
high above the citadel
of commanding triumph
that we have built together.
From this joyous vantage,
let us turn our gaze once more
to distant, eternal vistas of life!

July 21, 2001

August 15—The dawn of a new day

August 15, 1945—
The day the Japanese nation,
led by arrogant, foolish leaders,
fell in defeat.

A day that marked the start
of a new era.
A day when the people's hearts
began to pulse again with joy
toward a new future.

A day of penitence
recalling the senseless
battlefield deaths
of so many millions
of loved ones.

A day of eternal parting
from sweethearts and lovers.
A day of tears
for mothers who would
never again see their dear children.
A day of hopeless heartbreak,
learning that young sons
—the future hope of their families
and society as a whole—
were never to return.
A day of anguished grief
as fathers, too, shed bitter tears...
The fifteenth of August—
Ah, August 15!

Stumbling in flight
from the raging flames
of aerial assaults,

so many died
in a lethal hail of lead.

Who was responsible?
Who would pay
or make amends
for these crimes?

Untold numbers of noncombatants
perished in the air raids—
running helter-skelter
through the fierce flames,
their hearts filled
with biting sorrow
and bitter outrage
at the stupidity of war.

Because of the war,
for the sake of their country,
so many men died,
so many women too,
serving with the troops
in the battlefields.

It is wrong to view
the service and suffering of war
solely in terms of men's lives.
We must never forget
the courage of the women
who died in the dedicated
service of their country.

More important
than debating where
the souls of the fallen
should be enshrined
is that we never forget
the precious reality
of their lives.

Everyone is equal
in their humanity.
If we focus on this fact
—this principle, this law—
false distinctions disappear
and there is no reason
for fighting or conflict.
The challenge of the twenty-first century
is to firmly embrace this philosophy
of fundamental humanism
and to spread it throughout the world.

Even now these sights
are burned indelibly
in my heart.
In the midst of an air raid
in the middle of the night
an elderly couple shaking with fear
as they fled weaving their way
through the streets.

Also unforgettable
was this pitiful sight—
a group of middle-aged men,
apparently of some standing,
scampering in desperate rout
like trapped and panicked prisoners...

Our family saw
my four elder brothers,
all in the prime of life,
called away to war.
All four were made tools
of Japan's invasion of China.
My eldest brother
was sent to fight in Burma,
where he died in battle.

With heavy steps
my aged parents
waited and waited,
wondering when, oh, when
would he and
their other three sons

to the icy blasts
of a northern wind.
Everywhere the sight
of decent people
looking like those condemned
to climb the gallows stairs
at the unfeeling command
of brutal assassins.

It was a bitter outrage.
While hardship and suffering
were forced on ordinary citizens,
a handful of politicians
—the hypocrites in power—
seemed to mock us
dismissing and deriding us,
looking down on us
with intolerable arrogance.

None of us had wanted
this war.
We had never
accepted or supported it.

Yet over time
almost without noticing,
we were all influenced,
maneuvered and brainwashed
to extol the glories of war.

The human heart holds
terrible possibilities.
More terrible still
are those who use their power
to mold and manipulate
people's minds.

On August 15,
Japan was defeated,
utterly and totally defeated.

The haughty pride of Japan
was beaten and crushed
by the bombs and blades
of the counterassault.

Without doubt
there were many wise
and clear-sighted citizens
who actually cheered
their country's defeat.

Ordinary people had longed only
for a moment's peace of mind.
It was only natural that
they should want to see
divine retribution
—the cutting lash

of sharp remorse—
meted out on the heartless leaders
who had inflicted
this slave-like subjugation.

Ah, August 15, 1945!
That day the summer sky
was bright and brilliant.

At noon there was
a radio broadcast announcing
Japan's defeat.
Invincible Japan,
so certain of victory,
had been thoroughly beaten.
Many wept,
but far more, no doubt,
felt relief
deep in their hearts.

The summer sky,
where once we had watched
enemy planes,
was now incredibly quiet,
and red dragonflies
flitted gaily through the air.
Japan, which had declared itself
the invincible land of the gods,
lay in utter ruin.

My family had been forced
to evacuate our home,
to stay with relatives
in Nishi Magome.
However, this refuge,
this house set amid peaceful fields,
took a direct hit
from an incendiary bomb.
With all our worldly

possessions inside,
it was instantly engulfed in flame.

With our relatives' consent,
my father constructed a tiny hut
on the same lot,
with a small sheet
of scorched tin for a roof.
We had no mosquito netting,
so now, instead of bombs,
we faced the assault
of squadrons of mosquitoes.

On that day of August 15,
my father, face flushed with emotion,
murmured to himself,
"My sons will now return.
My eldest, Kiichi,
my second, Masuo,
my third, Kaizo,
and my fourth, Kiyonobu,
are coming home.
One from Burma,
three from China—
they're coming home."
He uttered these words,
breath catching painfully
in his chest,
as one awakening
from a dream.

My diminutive mother
prepared dinner,
excited as a young girl:
"How bright it is!
Now we can keep the lights on!
How lovely and bright!"

That summer,
my father was fifty-seven,
my mother forty-nine,
and I was seventeen.

August 15 was the day,
the moment we emerged from a
deep and hellish gloom,
regaining as a family
some happiness and cheer.

Although some of my siblings
wept at Japan's defeat,
deep inside everyone was relieved:
How good, they thought,
how good that the war
is over at last.

Eventually
the sad news came—
my eldest brother
was dead,
killed in action in Burma.

While many were discharged
and returned quickly
to their homes,
one year passed,
and then another,
before each of my
three surviving brothers
managed to return home
quietly alive.

All three,
unable to feel
the new era's hope,
returned dazed

with forced smiles
on their faces.

"Thank goodness!"—
beyond this simple
phrase repeated,
parent and child
could find no words to share.

Our home-life shattered,
our family tossed down
to misery's depths...
But we were hardly alone,
countless people wept tears
of anguished suffering
and heaving grief.
Each year I greet
this day of August 15
my heart filled with outrage.

The years of youth,
which should be
the time in life
most burning and blossoming
with hope,
were ruined, distorted and despoiled,
the purest sentiments
crushed underfoot.
With the coming
of this day each year
my sorrow at the pain and loss
turns to boiling rage.

August 15—
Is this not the day each year
when Japan's leaders
should prostrate themselves
before the people?
Is this not the day

when you should
vow to consecrate your lives
to the people
to the cause of peace,
the day when you should
promise to work
with unstinting devotion
for the happiness
of all people?

With what words
would those eminent scholars
who had extolled war's glories
now apologize,
their heads bowed low
before their youthful students?

The famous who,
festooned with honors,
had sung war's praises—
now bowing deeply in apology
to the common people,
backs bent and
shoulders drooping.
No doubt there were many
who could feel only
contempt at this sight.

We experienced the truth
that demonic evil
plainly contains
the seeds of its own destruction.

Those who would lead
must never, for all eternity, forget
the pain and suffering
—the dank prison torture—
undergone by people everywhere

because of bombardment,
military assault and warfare.

Royalty are human.
The immensely rich are human.
The great and powerful are human.
And we, we ordinary citizens,
are human.
Nothing can therefore justify
causing people to live in fear,
to be tossed by tempests of misery,
to have poison forced
into their sacrosanct bodies,
simply to benefit
the powerful few.

The nineteenth-century Ukrainian poet
Lesya Ukrainka wrote:
    The predawn light,
    heralding the sun's arrival,
    dispels the darkness of night.
    In that time
    when the sun has not yet risen—
    the predawn light blazes
    and illuminates the sky.
    You who are awake, arise!
    The time to fight is here!

We have arisen!
We have arisen
for the goal of world peace
which we call kosen-rufu!
But even as they gave everything
for the cause of truth and justice,
our mothers and fathers
were subjected to abuse and insult
from the prejudiced and closed-minded.
Relatives and friends, likewise,
experienced slander and scorn.

Day after day,
those who came before us,
made noble by their dedication,
took on the arduous challenge
to scale the daunting heights
of this quest for peace.
We will carry on
the work of those noble pioneers,
reaching the goal without fail!

This is the path of humanity.
It is the path of faith.
It is the path of peace,
the path of truth and justice.

August 15—
We must never forget
the painful misery of that day.
We must never forget
the desolation of that day.
And we must never forget
that humiliating awakening
to the folly of slavish obedience.

August 15—
Let us make this day
a day praised by all
the people of Asia.
Let us make this day
a day respected by all
the world's citizens.

This day of
August 15, 2001—
this is a day of fresh departure
for the youth of the new century.
It is a day
to be eternally commemorated

as a day of peace,
as the start of a new era of life.

August 14, 2001

Recalling the day, fifty-four years ago,
when I first met my mentor, Josei Toda,
with palms pressed together in prayer

This translation, by Andrew Gebert, was first published in *Fighting for Peace* (2004).

August 15, 1945, was the day the Japanese government announced it was accepting the terms of the Potsdam Declaration, signaling its surrender and the end of World War II.

Nishi Magome: a quiet residential area in Tokyo's Ota Ward.

Lesya Ukrainka (1871–1913): Ukrainian poet, writer and social activist.

"The predawn light": trans. from Ukrainka, "Predrassvetnye ogni" (Predawn Lights) in *Biblioteka vsemirnoi literatury*, Series 3, vol. 157, p. 305.

Salute to the smiling faces of the twenty-first century

This poem is dedicated to my dear young friends of the Beyer Elementary School

Each of you
is a most excellent
scientist.

"Why is the sky blue?"
"How does a magnet
attract iron?"
"Why did all
the dinosaurs die?"
"What is it like
at the edges of space?"

The mind that questions,
that asks "why?" and "how?"—
this is the very heart of science.

A child looks up
at the open sky
across which a condor
leisurely, serenely wings its way,
and wonders:
"How come you can fly like that?
Yes! I also want to fly!"

This is the dream
that lived in
the hearts of children
for hundreds,
for thousands of years.

It was the power of this dream,
the blue sky mirrored in your eyes

as you followed birds
flying freely through the skies...
Yes! The airplane was invented
through the power of your dreams.

Each of you
is a born poet.

Spreading wide the wings
of imagination
toward distant hills
under a rainbow's arch,
you wonder:
"What are the cities like
beyond the horizon?"
"What kind of people
might be living there?"

Looking up at an endless
night sky you ask yourself:
"What shapes would form
if I drew lines between each
of those sparkling gem-like stars?"

Spinning a cloth of thrilling tales
across the eternal reaches
of space and time,
you prove again
that you are all indeed
true poets.

Each of you
is a brilliant
philosopher.
"Why am I me?
Couldn't I have been you instead?"
"How did I come to be born
into this family?"

"Where did I come from and
where am I going?"

Gazing at yourself
in a mirror,
you secretly ponder
the mystery of being—
In your heart
you are always aware
of this one great problem,
which has troubled
the world's deepest,
most famous thinkers.

More than anyone
you are true philosophers,
a shining crystal
held deeply in your heart.

The perfect clearness
of your gaze
surprises adults,
reminds them
who they really are.

The question in
your innocent eyes
will certainly shake
the world from its sleep.

And each of you
is a citizen of the world
bringing people together.

Neither the color
of a person's skin
nor the color of their eyes,
nor their nationality
makes any difference to you.

The one who's good at baseball
and the one with a disability
support and help one another,
smile at each other
here in the world of children.

What is the most precious
of all treasures?
It is nothing other
than the life in each of you,
the smile on every one of you!

A lively, smiling face—
this is the passport
of a global citizen
making friends with people
everywhere.
Each of you was born
into this world
carrying such a passport.

Let us create a world,
a time, a century
in which simply being human
is reason enough
to greet each other
with a smile.

Each of you
will play a leading role
in the twenty-first century.
The mountain peaks of courage
soar high within your heart!
A rainbow of hope
shines bright within you!
Within each of us,
yes, within our lives
is an infinite treasure
waiting to be unlocked!

Rise up!
Go forward!
So that you may grasp
the limitless treasures of the heart.
So that you may become yourself,
who you most truly are.

The writer Henry David Thoreau called out—
Explore your own life!
If you advance confidently
in the direction of your dreams,
if you work to live the life
you have imagined,
you will find greater success
than you had ever hoped for—

When life is hard,
when you are hurt or sad…
Plant both feet firmly on the ground,
throw back your shoulders
look out to the wide skies
and take a deep, full breath of air.

The earth and skies
are your friends,
they are on your side.
So long as the sun
is shining up above
and the earth is supporting us
from below,
we have absolutely nothing
at all to fear.

In the beautiful Makiguchi Garden
made by your own hands
are the trees you planted
in honor of Tsunesaburo Makiguchi
and myself.

Never giving up
no matter what others did to him,
Mr. Makiguchi always worked
so that people could enjoy
peace and happiness.
Indeed he should be called
one of the great men of our times.
Please know that
his care and concern
are with you always.

With a heart filled with joy
I salute and respect you.
Your bright faces are
lit with the hopes and smiles
of the twenty-first century.

Your growth is
the hope of all humanity,
all people everywhere.
And for that reason
I will do everything I can
to protect and support you.

Let us go forward together
toward the rainbow of peace
shining above the mountains
of the new century.

Hand in hand
let us walk,
singing with voices
bright and clear
the songs of hope resounding!

August 24, 2001

The Beyer Elementary School in San Diego, California, designated the author and his wife, Mrs. Kaneko Ikeda, honorary principals of the school in 2001. An engraving of this poem stands outside the school's campus. August 24 is the anniversary of the author joining the Soka Gakkai.

If you advance confidently: see Thoreau, *Walden and Civil Disobedience*, p. 372.

The promise of a majestic peace

Long have I walked
the roads of this world,
leaving behind
so many memories,
creating my own history.

I have no regrets.
For in my justice-loving heart
has burned the flame
of compassionate determination
to rid the world
of fear and war.

Nameless,
I have known the joy
of innumerable struggles,
the diverse, resounding cheers
of so many friends.

I have forged
broad new paths for peace.
With the passion of my youth,
with brightly burning eyes,
I sought to create
an ideal world
such as people have dreamed of.

I have always stood,
have always walked,
have always fought,
in the light of happiness
that is the Mystic Law.

Closing tired eyes,
I recall how

I ceaselessly raised
the cry of justice,
scarcely pausing
for a breath.

Worldwide kosen-rufu
signifies world peace.
Nothing remains to me,
I have no other wish,
than the realization
of that dream.

However trying
the realities
of daily life,
the motivation of my heart
has always been
the world's peace.

There have been
bright and beautiful
seasons of spring.
There have been days
when the closing fog
obscured everything.
These memories
are already part
of the distant past,
and yet they are the source
of an energy that is
deep and powerful
and wondrous.

In the words
of the American poet
Walt Whitman:
    I would be the boldest and truest
    being of the universe.

I know that
with the coming
of each new day,
I have prayed
and taken action
for the peace of the world.
Thus my heart
is fulfilled and satisfied.
Like the stars
that sparkle
in the highest reaches,
I know that I have won.

Peace is humanity's greatest,
most solemn undertaking.

While the limitless progress
of scientific advance
has enhanced the means
of killing people,
still the promise
of a majestic peace,
the kind required for us
to live humanely
—and the determination
to realize such a peace
in perpetuity—
remains unfulfilled.

Albert Einstein
stated that
human beings must
continue to fight.
But they must fight
for something whose value
justifies the struggle.
And he declared that
their "arms" should be
"weapons of the spirit."

Vacant stares fixed
on piteous, desolate ruin.
For what purpose
have we lived?
To what end
this violent strife?
The only response
is the howling
of an infinitely empty wind.

The unsound nature
of those who
continue to bring
this sorrow and suffering
to people like us
—we who have had
no say whatsoever
in any of this—
it is this nature
that we must absolutely
transform and change.

A statesman
once declared
that peace is not found
in the interval between wars,
that peace does not mean
the mere absence of war.

The utter brutality
that can casually
rob others of life!
The madness and folly of power
pillaging the last scraps
of happiness!

Demonic authority
that strips everything
from those honest,

good-natured people
who have exerted
every effort to live,
carrying in their hearts hope
for the simple
happiness of spring.

In the contemptuous glare
that does not recognize
people as people,
the human heart is absent;
there is only something
monstrous and bestial.

For both victor
and vanquished,
war leaves only
a sense of endless futility.
Whose responsibility is this?
The answer should be clear,
and yet it is not.

Our happiness,
our peace,
must be inviolable.
We must never permit
our right to happiness,
our right to peace,
to be abused or trampled
by those possessed
by cold brutality.

Even in the depths
of the darkest night,
when all is obscurity
and decline,
we must never allow
the light of peace
to be extinguished.

Whatever the sway,
the back and forth
of clamoring debate,
of slanderous abuse,
keep the sun of peace
shining bright and firm
in your proud, triumphant
and tireless soul!

Those who would run and flee
may do so.
The treacherous
may do their worst.
Those who would loose
the poisoned darts
of calumnious envy
may do as they please.

Champions whose wealth
is their commitment to humanity,
monarchs working for peace,
fear nothing, nothing at all.
For our spirits
are eternal and indestructible.

Today again
the night comes.
So many people
are weeping
in the gloom.
All are huddled
fearful and silent
in the lightless dark.

Nowhere are there any
brightly lit homes.
No—
each person's very soul
is oppressed by darkness.

Hearts fraught,
weighted down
with an indescribable burden—
how much longer
will this exhaustion continue?
When will it become possible
to feel hope or happiness?

It isn't fair, it isn't right.
Why are we tormented
and made to suffer?
Why do those with the power
to do so make no
attempt to help us?
Ah, to quickly leave
this life behind!

What in the world
is this life all about?
For what purpose
have we been living?
Surely it is not
to wage war,
to suffer like this,
to tremble in terror
or to wail out loud.

We should like
to see the day
when menacing tyranny
takes flight
and runs away.
And we wish
to tell future generations
how the potent flames
of our joyous commitment
to justice
burned high.

The agony of days
under merciless
aerial attack.
The unbearable sorrow
of ordinary citizens
fleeing in confusion,
desperate to survive.
The carnage of war
has changed all
of life's joys
instantly to sadness.

Without a moment's hesitation
war has cruelly torn
happiness and peace
from the beautiful hearts
of families living earnestly,
from the inner nobility of their lives.

The glory of which
we dreamed
has been completely
and utterly destroyed.
It isn't fair, it isn't right.
We envy the birds
who can fly from here.

Even in daytime,
there is darkness
in the depths of our lives.
Night brings the further dark
of horror and pain.
Time's passage
brings only more
trembling in terror
at the accusatory tone
of the enemy's voice.
The regal spirit of peace,
the crown of life's dignity,

has been debased to something
worse than servility.

You who arrogantly
abuse your power!
How do you plan
to compensate
for grinding into the earth
the hopes and dreams
of honest citizens?

Citizens of loyal heart
have been cast aside.
And the powerful,
as if having pulled off
a brilliant performance,
recognizing no existence
other than their own,
commit grave
and eternally enduring
crimes against
the dignity of life.

The undying wish
of ordinary citizens
is for real and lasting peace.
Never become
a person of sad,
unprotesting silence!

The Ancient Greek poet
Sophocles proclaimed:
    If there is truth in one's words
    one possesses the greatest strength.

We must give full
and unrelenting voice
to the call for justice
in order to realize peace,

in order to achieve happiness.
In such actions above all
will be found
a bright and happy future.

There is absolutely
no place in our world
for bloodstained children.
Such are the monstrous deeds
of those who have
abandoned their humanity.

Those who wield power
must never use it
to wreak tragedy,
to fill people's lives
with agony and grief.
No one,
absolutely no one,
has the right to do that.

To transform
days of tragedy
into days of happiness,
days of anguish
into days of peace.

The purpose of our lives
is for all to spend our days
smiling happily.
This is the real responsibility
of those in positions of power.

Political leaders!
Do not harm
the already despairing,
but make it possible
for them to experience
heartfelt joy.

Your purpose
must be to enable
the people's
efforts and struggles
to blossom in happiness.
It must be to create
the peaceful stage
on which they may enjoy
the dance of life.

To this end,
you must respect the people
and you must earn their trust.
"The people are emperor."
Now more than ever,
engrave these words of
Sun Yat-sen
deeply in your heart.

Thus will you qualify yourselves
to be true world leaders,
champions of the sovereign people.

In Einstein's impassioned cry:
    We must try to awaken in people
    a sense of solidarity that will not stop
    at national borders.

History is in
ceaseless motion.
And with it the people's
wisdom and discernment grow.
Do not overlook the fact
that with every passing day
they stretch their wings
and stroke through the air
with ever greater wisdom.

Ringleaders of violent turmoil
plunge all

into the deepest pits of misery,
leaving them
weeping there.

"Evil leaders depart!"
This is the cry
of all people everywhere.

Our desire is to walk
with our intimate friends
beneath the cherries' full bloom,
inhaling the fragrance of peace,
caressed by warm breezes
and sharing our hopes
in pleasant conversation.

Strike the bell signaling
the arrival of peace!
Firmly sound the resonant chimes
announcing peace,
announcing victory
to people everywhere.
From a dark and blackened sun
raise your sights,
and regard the brilliant
sun of peace!

April 2, 2003

At Tokyo Makiguchi Memorial Hall

This translation, by Andrew Gebert, was first published in *Fighting for Peace* (2004).

"I would be the boldest": Whitman, "Excelsior," in *Leaves of Grass*, p. 588.

human beings must continue: see Einstein, *Einstein on Peace*, p. 126.

If there is truth: see Sophocles, *Fragments*, p. 413.

Sun Yat-sen (1866–1925): Chinese political leader who established the Nationalist Party in China. He became the first president of the new Republic of China in 1911.

We must try to awaken: see *Einstein on Peace*, p. 77.

The triumph of the human spirit

Brisk morn in the New World,
the light of dawn
dyes the eastern sky crimson,
brightening endless expanses
of canyon and plain.
The pale mysteries of
obscuring mists
quietly disperse,
revealing the green forest,
its colorful flowers and towering trees—
trees that stretch high into the heavens,
with more than a century of growth,
whose regal bearing speaks of
triumph in struggle after struggle.
Early rising birds dance and sing,
dewdrops on leaves flash gold,
as everything that lives
breathes deep the morning air.

The wind rises to carry off
the fresh energy of growth
—the abundant, vital pulse
arising from these magnificent woods—
transporting it to the clustered skyscrapers,
the very heart of civilization.

Towering timbers of the spirit,
Ralph Waldo Emerson,
Henry David Thoreau,
Walt Whitman—
friends bound by a deep and mutual respect,
Ralph Waldo Emerson,
Henry David Thoreau,
Walt Whitman—
ceaselessly issue the generous

cry of their souls,
a call redolent with the
vastness of nature,
into the endless firmament
of humanity.

Proud banner-bearers of the
American Renaissance!
Before their emergence,
the word *I* never had so proud a ring,
the words *to live* were never spoken
with such earnest dignity and grandeur.

Literature is a clear mirror
reflecting the human heart.
It is only when the right person
gives it voice
that the written word can shine
with its true, original brilliance.

The poetry of these men
was never authoritative revelation
conferred from oracular heights.
Rather, their words were like
treasured swords
forged in the furnace of the soul
day by day, blow by blow,
amidst the onslaughts of
suffering and trial.

It is for just this reason that
they have continued to offer
to so many people
—in different lands
and different times—
the strength and courage to live
when they confront the implacable
challenges of life.

"Camerado, this is no book,
Who touches this touches a man…"
In these words of Whitman,
fearless poet of the people,
we hear the confidence and pride
that gave birth to
the American Renaissance.

Although they be words on paper,
each phrase and line
earnestly addresses
the innermost being and concern
of every one of us as we face
the unavoidable sufferings
of birth, of aging,
of illness and of death.

"Nothing is at last sacred
but the integrity of your own mind."
Emerson's declaration of
spiritual independence
resounds like a proud,
solemn cry of triumph,
a paean to the
dignity of humankind.

Having left behind
the distractions of the city,
Thoreau began his life in the woods,
on the pristine shores of Walden Pond:
"Only that day dawns to which we are awake.
There is more day to dawn.
The sun is but a morning star."

It is in the vigorous spirit
of taking on new challenges
that youth has always found
its defining pride and place.

As they grappled with
the realities of their times,
Emerson, Thoreau and Whitman
never silenced their leonine roar.
The crisp clarity of their call
aroused long-stagnant minds
urging a complacent society
toward vibrant transformation.

Now a century and some decades later,
their courageous call of conviction
still echoes and resounds—
deep, strong and everlasting.

The workings of nature
are infinite and enduring.
The wisdom that issues
from nature's spring
is likewise limitless.
These great leaders of the
American Renaissance
took untold pleasure
in their dialogues with nature,
drawing from it
the nourishment to live,
the energy to sound
loud alarms for their age.

The word *renaissance* signifies
the radiant triumph of the human spirit,
the full flowering of
the infinite power and potential
of a single individual,
the grand undertaking of constructing
a magnificent sense of self,
a new society.

When the chords of the human heart
resonate with the august tones

of nature's ensemble,
we perform a wondrous symphony of life
whose rhythms vibrate
into eternity.

The same primal laws
permeate the stars that sparkle
in distant constellations
and the inner cosmos
of the individual life;
they are two and yet not two,
indivisibly interwoven...

On the azure expanses
of this oceanic renaissance,
the freely intermingling
wind and light
of East and West
generate ever-spreading waves
of harmonious union.

Each form of life
supports all others;
together they weave
the grand web of life.
Thus there really is
no private happiness
for oneself alone,
no sorrow
belonging only to others.

An age in which
all the world's people
enjoy the mutually recognized
dignity of their lives,
savoring days of happiness
in a peaceful society...

Such is the world of which
Emerson, Whitman and Thoreau dreamed.
This is the path humanity must pursue in the
twenty-first century.

Let us set out in quest
of the dawn of a new renaissance,
guided on this
vivid journey of inquiry
by two great American scholars.

Together we advance
in the thrilling adventure
to explore the inner human cosmos,
to find new sources of our creativity,
our planet's fresh dawn!

In Whitman's words:
"Allons! we must not stop here."

Let us press on together,
my friends and companions.
And let us sing songs of praise
to life's beauties and wonders
as we go.

July 3, 2006

In boundless gratitude for the literary training
I received from my mentor

Written for the book *Creating Waldens: An East–West Conversation on the American Renaissance*, the author's dialogue with Ronald A. Bosco and Joel Myerson.

"Camerado, this is no book": Whitman, "So Long!" in *Leaves of Grass*, p. 611.

"Nothing is at last sacred": Emerson, "Self-reliance" in *The Selected Writings of Ralph Waldo Emerson*, p. 148.

"Only that day dawns": Thoreau, *Walden and Civil Disobedience*, p. 382.

"Allons!": Whitman, "Songs of the Open Road" in *Leaves of Grass*, p. 302.

Pampas grass, the poet's friend

The pampas grass
lifts its hands
in invitation.
In the sacred solemnity
of the morning light,
in the burnished
sparkle of sunset,
the pampas grass beckons:
"Happiness awaits you here!"
"Victory awaits!"

No one raises
loud cheers for
the pampas grass.
This is because
they do not understand
the noble spirit
with which it strives,
with its slender stalk of life,
to offer the gift
of heartfelt courage
and happiness
to all.

Poets, however,
are your friend and fellow
applauding and
praising you.

Without you,
the autumn would
be desolate,
so many landscapes
would be denuded.

For the pampas grasses
embody the spirit
of poetry
and friendship.

In the morning
they call out brightly:
"This way, everyone, this way!"
At the height of day
they extend their invitation
to all engaged
in important, invaluable efforts.
In the evening
rustling in the breeze
they commend the triumph
of our day's work and
invite us to an easy rest,
assure us in whispers
that they will watch over us
in our sleep,
offering their prayers
in great numbers.

The pampas grasses
have life,
they are life.
They gesture with a
nearly human wisdom.

Never demean
the pampas grasses!
Never look on them and laugh.
For they offer comfort
to the greatest hearts.

A single reed
of pampas grass
feels forsaken and alone.
They thrive in

large and vibrant families
mutually assisting,
flowering with rich confidence.

Pampas grasses
are never just the pair
of parent and child.
They are always surrounded
by children, relations and friends
in great numbers.
To see them smiling,
conversing together,
they may appear frail.
But in the core of their being
they are stronger than
the mightiest tree.

The pampas grasses
sway with supple strength.
The sight of them—
their beckoning gestures
invite us
to be people of inner nobility,
to be deeply caring
and good-natured,
to work tirelessly to
bring into being
that which is
beneficial and just.

Flowers too
are lovely.
Beautiful also
are the fruits
that adorn
people's tables.

But the pampas grass
must sing their own song!
The pampas grass
whose slender stems
gleam more brightly
than any sword,
living out their lives
in serene delight.

You have something
to teach us all.
We must learn
what this fresh
new lesson is.
We must learn
the meaning you
seek to convey with
your beckoning gesture.

In you we find songs
and poetry
and humor.

While your unbroken
silence may suggest
solitude,
you have vowed
never to be defeated
by the fiercest storm.
And for this
I hope people
will love you.

You call out
to people,
to the joyful
and the suffering,
and remind them
that there is something

they must call to mind
at the sight of you
unconquered by any gale.

The full moon casts its gaze
on the swaying pampas grass.
Innumerable stars watch you.
So does the sun,
the wind and people too.
The pampas grass
is a triumphant victor
always living courageously,
wholeheartedly.

All who are witness
to the proud sight
of the pampas grass
exult with you
as you call out
your hands raised high:
"We have won!"
"We have won!"

Your name in Japanese
—*susuki*—
is said to derive
from words meaning
a tree that stands
straight and tall.

In his writings,
Nichiren describes
the Lotus Sutra's
most solemn ceremony
of transmission
from mentor to disciple
in this way:
      Crowding four hundred
      ten thousand million

nayutas of worlds,
like the grasses of Musashino Plain
or the trees covering Mount Fuji.

Ah, pampas grass!
Though valiant and brave,
still you bow your heads
with humility.

Your beckoning gesture
is an invitation to happiness,
an admonition
to avoid impatience,
a quiet command
to fulfill
a meaningful role.

Pampas grass!
I urge you on,
you who live
so bravely and so fully,
who flower in
the fullness of courage!

August 27, 2007

"Crowding four hundred": Nichiren, *The Writings of Nichiren Daishonin*, vol. 1, p. 911.

nayuta: an Indian numerical unit. According to one account, it refers to 100 billion (10^{11}), and to another, 10 million (10^7).

Musashino Plain: a wide plain encompassing present-day Tokyo and Saitama Prefecture.

In praise of morning glories—
a flower loved by all

This morning again
the morning glories
—blue and scarlet—
are in bloom.
It is my wish
each morning
to be able to
offer just such
a bright and cheerful
refreshing smile
to the world.

The blue blossoms are princes,
the scarlet ones princesses!
Morning glories
will always be
happy and graceful
princes and princesses.

Their name is celebrated
in the poems of
The Collection of Ten Thousand Leaves.
Opening fully
in the early dawn,
morning glories
were beloved
by the people of
that rustic era,
and later in
the sophisticated
aristocratic Heian culture.

Lady Murasaki,
the author of *The Tale of Genji,*

famously entitled one
of her novel's chapters
"Morning Glories."

In her reflections
in *The Pillow Book*,
another court lady, Sei Shonagon,
counted the morning glory
among the foremost of
late-blossoming flowers.

One lady indicated
the blue and scarlet blossoms
of the morning glories and
exclaimed, "Ah, such beauty!"

In the sight of
morning glories blooming
we see hope
and nature
and humanity
and the energy of life,
deep and heartfelt communication,
the serenity of a peace
that is beyond words.

This flower
has been loved
by people in all ages.
Few flowers have held
such an intimate place
in ordinary people's lives.

Originating in the tropics
morning glories have
spread throughout the world.

They are said to have reached Japan
through China, a country to which
we are always so indebted.

Gazing on morning glories,
the poet laureate
sings their praise.
For they are poetry
incarnate.

In Goethe's words:
    What shall always bring us together?
    Love.

When we regard
the morning glories
we do so with love.
The noble-minded
are naturally drawn
to all they see
and inspired to
poetic flight.

The renowned haiku poet
Matsuo Basho wrote:
    I am a man
    who has his breakfast
    with the morning glories.

He is said
to have addressed this
to a young disciple
who was leading a disorderly life—
your teacher awakens
early each day
and eats a proper breakfast
gazing at morning glories
before starting the day's work...

A well-ordered life—
this is the rhythm that ensures
the triumphant blossoms
of morning glories
will flower in our hearts.

Oh, morning glories!
With your serene
and virtuous beauty
give strength
to the unhealthy,
troubled people of the world;
empower them to spread
fair and mighty wings
forever and a day!

Kobayashi Issa wrote this wry verse:
    The visage of the morning glory—
    human faces somehow leave
    so much to be desired.

He seems to be saying that
compared to this handsome flower
the human face appears
imperfect and incomplete.

Like morning glories
brightly lit by the rising sun,
let us set out
with a beaming visage
and fully live each day.

With each new
and coming year
the poet hopes to see
the princes and princesses
of morning glories!
He always looks forward
to their next encounter.

I offer my earnest thanks
to my friends with radiant smiles
who planted and raised these
noble flowers,
these princes and princesses
of happiness.
Thank you! Thank you!

August 27, 2007

The Collection of Ten Thousand Leaves (Jpn *Man'yoshu*): the oldest existing short poem anthology in Japan, compiled in the mid-eighth century. It was a time when not only the nobility but ordinary people as well freely expressed their feelings in the form of short poems.

The Heian period (794–1185): the era that followed the Man'yo period.

Lady Murasaki or Murasaki Shikibu (late tenth to early eleventh century): Japanese novelist, poet and lady-in-waiting at the imperial court during the Heian period. Her masterpiece, *The Tale of Genji*, is considered the world's first novel.

Sei Shonagon (*c. 966–c.* 1017): Japanese court lady and author of the famous essay *The Pillow Book*.

"What shall always bring us together?": trans. from Goethe, "Aus den *Briefen an Frau v. Stein*" in *Werke: Hamburger Ausgabe in 14 Bänden*, vol. 1, p. 128.

Matsuo Basho (1644–94): Japanese poet recognized as a master of brief and clear haiku.

"I am a man": trans. from Matsuo, *Basho haikushu*, p. 53.

Kobayashi Issa (1763–1827): Japanese poet regarded as one of the four great haiku masters.

"The visage of the morning glory": trans. from Maruyama, *Kobayashi Issa: Hito to sakuhin*, p. 227.

Salute to poets

*Offered with deepest respect to the wise members
of the World Congress of Poets, who struggle daily
for the cause of peace and humanity*

There is a power in words,
an infinite power
to revive, restore
and make life blaze anew.

There is a life in poetry,
a limitless, eternal life
that can stir and arouse
a society to new vibrancy.

Poets!
Reflected in
your clear eyes
—like the still waters
of a lake—
we can see:
Clusters of people
fleeing in confusion
through a field of battle.
A wailing mother
tenderly cradling
a tiny corpse.
An infant,
starving, emaciated,
weakened and awaiting death.
The trembling fist
of a young boy,
who writhes beneath
the crushing weights of
discrimination and hate.

Poets!
Through your keen ears
we can hear,
as in an echoing valley:
The self-mocking sighs
of young people
filled with mistrust and isolation,
who sense no future
as they wander aimlessly
through thronging crowds.
The painful cry of Earth herself,
oceans and atmosphere polluted,
stripped and denuded of green,
bound by atomic burdens,
crying in distress
as she continues to revolve
on her grinding axis.

Poets!
Poets whose fine hearts
feel the full torment
of people's pain!

War, nuclear weapons,
environmental destruction,
discrimination,
the trampling of people's rights—
all these problems
are caused and created
by human beings.

Thus there is
no misery or cruelty
beyond our power
as humans
to resolve.

All people, everyone,
crave and thirst

for peace,
everyone seeks and pursues
the goal of happiness.

All people
hold within themselves,
in their hearts,
a golden sun
that can brightly light their own lives
and shed far and wide
warm and brilliant beams
of friendship and fraternity.
This inner luster
of life itself,
is the ultimate
font and source
of new creation.

Poets!
Now is the time
to raise your voices,
to call forth and awaken
the sun sleeping
in the hearts of people
the world over.

Society is awash
with false discourse;
with propaganda
that incites
xenophobic rejection;
with low and ugly rumor
whose sole purpose is
to degrade and demean;
with shrieked abuse that
destroys dignity,
tearing into the heart
like a lethal blade.

This flood
of deceptive, vacuous
and violent language
has caused people
to treat all words and language
as suspect.
Words are
the human heart
and this doubt
has driven people
into the dark and rampant isolation
of cynicism and fear,
distrusting everything
including society
and humanity itself.

Ah, poets!
Now is the time
to use the words
of compassion and truth,
the words of universal justice
that roil and seethe within your heart,
to use these words to dispel
the dark and heavy clouds
of language laden with
false and evil intent,
to stir new winds
of hope and courage,
to bring about a
new and golden dawn!

Mahatma Gandhi declared:
    A poet is one who can call forth
    the good latent in the human breast.

Ah! The innumerable
cruel fissures that split
and divide our
blue planet.

Divisions based
on differences
of ideology,
of state,
of national and ethnic
identity,
of religion,
of class.
The absurd, horrific
and repeated reality
of people
turned against people,
viciously discriminating,
resenting, wrangling
and hating each other.

The deepest evil,
the ultimate source
of all conflict and tragedy,
is the dividing heart.
Preoccupied with difference,
it drives people
to reject and exclude
others.

But this very Earth,
this lovely planet,
is a garden rich
with the full and gorgeous
blossoming of diversity.

It is difference
above all
that makes each
flowering tree
—cherry, plum, peach and damson—
uniquely valuable.
Difference is
the quality that

enables us
to learn from each other,
to complement and fulfill each other,
to respect and honor each other.

Poets!
Let us throw new bridges
across the gulfs dividing
people's hearts!
With the cries that issue
from your soul
turn the gears of history:
away from suspicion and toward trust
from divisiveness to harmony
from war to peace.

We are all human beings.
The poetic spirit
beats and throbs
in our veins!

All people are in fact
sisters and brothers
capable of mutual love,
of coming together
in harmonious unity.

All people
have the right
to live out their lives
in happiness and dignity.

Poets, arise!
Wait for no one,
but stand up resolute
and alone!

With our words
and with our actions,

let us till and turn
the sprawling expanse,
the desert aridity
of people's hearts.

The voice of the poet
who has chosen to stand alone
calls out to and resounds with
the voice of another
self-sufficient poet.
A single ripple
elicits ten thousand waves.

When our cries of justice
swell to a symphony
extolling humanity and life
and when its resonant tones
reach all corners of the Earth,
wrapping and cradling it…

Then the deep red glory,
the dawning sun
of peace for all people everywhere,
will rise and lift
into the sky.

Dedicated to the Twenty-seventh World Congress of Poets, held in Chennai,
India, September 1–6, 2007. The World Congress of Poets was established
in 1969 in Manila under the auspices of the World Academy of Arts and
Culture for the promotion of world peace and mutual understanding
through poetry. The World Academy of Arts and Culture conferred the title
of Poet Laureate on the author in July 1981.

"A poet is one who can call forth": Gandhi, *An Autobiography*, p. 250.

cherry, plum, peach, and damson: refers to the Buddhist principle that likens
each individual to a beautiful flower that has its own unique mission and
potential.

Glossary

BODHISATTVA   One who aspires to enlightenment, or Buddha-hood, and carries out altruistic practices. It also indicates a state of life characterized by compassion. The bodhisattva ideal is central to the Mahayana Buddhist tradition as the individual who seeks happiness both for him- or herself and for others.

BODHISATTVAS OF THE EARTH   An innumerable host of bodhisattvas who emerge from beneath the earth as described in the fifteenth chapter of the Lotus Sutra. The Buddha, Shakyamuni, entrusts to them the task of propagation of the essence of the Lotus Sutra in the time after his death. Nichiren regarded those who embrace and propagate the teaching of the Mystic Law as Bodhisattvas of the Earth.

BUDDHA   Literally Awakened One; one who perceives the true nature of all life and who leads others to attain the same enlighten-ment. The Buddha nature or condition of Buddhahood exists within all beings and is characterized by the qualities of wisdom, courage, compassion and life force. Historically this indicates Shakyamuni, the founder of Buddhism.

BUDDHIST GODS   The heavenly gods or benevolent deities that protect the correct Buddhist teaching and its practitioners. Forces in life that function to protect the people and their land and bring good fortune to both.

DAIMOKU   The practice of chanting Nam-myoho-renge-kyo with belief in the fundamental law of the universe expounded by Nichi-ren. See Nam-myoho-renge-kyo.

DAISHONIN *see* NICHIREN.

DHARMA   The teachings or universal law of enlightenment taught by the Buddha.

GOHONZON   The scroll that serves as the object of devotion in Nichiren Buddhism. SGI members chant Nam-myoho-renge-kyo to a Gohonzon enshrined in their own homes in order to bring forth the life state of Buddhahood from within.

GONGYO   One of the basic elements of the practice of Nichiren Buddhism. It consists of chanting Nam-myoho-renge-kyo and reciting portions of the Lotus Sutra (from the "Expedient Means" and "Life Span" chapters). Gongyo literally means to "exert [oneself in] practice," and is performed twice a day by members of the SGI.

HUMAN REVOLUTION   The term used by Josei Toda to describe a fundamental process of inner transformation whereby each individual can unleash the full potential of their lives and take control over their own destiny.

JIYU   Literally, "to emerge from the earth," *see* BODHISATTVAS OF THE EARTH

KOSEN-RUFU   A Japanese phrase literally meaning "to declare and spread widely." It refers to the process of securing lasting peace and happiness for all humankind by establishing the humanistic ideals of Nichiren Buddhism in society. Kosen-rufu is often used synonymously with world peace, and more broadly could be understood as a vision of social peace brought about by the widespread acceptance of core values such as unfailing respect for the dignity of human life.

LOTUS SUTRA   Widely regarded as one of the most important and influential sutras, or sacred scriptures, of Buddhism, forming the core of the Mahayana school. In the sutra, Shakyamuni reveals that all people can attain enlightenment and that Buddhahood—a condition of absolute happiness, freedom from fear and from all illusions—is inherent in all life.

MAKIGUCHI, TSUNESABURO (1871–1944)   A reformist educator, school principal and author of works on geography and educational theory. He started to practice Nichiren Buddhism in 1928, and in 1930 founded the Soka Kyoiku Gakkai (the forerunner of the Soka Gakkai). He was detained and incarcerated from July 1943 until his death in prison in November 1944 as a result of his opposition to Japan's wartime militarist government.

MYSTIC LAW   The ultimate law, principle or truth of life and the universe in Nichiren's teachings; the Law of Nam-myoho-renge-kyo.

NAM-MYOHO-RENGE-KYO   An invocation established by Nichiren on April 28, 1253. The title of the Lotus Sutra in its Japanese translation is Myoho-renge-kyo. To Nichiren, Nam-myoho-renge-kyo was the expression, in words, of the law of life which all Buddhist teachings seek to clarify. Practitioners of Nichiren Buddhism chant Nam-myoho-renge-kyo as their core Buddhist practice. This is sometimes described as chanting daimoku.

NICHIREN (1222–82) A Buddhist reformer who lived in thirteenth-century Japan, often referred to by the honorific title "Daishonin" or "great sage." His intensive study of the Buddhist sutras convinced him that the Lotus Sutra contained the essence of the Buddha's enlightenment and that it held the key to transforming people's suffering and enabling the peaceful flourishing of society. Nichiren established the invocation of Nam-myoho-renge-kyo in 1253. His claims invited an onslaught of often violent persecutions from the military government and the established Buddhist schools. Throughout, he refused to compromise his principles to appease those in authority.

SOKA GAKKAI Literally, "Society for the Creation of Value," a Japanese lay Buddhist movement based on the practice of Nichiren Buddhism, founded in 1930 by Tsunesaburo Makiguchi and Josei Toda. Originally called Soka Kyoiku Gakkai (Value-Creating Education Society), it expanded rapidly in postwar Japan to become one of the world's largest lay Buddhist movements.

SOKA GAKKAI INTERNATIONAL (SGI) Founded by Daisaku Ikeda in 1975, a worldwide network of lay Buddhists dedicated to a shared vision of a better world through the empowerment of the individual and the promotion of peace, culture and education based upon the teachings of Nichiren.

SHAKYAMUNI (GAUTAMA SIDDHARTHA) Also known as the Buddha or Awakened One. The historical founder of Buddhism. Born in what is now Nepal some 2,500 years ago, he renounced his royal upbringing to embark on a spiritual quest to understand how human suffering could be ended. While in deep meditation, he experienced a profound awakening, or enlightenment. He then traveled throughout the Indian subcontinent sharing his enlightened wisdom, promoting peace and teaching people how to unleash the great potential of their lives. The Lotus Sutra is said to contain his ultimate teaching: the universal possibility of enlightenment.

THREE EXISTENCES Past existence, present existence and future existence. Used to indicate all of time from the eternal past, through the present and into the eternal future. In Buddhism, the three existences represent the three aspects of the eternity of life, linked inseparably by the inner law of cause and effect.

TODA, JOSEI (1900–58)   An educator, publisher and entrepreneur who became the second president of the Soka Gakkai and the mentor of Daisaku Ikeda. Along with Tsunesaburo Makiguchi, Toda was incarcerated during World War II for his criticism of the government's wartime policies. After the war, he rebuilt the Soka Gakkai into a dynamic popular movement with members throughout Japan.

TREASURE TOWER   A massive tower or stupa adorned with treasures or jewels described in the eleventh chapter of the Lotus Sutra. It indicates the enormity, profundity and dignity of both the universal law of life, Nam-myoho-renge-kyo, and individuals who inherently possess the law within their lives.

Bibliography

Beethoven, Ludwig van, *Symphonien Nr. 6–9* [Symphonies No. 6–9] (Farnborough: Gregg Press, 1966).

Burton, Sir Richard Francis, *The Kasidah of Haji Abdu El-Yezdi* (Lenox: Hard Press, 2006).

Caine, Hall, *The Eternal City* (New York: Appleton, 1901).

Einstein, Albert, *Einstein on Peace*, ed. Otto Nathan and Heinz Norden (New York: Avenel Books, 1981).

Emerson, Ralph Waldo, *The Selected Writings of Ralph Waldo Emerson*, ed. Brooks Atkinson (New York: Random House, 1968).

Gandhi, M. K., *An Autobiography or The Story of My Experiments with Truth*, trans. Mahadev Desai (Ahmedabad: Navajivan Trust, 1927).

Goethe, Johann Wolfgang von, *Faust: Parts One and Two*, trans. George Madison Priest (Chicago: Encyclopaedia Britannica, 1952).

———, *Werke: Hamburger Ausgabe in 14 Bänden* [Works: Hamburg Edition in 14 Volumes], 14 vols (Munich: Deutscher Taschenbuch Verlag, 1998).

Hugo, Victor, *Les Contemplations* [Contemplations], 2 vols (Paris: Hachette, 1877).

———, *The Rhine* (New York: John Wiley, 1848).

Ikeda, Daisaku, *The Human Revolution*, 2 vols (Santa Monica: World Tribune Press, 2004).

Kant, Immanuel, *Critique of Practical Reason*, trans. and ed. Lewis White Beck (New York: Macmillan, 1993).

Kierkegaard, Søren, *Søren Kierkegaards skrifter* [The Writings of Søren Kierkegaard], ed. Niels Jørgen Cappelørn, 28 vols (Copenhagen: Gad, 2000).

Lectures on the Sutra: The Hoben and Juryo Chapters, rev. edn. (Tokyo: Nichiren Shoshu International Center, 1984).

Leonardo da Vinci, *The Notebooks of Leonardo da Vinci*, comp. and ed. Jean Paul Richter, 2 vols (New York: Dover Publications, 1970).

Makiguchi, Tsunesaburo, *Makiguchi Tsunesaburo zenshu* [The Complete Works of Tsunesaburo Makiguchi], 10 vols (Tokyo: Daisan Bun-meisha, 1980–97).

Martí, José, *Obras Completas* [Complete Works], 26 vols (Havana: Editorial Nacional de Cuba, 1963–73).

Maruyama, Kazuhiko, *Kobayashi Issa: Hito to sakuhin* [Kobayashi Issa: His Life and Works] (Tokyo: Ofusha, 1971).

Matsuo, Basho, *Basho haikushu* [Collected Haiku of Basho], ed. Shunjo Nakamura (Tokyo: Iwanami Shoten, 1971).

Melville, Herman, *Moby Dick; or, The Whale* (Chicago: Encyclopaedia Britannica, 1952).

Nichiren, *Nichiren Daishonin gosho zenshu* [The Complete Writings of Nichiren Daishonin], ed. Nichiko Hori (Tokyo: Soka Gakkai, 1952).

———, *The Record of the Orally Transmitted Teachings*, trans. Burton Watson (Tokyo: Soka Gakkai, 2004).

———, *The Writings of Nichiren Daishonin*, ed. and trans. Gosho Translation Committee, 2 vols (Tokyo: Soka Gakkai, 1999–2006).

Rizal, José, *El Filibusterismo* [Subversion], trans. León Ma. Guerrero (London: Longman, 1965).

———, *The Philippines a Century Hence* (Manila: Philippine Education, 1912).

Rolland, Romain, *Beethoven*, trans. B. Constance Hull (London: Kegan Paul, Trench, Trubner, 1919).

Sophocles, *Fragments*, ed. and trans. Hugh Lloyd-Jones (Cambridge MA: Harvard University Press, 1996).

Symonds, John Addington, *A Short History of the Renaissance in Italy* (New York: Charles Scribner's Sons, 1898).

Tagore, Rabindranath, *The English Writings of Rabindranath Tagore*, ed. Sisir Kumar Das, 4 vols (New Delhi: Sahitya Akademi, 1994–2007).

Thoreau, Henry David, *Walden and Civil Disobedience* (New York: Penguin Books, 1983).

Tyutchev, Fyodor Ivanovich, *Poems and Political Letters of F. I. Tyutchev*, trans. Jesse Zeldin (Knoxville: University of Tennessee Press, 1973).

———, *Poems of Night and Day*, trans. Eugene M. Kayden (Boulder: University of Colorado, 1974).

Ukrainka, Lesya, *Biblioteka vsemirnoi literatury* [World Literature Library], Series 3, vol. 157 (Moscow: Khudozhestvennaya Literatura, 1968).

Wakayama, Bokusui, *Wakayama Bokusui zenshu* [The Complete Works of Bokusui Wakayama], 13 vols (Shizuoka: Zoshinkai Publishers, 1992–93).

Whitman, Walt, *Leaves of Grass* in *Complete Poetry and Collected Prose* (New York: The Library of America, 1982).

Zhou Enlai, *Shuonrai senshu* [Selected Works of Zhou Enlai], 2 vols (Beijing: Foreign Languages Press, 1989).

Appendix

The poems in this volume and their Japanese titles

The numbers following the Japanese titles refer to the volume and page numbers of the *Ikeda Daisaku zenshu* (The Complete Works of Daisaku Ikeda). For poems which are not included in the *Ikeda Daisaku zenshu* at this point, the original Japanese-language details are provided. The dates that follow the titles indicate the year the poem was written.

"Blossoms that scatter," *Chiru sakura* (散る桜) (1945), vol. 39, p. 220.

"Fuji and the poet," *Fuji to shijin* (富士と詩人) (1947), vol. 39, p. 214.

"Morigasaki Beach," *Morigasaki kaigan* (森ケ崎海岸) (1947), vol. 39, p. 223.

"Offering prayers at Mount Fuji," *Fuji ni inoru* (富士に祈る) (1950), vol. 39, p. 209.

"I offer this to you," *Nanji ni sasagu* (汝に捧ぐ) (1951), vol. 39, p. 348.

"Travelers," *Tabibito* (旅人) (1952), vol. 39, p. 217.

"Spring breezes," *Harukaze* (春風) (1950s), vol. 39, p. 293.

"Autumn wind," *Akikaze* (秋風) (1950s), vol. 39, p. 297.

"Daybreak," *Reimei* (黎明) (1966), vol. 39, p. 371.

"The crisp day we parted," *Sawayaka na wakare no hi ni* (爽やかな別れの日に) (1967), vol. 39, p. 198.

"To my young friends," *Wakaki tomo e okuru* (若き友へ贈る) (1970–71), vol. 38, p. 43.

"Pampas grass," *Susuki* (芒) (1971), vol. 39, p. 193.

"The people," *Minshu* (民衆) (1971), vol. 39, p. 157.

"Weeds," *Zasso* (雑草) (1971), vol. 39, p. 130.

"Mother," *Haha* (母) (1971), vol. 39, p. 141.

"Song of the crimson dawn," *Kurenai no uta* (紅の歌) (1981), vol. 39, p. 459.

"Youth, scale the mountain of kosen-rufu of the twenty-first century," *Seinen yo—nijuisseiki no kofu no yama o nobore* (青年よ　21世紀の広布の山を登れ) (1981), vol. 43, p. 393.

"Days of value," *Kachi no hibi* (価値の日々) (1985–87), vol. 38, p. 7.

"My mentor, Josei Toda," *Waga shi—Toda Josei sensei* (わが師　戸田城聖先生) (1986), vol. 68, p. 151.

"Arise, the sun of the century," *Seiki no taiyo yo nobore* (世紀の太陽よ昇れ) (1987), vol. 40, p. 16.

"Toll the bell of the new renaissance," *Aratanaru runesansu no kane* (新たなるルネサンスの鐘) (1987), vol. 40, p. 240.

"Dunhuang," *Tonko* (敦煌) (1987), vol. 41, p. 67.

"Like Mount Fuji," *Fuji no gotoku ni* (富士のごとくに) (1987), vol. 41, p. 104.

"The lion's land, Mother India," *Shishi no kuni—haha no daichi* (獅子の国　母の大地) (1987), vol. 41, p. 9.

"Youthful country with a shining future," *Wakawakashiku mirai ni hikaru kuni* (若々しく未来に光る国) (1988), vol. 40, p. 467.

"Be an eternal bastion of peace," *Eien tare "heiwa no yosai"* (永遠たれ"平和の要塞") (1988), vol. 40, p. 558.

"Embracing the skies of Kirghiz," *Kirugisu no sora o idaite* (キルギスの空をいだいて) (1989), vol. 42, p. 527.

"Banner of humanism, path of justice," *Jindo no hata—seigi no michi* (人道の旗　正義の道) (1990), vol. 41, p. 393.

"Mother of art, the sunlight of happiness," *Geijutsu no haha—sachi no taiyo* (芸術の母　幸の太陽) (1990), vol. 41, p. 405.

"Shine brilliantly! Crown of the Mother of the Philippines," *Santare! Firipin no haha no kanmuri* (燦たれ！フィリピンの母の冠) (1991), vol. 41, p. 457.

"May the laurels of kings adorn your lives," *Kimi ni "oja no gekkeikan" o* (君に「王者の月桂冠」を) (1991), vol. 41, p. 326.

"Like the sun rising," *Noboriyuku taiyo no yoni* (昇りゆく太陽のように) (1992), vol. 43, p. 87.

"Cosmic traveler, our century's premier violinist," *Uchu kara no tabibito* (宇宙からの旅人) (1992), vol. 43, p. 98.

"The sun of jiyu over a new land," *Shinsei no tenchi ni jiyu no taiyo* (新生の天地に地涌の太陽) (1993), vol. 43, p. 28.

"Salute to mothers," *Haha ni saikeirei* (母に最敬礼) (1995), vol. 43, p. 374.

"Unfurl the banner of youth," *Hirugaere—seinen no hata* (翻れ　青年の旗) (1998), vol. 43, p. 382.

"The poet—warrior of the spirit," *Shijin—tamashii no senshi* (詩人　魂の戦士) (1998), vol. 47, p. 285.

"May the fragrant laurels of happiness adorn your life," *Sachi kaore—midori no eikan* (幸薫れ　緑の栄冠) (1999), vol. 43, p. 418.

"The noble voyage of life," *Homare no jinsei koro* (誉れの人生航路) (1999), vol. 43, p. 340.

"Standing among the ruins of Takiyama Castle," *Takiyama joshi ni tachite* (滝山城址に立ちて) (2000), vol. 43, p. 428.

"The path to a peaceful world, a garden for humankind," *Sekai heiwa no michi—jinrui no hanazono* (世界平和の道　人類の花園) (2000), vol. 44, p. 495.

"Together holding aloft laurels of the people's poetry," *Minshu shijin no keikan o tomoni* (民衆詩人の桂冠を共に) (2000), published in the December 25, 2000, issue of the *Seikyo Shimbun*.

"Eternally radiant champion of humanity," *Fumetsu no kagayaki—ningen no eiyu* (不滅の輝き　人間の英雄) (2001), vol. 46, p. 212.

"August 15—The dawn of a new day," *Reimei no hachigatsu jugonichi* (黎明の八月十五日) (2001), vol. 46, p. 36.

"Salute to the smiling faces of the twenty-first century," *Nijuisseiki no kibo no egao ni keirei!* (21世紀の希望の笑顔に敬礼！) (2001), published in the September 6, 2001, issue of the *Seikyo Shimbun*.

"The promise of a majestic peace," *Heiwa yo! Kofuku yo! Eien naru sekai heiwa o inori utau* (平和よ！幸福よ！永遠なる世界平和を祈り詩う) (2003), vol. 49, p. 353.

"The triumph of the human spirit," *Ningen seishin no atarashiki gaika* (人間精神の新しき凱歌) (2006), published in *Utsukushiki seimei—chikyu to ikiru tetsujin Soro to Emason o kataru* (Creating Waldens, An East–West Conversation on the American Renaissance), p. 2.

"Pampas grass, the poet's friend," *Shijin no tomo—susuki o utau* (詩人の友　芒を謳う) (2007), published in *Heiwa no hata* (Banner of Peace), p. 763.

"In praise of morning glories—a flower loved by all," *Mina no hana—asagao o tatau* (皆の花　朝顔を讃う) (2007), published in *Heiwa no hata* (Banner of Peace), p. 757.

"Salute to poets," *Shijin—banzai!* (詩人　万歳！) (2007), published in the September 5, 2007, issue of the *Seikyo Shimbun*.